A Posthuman Perspective on Media Technologies and Media Literacy

A Posthuman Perspective on Media Technologies and Media Literacy

Herschel Glavin

STATES
ACADEMIC PRESS
www.statesacademicpress.com

States Academic Press,
109 South 5th Street,
Brooklyn, NY 11249, USA

Visit us on the World Wide Web at:
www.statesacademicpress.com

ISBN: 978-1-63989-709-4

Cataloging-in-publication Data

A posthuman perspective on media technologies and media literacy / Herschel Glavin.
p. cm.
Includes bibliographical references and index.
ISBN 978-1-63989-709-4
1. Mass media--Technological innovations. 2. Mass media and technology. 3. Media literacy.
4. Mass media--History. I. Glavin, Herschel.
P96.T42 P67 2023
302.23--dc23

Table of Contents

Preface

I am honored to present to you this unique book which encompasses the most up-to-date data in the field. I was extremely pleased to get this opportunity of editing the work of experts from across the globe. I have also written papers in this field and researched the various aspects revolving around the progress of the discipline. I have tried to unify my knowledge along with that of stalwarts from every corner of the world, to produce a text which not only benefits the readers but also facilitates the growth of the field.

Media literacy is a broad perception of literacy which encompasses the ability of analyzing and accessing media messages. It also includes the ability to act, create and reflect using the power of communication and information to instigate a change in the world. Media literacy is considered as a collection of competencies which are necessary for citizenship, work and life, and is not limited to a single medium. Media literacy education is a method for improving media literacy competencies. It aims to raise awareness of media influence and encourage people to take an active role in both producing and consuming media. Inquiry-based pedagogy model is frequently used in media literacy education, which inspires individuals to ask questions regarding the things they read, see and hear. This book brings forth a posthuman perspective on media technologies and media literacy. It is appropriate for students seeking detailed information in this area of study as well as for experts. This book is a vital tool for all researching and studying this field.

Finally, I would like to thank all the contributing authors for their valuable time and contributions. This book would not have been possible without their efforts. I would also like to thank my friends and family for their constant support.

Herschel Glavin

1

Discussing the Relationship between Humans and Media Technologies

We are immersed in a world mediated by information and communication technologies (ICTs), both hardware (smartphones, smartwatches, home assistants) and software (algorithms, software programs, and infrastructures such as Facebook, Instagram, Twitter, Snapchat). We are transformed by these media, whether we have invited them into our lives or not. We subsequently perceive and engage with the world through these transformations. However, media literacy for the most part does not provide clear assistance in helping us become aware of these effects.

Thus far, media literacy has focused mainly on developing the skills to access, analyze, evaluate, and create media *messages,* and has not focused sufficiently on the impact of the actual technological medium, how it enables and constrains both messages and media users. Additionally, a more fully developed media literacy would situate media investigations in such a way as to allow for a deeply practical analysis without losing a holistic, theoretical perspective. In order to accomplish this, a concise transdisciplinary approach comprised of a general framework and specific instrument is proposed. This approach is based on an interdisciplinary study of postphenomenology, media ecology, philosophical posthumanism, and complexity theory.

The framework of the approach described in this book uses six groupings of relations: technological, sociocultural, time, space, mind, and body, with a main emphasis on technological relations. How these relations, as well as their interrelational effects, participate in the constitution of the human subject is explored through an analysis of a museum selfie, which contributes to the development of a pragmatic instrument that can be used for media literacy.

The pragmatic instrument helps bring to the foreground the contributing influences that are continually constituting human subjects in everyday media environments, thus allowing people to make more informed decisions on which media they invite into their lives. The human subject is understood here as a *posthuman* subject, as opposed to the standalone, exceptional being with roots in the Enlightenment. The posthumanist approach understands the human subject as constantly *becoming* through the myriad of constituting relations in their life. While it is not possible to completely understand the complexity of all interrelations that constitute us, the more we can become aware of how we relate with the world through these transformed aspects of our selves, the greater chance we will have for reclaiming some of our agency, which arguably is the main goal of media literacy.

In this chapter I provide an overview of the current trend of an ever-increasingly media-saturated world and how media literacy currently responds. I discuss the importance of the technological medium, the technological relation, and describe the importance of better understanding the human subject. I share the overall structure of this book and briefly touch upon the various fields that will be addressed.

Situating the Research

My own personal research interest began by focusing specifically on the effect of ICTs on museum visitor experience. Investigating the mediating relations between humans and technologies led me to an approach in philosophy of technology called postphenomenology. While this helped me to understand the mediating role of technologies, it also raised unanswered questions as to exactly how the subject was being transformed in its relation with technology. This then led me to broaden my focus and attempt to more completely understand the subject as embodied and situated in a complex network of a multiplicity of relations, one group of these relations being technological. This led me to develop an approach that reflects this interrelationality and that can be an effectively used for media literacy.

It is fairly common for people in the developed Western world to live in a media-saturated environment. However, far from being new, this trend began in earnest with Gutenberg's invention of the printing press,[1] which eventually led to an exponential increase in literacy and a democratization of information, education, and knowledge (Martin & Cochrane, 1994; Ong, 2012; Postman, 2006; Strate, 2014). The printing press paved the way for communication through mass replication and broad dissemination. Today, as we[2] enter into the second decade of the twenty-first century, there is a ubiquity of screened-communication technologies that allow us, for the most part, to communicate whenever and wherever the mood strikes. The ubiquity of ICTs such as smartphones, tablets, and laptops—sometimes referred to as *technomedia* (Han, 2008)—is the everyday environment within which we live, and this has become 'normal' and unremarkable for a large part of the world—simply part of how things are. Unless noted otherwise, the ICTs I refer to are digitally networked devices that are prevalent in much of the world today.

In the United States, 'Digital media use has increased considerably, with the average 12th grader in 2016 spending more than twice as much time online as in 2006' (Twenge et al., 2019: 329). In the European Union (EU), while television is still the most commonly used medium—84% watch it every day or almost every day and 94% watch it at least once per week—the number of people who use the internet is catching up, with 65% of EU citizens using it daily or almost daily and 77% using it at least once per week (European Commission, 2018: 4). And throughout the world, a 2017 Pew Research global survey showed that while smartphone ownership has remained steady for developed nations—at around 72%—it is increasing in developing nations, growing from approximately 25% in 2013/2014 to 42% in 2017 (Poushter et al., 2018: 4).

---

1 It was not the production of books (since books were already being produced), but rather the re-production that printing enabled, making it possible for a large number of people to own a copy of a certain book title.

2 Unless otherwise noted, general pronouns such as 'we' refer to the majority of people living in the contemporary developed Western world.

This environment of ubiquitous ICTs brings many benefits. With our GPS-enabled smartphones we rarely become lost. Finding a place to eat in an unfamiliar town, a place with good reviews and the cuisine of our choice, is now quite easy. Keeping in touch with a large number of friends is as simple as checking our social media feed. By allowing notifications to be sent to us, updates from our 'friends' are delivered directly to our phones, where we can simply glance down to attend to them. These ICTs enable a robust interconnection with our sociocultural world.

In this saturated media environment, the media tend to disappear into the background of our awareness.[3] They become part of the environment in which we live. This immersion, as Figure 1.1 reflects, is especially visible with the number of smartphones in use and how often people are engaged with them. As Galit Wellner (2016) describes, smartphones have a wall/window trait. They create an inclusive 'window' to a virtual world and community while also creating an alienating 'wall' to whatever and whomever is in the person's immediate surroundings. This reflects the idea that all technologies are non-neutral and have both enabling and constraining aspects to them (Ihde, 1990).

Fig. 1.1 *Waiting for the train.* Brussels-Luxembourg station, Brussels. Photo by author (2019), CC BY-NC 4.0.

While many people embrace the changes and innovations in media technologies, others are questioning, pointing out the drawbacks and costs of such changes. The Center for Humane Technology warns, 'The companies that created social media and mobile tech have benefited our

3 See Marshall McLuhan's use of figure/ground in Logan, 2011; McLuhan et al., 1977.

lives enormously. But even with the best intentions, they are under intense pressure to compete for attention, creating invisible harms for society' (Center for Humane Technology, n.d.). There is increasing concern about the amount of influence that the dominant GAFAM[4] (Google, Amazon, Facebook, Apple, and Microsoft) technology companies have (cf. Harris 2019, 2020; Hill, 2019; Twenge, 2017). Additionally, we should not only be concerned with these companies and the content of media messages, but we also should pay attention to the actual technology itself. While there have been certain fields of media studies that focus on the technology or medium (media ecology, mediatization,[5] medium theory), the field of media literacy has mostly avoided addressing the effects of the technological medium in a rigorous manner.

For all that, our daily lives are interconnected with more than media technologies. There are sociocultural relations such as normativity, power, and language. There are both positive and less than positive issues with our minds and bodies that influence how we relate with media technologies. In addition, we are always located within a specific time and place, both of which relate to media technologies (Innis, 2008). These groups of relations interrelate and inter-influence each other, contributing to the creation of the ever-changing human subject. Salman Rushdie (2006) posits, 'To understand just one life, you must swallow the world' (145). I take this to mean that everything is interconnected, and in order to really know something, we must realize how it is interconnected with everything.

To put this another way, in order to understand any one mediating technology, we must understand all the mediating interrelations that affect us as human subjects. While achieving this level of comprehension is implausible, it alludes to the complexity and challenge of fully understanding the effects of media technologies on a human subject. The more we can understand about these complex interrelations, the greater chance we will have for reclaiming some of our agency, which I believe is one of the primary goals of media literacy. Therefore, in an age of ubiquitous smartphones and other communication technologies,

4 Microsoft is not always included, making it GAFA.

5 Adolf (2011) states 'mediatization research is about the inherent, the structural role *of the media system as a whole* for the way we organize and (re)produce our social relations' (154).

implementing the approach developed in this book can enable media literacy to identify and situate the complex interrelations, such as the sociocultural (normativity, power, language) and the technological, which contribute to the continual constitution of human subjects.

Media Literacy

The field of media literacy attempts to help educate people—especially the young—in order to become more skilled and aware users of media by primarily looking at 'four components: access, analysis, evaluation, and content creation' (Livingstone, 2004: 5). Sonia Livingstone describes how these components work together as a dynamic learning process. She outlines how learning to create content helps one better understand and analyze professionally produced content, and the 'skills in analysis and evaluation open the doors to new uses of the internet, expanding access, and so forth' (5).

Media literacy is vital to our everyday engagement with ICTs *because* of their everydayness (Kim, 2015; Onge, 2018). The field of media literacy attempts to shed light on how we use, and are potentially used by, media. With media technology everywhere in our lives, it becomes ordinary; commonplace. These technologies are part of the fabric of our existence, the ordinary environment within which we exist. For example, according to a recent Nielsen report, the average adult (over eighteen years of age) in the U.S. spends around 10 1/2 hours each day involved with some kind of media[6] (Nielsen, 2019: 3). We live in this mediatized environment and now, more than ever, it is important to have a comprehensive media literacy program that helps us better understand the effects of our media-rich environment. With this in mind, I explore the current approaches in media literacy.

Four Approaches to Media Literacy

Media literacy focuses on education in order to help people, especially youth, develop the skills to create (produce) with media technologies, as well as to critically analyze and evaluate media and media messages.

6 Nielsen (2019) defines media as 'TV, TV-connected devices, radio, computers, smartphones, and tablets' (3).

Rather than creating grand sociological theories, the focus of media literacy is mostly pragmatic, concerned with helping the *user* improve their 'ability to access, analyze, evaluate and create messages across a variety of contexts' (Livingstone, 2004: 3). Douglas Kellner and Jeff Share (2005; 2007) identify four specific approaches to media literacy: media arts education, the media literacy movement, a protectionist approach, and critical media literacy. While these approaches —which I will briefly describe next—can be perceived as individual approaches, in practice they can be combined with each other, which offsets some of the drawbacks inherent in each approach when used independently.

The approach of media arts education focuses specifically on helping teach students 'to value the aesthetic qualities of media and the arts while using their creativity for self-expression through creating art and media' (Kellner & Share, 2007: 7). Here, media is a skill to be learned. The approach of the media literacy movement has ties to print literacy and focuses on the competencies needed in order to be perceived as being 'literate'. Kellner and Share (2005) state that media literacy 'attempts to teach students to read, analyze, and decode media texts in a fashion parallel to the advancement of print literacy' (372). Both of these approaches tend to perceive media in a neutral manner.

However, the protectionist approach typically perceives media technologies in a more determining manner. Some philosophers and media theorists approach media and technology as something that people, especially children, should be protected from. There are valid concerns for a protectionist approach to focus on. Jean Twenge et al. (2018) find, 'Adolescents who spent more time on screen activities were significantly more likely to have high depressive symptoms or have at least one suicide-related outcome, and those who spent more time on nonscreen activities were less likely' (9). Educating people on possible dangers and negative effects of media falls within this protectionist approach.

The approach of critical media literacy has increased the scope of media literacy by adding the critical study of how messages contain underlying stereotypes, marginalization, and exploitation. Livingstone (2004) writes, 'to focus solely on questions of skill or ability neglects the textuality and technology that mediates communication. [...] there is not only skill involved but also an interpretive relationship with a complex, symbolically-encoded, technologically-mediated text' (8). This addition improves the ability of media literacy to explore and bring to light important issues that are embedded in media messages (Kellner & Share, 2005; Lemke, 2006). On the whole, critical media literacy continues to focus on the symbolic content of the message. While this is important, I believe that if the borders of media literacy can be expanded to include the influence of the actual technological medium as well as the broader context within which the media are used, then a space is created for media literacy to be even more inclusive and effective.

These four approaches will be discussed in more detail in Chapter 2. The approaches are representative of what is currently happening in media literacy. However, this is not meant to imply a comprehensive reflection of the entire field, which is constantly developing. I will endeavor to include a few of the voices that are encouraging the development of the field. I believe that media literacy can benefit by expanding, and the goal reflected by my research is to create an inclusive and situating approach to do just that.

Benefits of Expanding Media Literacy

Supporting the expansion of media literacy, David Morley (as cited in Krajina et al., 2014) says, 'Media questions are important, then, but they only seem to me to be really significant if they are set in a far wider frame, rather than focusing just on media technologies themselves' (684). One way to increase this frame is through domestication theory,[7] which parallels aspects of media literacy. Roger Silverstone (1994, 2006) developed domestication theory. Together with Morley, Silverstone began researching television 'in a broader framework' (Morley & Silverstone, 1990: 31) in order to understand 'the meanings of both texts and technologies, [...] as emergent properties of contextualized audience practices' (32). Domestication theory focused beyond simply the text and analyzed 'a whole range of overlapping, determinate and indeterminate social and cultural practices which together define—for particular

7 From domestication theory arose the concept of *double articulation*, which 'provides an *inclusive* move from the *semiology* to the *sociology* of media use' (Silverstone et al., 1991: 219). Here, the media object (the television set being the one primarily studied) is examined as a material object embedded within a broader (domestic) context.

viewers at particular times in particular places—their relationship to the medium' (Silverstone, 1989: 108).

While domestication theory has worked fairly well theoretically, it has been criticized for the challenge of empirically applying the theory (Hartmann, 2006). Even with the inclusion of the media-as-object, domestication theory still lacks a robust way of investigating the effects of the medium. While domestication concerns itself primarily with social theory, it focuses less on educating the individual as media literacy does. What is still missing is a concentrated approach to investigating the effects of a specific medium on individuals and societies.

While domestication theory includes attention to media objects such as television sets, it often does so in an anthropological or ethnographic approach (cf. Horst, 2012; Lesage, 2013) with an emphasis on the context within which the object resides. Morley (2009) states, 'we need a new paradigm for the discipline, which attends more closely to its material as well as its symbolic dimensions' (114).

The study of media and communications can also have an interdisciplinary focus. Shaun Moores (2005) explains, 'media have to be understood in their broad social and cultural contexts' (3). He suggests that it is a common misconception that 'media studies are simply about "studying media" in isolation' (3). Contextualizing ideas from Moores and domestication theory counters a more narrowly defined approach to media literacy, and lends support to enhancing media literacy through a situating approach.

Beyond media literacy are other media-related fields researching the impact of ICTs. Some of these are areas that focus on the technological features of media, but their approach can often be more functional. Examples of this are digital literacy (Koltay, 2011; Nichols & Stornaiuolo, 2019); data literacy (Koltay, 2015); and the digital detox movement (Bauwens et al., 2019; Rauch, 2018; Ugur & Koc, 2015).

Additionally, there are disciplines that can provide insights outside of media and communications, which focus on the relation between humans and technologies; these include postphenomenology, actor-network theory (ANT), and the general field of philosophy of technology. Also, scholars like Rosi Braidotti, Katherine Hayles, and Donna Haraway offer viewpoints from within philosophical posthumanism that focus more on the human side of human-technology relations. They focus on concepts such as de-centering the human and making sure marginalized groups are included in any definition of 'human'.

The Non-neutrality of Technological Relations

In order to investigate the influence of the technological medium I implement two approaches: a microperceptual and a macroperceptual. The microperceptual approach focuses on the embodied and embedded perspective of a human subject. The macroperceptual approach focuses on the broader sociocultural context that the particular human subject exists within. Don Ihde (1990) says, 'There is no microperception (sensory-bodily) without its location within a field of macroperception and no macroperception without its microperceptual foci' (29). Both the microperceptual and macroperceptual views are entangled and necessary in order to comprehend overall the effects of media and to fully become media literate.

While the four approaches in media literacy (cf. above) are effective in what they do, there are several concepts from other fields of study that can help create a more robust approach. In order to better understand technological objects, and our relations with them, the fields of postphenomenology and media ecology excel at analyzing technologies, covering the micro level of the embedded and embodied human subject, as well as the sociocultural macro level respectively. Both also stress relationality as a means to understand how we are constituted and transformed by the technological relations in our lives.

Technological Mediation as Relation: A Micro Approach

Relationality is one of the foundational concepts of the posthuman approach that I develop as well as being fundamental to postphenomenology's concept of technological mediation. Technological mediation describes how our technological relations are not neutral, but without succumbing to technological determinism. Jan Bergen and Peter-Paul Verbeek (2020) say, 'technological mediation aims to take technological artifacts seriously, recognizing the constitutive role they play in how we experience the world, act in it, and how we are constituted as (moral) subjects' (1). Postphenomenology specifically analyzes the technological mediation using the formula: I-technology-world. As humans, we are never standalone beings but always in relation; these relations are non-neutral,[8] contributing to the *co-constitution* of our selves, the specific technology, and the world (cf. Ihde, 1990; Rosenberger & Verbeek, 2015; Smith, 2015; Van Den Eede, 2016; Verbeek, 2005). The term 'constitution' is used to describe the specific coming together or unique arrangement that takes place in the process of these relations.

Postphenomenology describes four types of technological relations: embodied (where we perceive the world *through* the technology, such as with eyeglasses); hermeneutic (where we *read* the technology to better understand the world, such as with a thermometer); alterity (where we interact with the technology as a *quasi-other*, such as with an ATM machine); and background (which affect us but mostly go unnoticed, such as a heating and cooling system for one's house). Postphenomenology excels at investigating the microperceptions experienced by people when they interact with the technologies in their lives. Postphenomenology also acknowledges macroperceptions, what Ihde (1990) calls cultural hermeneutics. However, the sociocultural component is not as emphasized in practice as the microperception. This is where media ecology can contribute to our understanding of technology as an environment.

Media Environments: A Macro Approach

Media ecology is a macro approach that describes media environments. This means that the approach often investigates the broader effects that media has on cultures and societies. Marshall McLuhan (1994) is the person most often associated with media ecology. McLuhan consistently attempted to get society's attention focused on the hidden influence of the medium that helped shape the media's content. His famous aphorism, 'The medium is the message' (7) was one such attempt. He often explained it through the figure/ground analogy where one's usual focus is on the figure (in this case the media's content) and the ground

8 The term non-neutral is used to indicate that a relation is not completely determining but also is not completely neutral.

(in this case the medium) goes unnoticed. While McLuhan popularized the study of media, the field of media literacy rarely works closely with his ideas.[9] Instead, media literacy was 'developed through the work of Len Masterman in England and Barry Duncan in Canada' (as cited in Jolls & Wilson, 2014: 68). Duncan (2010) credited the work of McLuhan for inspiring him in his study of media but still held that the primary focus of media literacy was to understand and study representation.

In contrast, media ecologists focus on understanding media as environments and how those environments affect society. Harold Innis (2008) writes about the differences that various mediums afford. For instance, Innis discusses the biases of media relating to time and space. He describes heavy media such as clay or stone tablets as being more permanent (able to move through time) but too cumbersome to move very well through space. Papyrus or radio is just the opposite; easy to move across space, but less permanent to move very far through time. This bias affects the type of content that can be 'carried' by the medium. For example, Innis criticizes radio as a medium that 'accentuated the importance of the ephemeral and of the superficial' (82). So, while it is important to analyze the content of media as critical media literacy does, it is also fruitful to analyze the medium itself.

Statements such as the above from Innis have contributed to the criticism that media ecology is technologically deterministic, with their focus on how media technologies influence individual and social behavior. However, before McLuhan popularized looking at the medium, media studies primarily focused on the content of media messages, heavily influenced by semiotics. As most people in media studies were already focused on the content, McLuhan worked to shed light on what was difficult to perceive, which he did by using dramatic and sweeping statements such as the already cited 'the medium is the message', or 'in all media the user is the content' (as cited in McLuhan & Zingrone, 1997: 266).

Most media ecologists have simply been trying to include the influence of the medium in the discussion and do not claim that the medium is all determining, only that it is not neutral. Lance Strate (2017: 34) states this quite clearly:

9 Ivan Kalmar (2005) suggests, 'if McLuhan's name no longer rings as it once did, it is because history has paid his ideas the compliment of making them commonplace' (227).

> The term *technological determinism*, [...] has been linked to the field of media ecology. For the most part, it is a label applied by critics, rather than a term used, let alone embraced, within the field. As there is no doctrine of technological determinism, or arguments that explicitly state such a position within our field, its use amounts to a straw man[10] argument used to dismiss media ecological scholarship, rather than subject it to serious consideration.

Which Human Subject?

While technological relations bring some agency to the technological object side of the human-technology relation, Tamar Sharon (2014) points out that disciplines such as postphenomenology focus more on 'breathing life into objects [...] than delving into the implications of having breathed life out of subjects' (9). Sharon proposes that we take a closer look at what is going on with the subject. As we focus on the effects of media on the subject, it is important to identify which human subject is being discussed. I am not referring to the ideal Enlightenment subject: autonomous and exceptional in the world, reflecting a subject-object duality. Instead, the subject is always-in-relation and is continually being constituted through a complex interrelated network of relations, what I refer to as a posthuman subject.

Rather than a *humanist* way of understanding the subject, I employ a *post-humanist* approach, using philosophical posthumanism, which is quite different from *trans*humanism. While transhumanism does focus on the entanglement of technology and the human, it does so from an 'ultra-humanist' (Onishi, 2011: 103) approach. The two fields use the term *posthuman* in two very different ways. Transhumanists use the word to describe an evolutionary shift for the human that they foresee occurring—primarily through technological means—into vastly more intelligent and efficient beings. Max More (2013) states that by 'thoughtfully, carefully, and yet boldly applying technology to ourselves, we can become something no longer accurately described as human—we can become posthuman. Becoming posthuman means exceeding the limitations that define the less desirable aspects of the "human condition"' (4).

10 Philosophical *strawmen* arguments are arguments where the person criticizing a concept first defines the concept without providing all of the context or nuances, allowing them to easily identify flaws.

Philosophical posthumanists, however, use the term posthuman as a way to distance themselves from the traditional idea of the human, based primarily on Enlightenment and modern ideas of the autonomous, standalone, and exceptional human individual. In this case, posthuman refers to a post-humanist, post-anthropocentric, and post-dualist approach to understanding the human (Ferrando, 2019). Posthumanism stresses that the subject is constituted through its relations, what Karen Barad (2007) calls *intra-action*, and will be explored more deeply in Chapter 4. The approach I develop is centered on the human subject as understood by philosophical posthumanism.

Situating Media Literacy with Intrasubjective Mediation

How can we keep everything straight? On the one hand, it is important to focus on specific technologies and how they affect the individual. On the other hand, it is important to focus on how the broader sociocultural relations—such as power, normativity, or language—affect us. There are technological and sociocultural environments all entangled and all contributing to our own constitution. Maren Hartmann (2006) points out the question that has not yet been solved: 'how to adequately research the complexity of the combination of media content and media context to paint a picture of the overall whole' (89).

One important word used throughout this book is 'situating'. The term 'situate' means, 'To put (something) in a (specified) context; to describe the circumstances surrounding (something)' (OED online, 4th definition). The approach developed is precisely dedicated to facilitating this. It creates a simple structure that can help guide the investigation into the complex interrelated processes that affect our relations with media.

The following research questions helped guide my understanding of the transforming impact of ICT technologies in our lives and also to inform the creation of the new approach developed. My research questions are as follows:

1. How can we specifically analyze and understand the interrelating micro and macro effects of media technologies on human subjects? [Chapters 3 and 4]

2. How do media relations interrelate with other relations—such as socio-cultural, time and space, and mind and body—in their constitution of the human subject? [Chapter 5]
3. How can an instrument be developed in order to tether our investigations, keeping us grounded to an overarching inclusive framework while we delve deeply into the specific relations that contribute to our constitution and enhance media literacy? [Chapters 5 and 6]

In order to help guide an investigation into the various relations, the approach developed leverages the concept of *intrasubjective mediation*, which is the idea that we are—and continue to be—mediated by the constituting aspects of all of our relations. The approach investigates both the current and continuing impact from relations, which in the case of media technology will help us to become more media literate by understanding the broader effects of media technologies. The framework serves to create a situating cartography,[11] which captures the main interrelating groups of relations that contribute to the constitution of the human subject. This supports Shaun Moores' (2016) call for a non-media-centric media literacy. By focusing on one aspect of media literacy, we can easily lose sight of others. By creating a situating instrument, we can tether our approach to the broader, encompassing framework while allowing our focus to narrow momentarily into each specific constituting relation.

Research Significance and Design

While the ubiquitous smartphone is likely the most common ICT that comes to mind for those in the Western globalized world, there are plenty of other technological devices (such as ebook readers and tablets), often networked, which make up the tapestry of our world today. Looking around at people, especially when they are in a forced pause—waiting for a doctor's visit, for a train, etc. (see Fig. 1.1)—often they are looking down at some technology rather than looking around and engaging with their immediate environment. They are immersed in technology

11 I use the term cartography as a facilitator of exploration rather than as a prescriptive map.

that virtually transports them elsewhere. Consider the following insight from Yoni Van Den Eede et al. (2017b: xxv):

> With the onset of mobile communication technology, media are no longer 'over there'; they are moving toward us, into us. Looking at the history of media, one perceives almost the evolution of an organism becoming more and more complex, diverse, and ubiquitous.

This technology can be a book, an ebook, smartphone, game console, or any of the other technologies that permeate our contemporary world. It is easy to become so distracted by the constant presence of technology in our lives that we do not recognize how many of our actions are being mediated in some way by these technologies. Instead, we tend to focus on posting and sharing, liking and commenting; simply living our mediated lives. The challenge for media literacy in this ubiquity and transparency is the fact that these mediating technologies are not registering in our awareness.

Use of Language

Though it is rather obvious to state that language[12] plays a key role in communication throughout this book, I want to take a moment to acknowledge its importance. Especially as I use words like 'human' in new ways (for instance the difference between what is referred to the human by humanists, transhumanists, or posthumanists). The specific words I use greatly affect the success, or lack thereof, of the ability to transmit ideas to the reader. Each word is a choice that has both benefits and limitations. Words are limited in their ability to faithfully represent the intended meaning behind them. In addition, words cut and separate; they are often thought of as individual carriers of meaning. Words also have historical use and cultural meanings attached. Different groups of people embody different ways of viewing the world and its relations, which affects a reader's understanding of particular words. An example of the challenge of using words is trying to describe an interconnected and interrelated *individual* when the word 'individual' has been used to

12 Semiotics, the study of words and language—sign and signifier—is mostly outside the scope of this book. However, it is quite important, so there is a place for it within the framework/instrument I develop.

imply autonomy and separation. Kenneth Gergen (2009: xxvii) describes this issue quite well:

> The very idea of individual persons is a byproduct of relational process. But how can I describe this process without using a language that inherently divides the world into bounded entities? To be more specific, by relying on common conventions of writing, I will invariably rely on nouns and pronouns, both of which designate bounded or identifiable units. The very phrase, 'I rely on you....' already defines me as separate from you. [...] Try as I may to create a sense of process that precedes the construction of entities, the conventions of language resist. They virtually insist that separate entities exist prior to relationship.

In this book I constantly struggle with words that divide and separate while I attempt to use them in ways that gather and combine. For instance, I often use the term 'subject' and refer to technological 'objects', but rather than meaning them in a dualist Cartesian split, I mean them to be constituted in relation to each other and not as standalone. Additionally, instead of using 'myself' or 'ourselves' I separate the terms from each other in order to highlight the self-subject that I am focusing on. My goal is to highlight, but not separate in any Cartesian sense.

I have also chosen to use the present tense when citing someone. I want to stress a current engagement with the concepts and words from people, even if those people are no longer living. My intention is to keep my philosophical approach as contemporary as possible, even when engaging with older philosophical ideas.

The words 'media' and 'medium' can also benefit from further explanation. While media is plural for medium, in today's contemporary Western world it is often used to refer to mass media, as in 'the media'. However, it is also used to refer to communication devices, as in technological media. For this book I will specifically use the term medium (or mediums for plural) to refer to the media technology that performs media content—examples being television, newspapers, and smartphones. I will use the term 'media' as a more general term and one primarily directed at content (unless used as 'media literacy').

I recognize that the term *posthuman* is one that can challenge some readers and may not be readily understood. However, I view this as beneficial since the comfort and ease which many find using the word *human* is exactly what the posthuman approach is trying to undermine.

By using *posthuman* I hope to bring the reader's attention to figuring out exactly what is meant. This questioning of human or posthuman is one of the main goals of the approach described in this book.

And finally, is the *approach* described best called an approach, a method, a cartography, a cartographic method, a framework, or an instrument? Each word carries the sediment of historical use and each reader will interpret these words through their own understanding. My goal is to make it as accessible as possible without either putting on academic airs or making it too specific. Deleuze's *cartography* is appropriate, and calling it a *posthuman cartography* would be fine for people in the field of posthumanism. However, there are different ways of using the term 'cartography'. One way is a prescriptive and controlled manner. This is the typical 'map', with lines of demarcation and separation, cutting a representation of reality into categories of differentiation. This is *not* the way I am using the term. Therefore, I ultimately decided to call it a 'posthuman approach' to stress its interrelational focus as well as to connect it with the various 'approaches' used in media literacy.

Designing Interdisciplinary Research and a Transdisciplinary Solution

My research is an interdisciplinary exploration of media technologies and how our relation with media contributes to the constitution of our subjectivity. Marilyn Stember (1991) defines *interdisciplinary* as bringing 'interdependent parts of knowledge into harmonious relationships through strategies such as relating part and whole or the particular and the general' (4). While the research I conducted has been interdisciplinary, the solution of the posthuman approach can be considered *transdisciplinary*. Wendy Austin et al. (2008) describes how transdisciplinary solutions can often emerge spontaneously from interdisciplinary research 'when discipline-transcending concepts, terminology, and methods evolve to create a higher level framework' (557). This reflects the process I experienced in doing this research.

The need for the original interdisciplinarity arose from my own research on museum selfies (Lewis, 2017); from this work, I realized the limitation of using only postphenomenology to investigate how my museum experience was being affected by the mediating technology that I was using. I felt that postphenomenology was not completely able to capture the complexity of constituting relations that I was experiencing, and there were more relations affecting my experience than the technological. This limitation led to more deeply exploring the concept of the human subject in its involvement with technologies than what postphenomenology provided. I discovered that by investigating several fields of inquiry, there were useful insights from each field for the overall development of my culminating approach. The fields I investigated, all being interdisciplinary themselves, were: postphenomenology, philosophical posthumanism, complexity, media literacy, and media ecology. However, as Van Den Eede (2016: 103) notes,

> Notwithstanding much feverish talk about inter- and multi-disciplinarity, real and substantial dealings between disciplines remain hard to come by. Paradoxically, that even counts for disciplines that are in themselves eclectic and composed of elements hailing from many different domains.

My initial research question of how technology affects the human subject steered me down several different paths, finally depositing me, in a circular fashion, back to my starting point. In fact, it was my investigation as to what was happening to me while taking a museum selfie that drove me to realize that I needed a new approach that did not seem to exist. An approach that would help me understand all of the influencing relations that were acting upon one another during my experience taking museum selfies.

In order to manage the expectation of the reader, it is important to note that my research does not reflect either a typical manuscript within continental philosophy or a typical book in media and communications studies. For example, many books in continental philosophy focus on a deep analysis of the writings of a specific philosopher, and in media and communications studies, at least where I was conducting my research in Brussels, it is most common to do an empirical study. Instead, my goal is to engage contemporarily with a variety of philosophers and philosophical approaches. Using the words of other philosophers and researchers honors the fact that they wrote the words and that the words spoke to me, but I take responsibility for using them for my own context and in my own way. Through this process I create an approach that is pragmatic and helpful in learning to understand the daily effects that media technologies have on us as human subjects.

The Layout of the Chapters

This book is divided into two parts. In Part I—Chapters 2 through 4—I develop the background concepts drawing upon media literacy, postphenomenology, media ecology, and philosophical posthumanism. However, the book does not need to be read by starting at the beginning. Some readers may want to skip the initial foundational chapters and simply get right to Part II—Chapters 5 and 6—where I develop the posthuman approach, both the overarching general frame, as well as a pragmatic instrument that shows how to implement the concepts into media literacy. Instructors who would like to use the approach without specifically framing it within media literacy can focus on Chapters 3 through 6. One option that I have used with university students is an hour lecture for each of the Chapters 3 through 6. This builds the foundation for then having the students use their specific technological relation in order to experientially engage with the instrument described in Chapter 6.

Specifically, Chapter 2 explores the various aspects of media literacy, from the five core concepts (cf. Fig. 2.1), to the four aspects outlined by Kellner and Share (2005, 2007). Additionally, I look to domestication theory, as first identified by Silverstone (2006; see also Haddon, 2007; Silverstone & Haddon, 1996), which leads to the idea of double and triple articulation of media technologies (Courtois et al., 2013; Livingstone, 2007). The concept of triple articulation emphasizes the content of the media, the medium itself, and the context that the media is used in. This facilitates the move for media literacy to go beyond the traditional four approaches and connects to the next chapter.

In Chapter 3, postphenomenology and media ecology emphasize analyzing the technological relations on micro and macro levels. I first investigate postphenomenology, which focuses on human-technology relations. This creates the foundational building block of my approach: the embodied relation. I explore various concepts that are articulated in postphenomenology, such as the non-neutrality of technology, multistability, sedimentation, and technological mediation as constitutive.

Secondly, I investigate media ecology, where the focus is specifically on the medium. I explore the idea of media as environments within which cultures can grow. Neil Postman (1970) states that media ecology studies information environments in order to 'understand how technologies and techniques of communication control the form, quantity, speed, distribution, and direction of information; and how, in turn, such information configurations or biases affect people's perceptions, values, and attitudes' (186). However, if media literacy is often too focused on the content, then media ecology can be accused of being too often focused on the medium, to the detriment of other influencing factors. There should be a balance and a manner to include all of the influencing relations; it is this gap that I intend to eventually fill through the approach developed.

In Chapter 4, the investigation focuses on the *subject* that is being constituted through the technological relations described in chapter three. I use philosophical posthumanism, as opposed to a humanist or transhumanist approach, to situate the post-humanist subject within a non-anthropocentric and non-dualist frame. Posthumanism also approaches the human subject as complex and always changing. I investigate the concept of complexity that is used in posthumanism—and occasionally used in media ecology—and I demonstrate how this term is fundamentally different from a mechanistic or causal approach to understanding the world.

With the background and fundamental concepts having been firmly established in the first four Chapters, the new framework is presented in Chapter 5. This framework allows for a clearer understanding of all of the relating and interrelating effects of media on the human subject, situating not only the technological and cultural, but the relations of time and space, as well as mind and body. I bring all the main concepts together in order to offer a comprehensive framework for situating media literacy.

In Chapter 6, I demonstrate how the framework can be employed by applying it to analyze a museum selfie. This leads to the development of a generic instrument for self-inquiry (or one could say an autoethnographic inquiry) into moments of media use, which can be used for enhancing media literacy. As previously mentioned, it was in trying to understand the constituting effect of museum selfies that I realized I needed a more inclusive approach in the beginning of my research. Within Chapter 6, the complex interrelationality of all of the contributing factors that occur while taking a museum selfie is demonstrated. The museum selfie is a contemporary phenomenon that captures many issues investigated in this research. I conclude by creating an exercise that can be used for teaching media literacy. This should be considered a starting point for further exploration into how this posthuman approach might be implemented for the purpose of media literacy education.

Concluding Thoughts

At the convergence of the fourth industrial revolution (Schwab, 2017) and the sixth mass extinction (Cafaro, 2015), we find our selves at a crossroads. Being media literate is but one fundamental aspect of life in a time of complex planetary existence. Being able to situate whatever we study is critical in order to maintain perspective and not fall prey to any one specific discipline or way of thinking. While I have attempted to be broad in scope for understanding media, media literacy, and communications, there are important ways of using media literacy that I only examine in a cursory manner, since a more comprehensive study is beyond the focus of a single book. Language is one such area. Signs and their ability (and inability) to transfer information, specifically looking into encoding and decoding, is a large area of research already established within media and communications; however, it is beyond the scope of this book. Ethics and normativity, both immensely important, are also only lightly touched upon because, in my opinion, the first important step before being able to ethically or morally judge is to have awareness of the situation. This book describes an approach that can help develop the awareness necessary that can then allow us to critically judge.

John Culkin (1967) concisely sums up the focus of this book with the words, 'We shape our tools and thereafter they shape us' (70). I investigate the transformative effects of the tools we use daily in our lives, specifically ICTs. The paradigmatic example of ICTs that I will often use throughout is the smartphone. These technologies permeate our existence, especially in the Western world. 'It takes less and less deliberate action on our part to engage with media or ICTs. No longer do we need to place ourselves behind a computer to go online; we carry "the online" constantly in our pockets or on our wrists' (Van Den Eede et al., 2017b: xvii). For many of the people in the Western world, everyday life is completely entangled with media technologies, so much so that these technologies are no longer in the forefront of our attention; they have faded into the background.

It is vital that media literacy steps in and plays a role in helping us become aware of the everyday media technologies in our lives and the influences they have upon our selves and society (cf. Kim, 2015; McLuhan, 1994; Silverstone 1994; Strate, 2017). As Catherine Adams and Terrie Lynn Thompson (2016) say, it is about understanding the digital and 'making its effects and affects visible' (2). In order to have a more comprehensive understanding of media literacy, we need a more complete understanding of how human subjects are constituted through all of their relations. We need to develop a right view, an orientation that allows us to better situate, and therefore more fully understand, our technological relations in order for us to make better decisions, to judge what and how to engage with the ubiquitous technologies in our everyday lives. The posthuman approach I have developed accomplishes this by situating the complex interrelating and constituting relations of human subjects and media technologies.

PART I

Interdisciplinary Concepts and their Location

2

Contextualizing Media Literacy in Communications and Education

> Literacy, meaning alphabetic literacy, is no longer the keynote of Western culture. That is to say that capital-L Literacy is obsolete, having been done in when we killed the reading public, the ground of literacy. As with the Hydra (once her head was lopped off, new heads sprang up in its place), so with Literacy: now we see dozens, nay entire litters of (small-'l') little literacies springing up spontaneously here and there with evident abandon. (McLuhan, 2009: 9)

It seems that everywhere we look in the modern Western world we see information and communication technologies being used, mediating our lives every day. We have become so accustomed to living with these extraordinary technologies that they have been rendered ordinary. New devices and technologies, after a brief though sometimes painful learning curve, begin to disappear from the center of our attention as we navigate the world *through* them. While media literacy focuses on educating people in order for them to become more aware and adept at consuming, using, and creating media content for specific outcomes (Aufderheide, 1993), it primarily attends to the content of the messages—both intended and unintended—especially concerning how human subjects are represented (Jolls & Wilson, 2014).

This chapter situates media literacy within the broader fields of communications and education. I investigate current ways of defining media literacy and call for an expansion of media literacy in order to include the medium and the context within which the messages are enacted. While more than a cursory overview of media literacy, this chapter will not exhaustively explore the field in its entirety. Rather, I give an overview of some of the current and historic aspects of media literacy and point out important areas that it often does not include. This provides a setting to bring in a framework and instrument of transdisciplinary concepts that can be used to enhance the field.

Focusing on the medium is a first step in broadening the scope of media literacy to include a broader context. While media literacy has focused mainly on media skills and representation (Jolls & Wilson, 2014; Masterman, 1989), this has left the study of the effects of the medium to outside fields such as medium theory (Meyrowitz, 1994; Qvortrup, 2006); mediatization (Adolf, 2011; Hjarvard, 2013, 2014; Lundby, 2014); media ecology (Anton, 2006, 2016; Logan, 2011; McLuhan, 1994; Postman, 1974, 2000; Strate, 2017; Van Den Eede, 2012, 2016); and even the study of the biography of things (Kopytoff, 1988; Lesage, 2013).

The next step after including the medium is to further expand media literacy to include the context within which we engage with media. I use the example of domestication theory in order to do so. By including the environment, the complexity of our media relations become more apparent, making the case for expanding our approach to media literacy to include, as Shaun Moores (2016) says, a non-media-centric media literacy. My goal is to describe the current field of media literacy, situating it at the intersection of communications and education. I make the case that expanding the focus beyond content to include the effects of the medium and context can help improve our understanding of the broader effects of media—both the drawbacks and benefits.

Communication Beyond the Transmission Model

Media literacy is a combination of media (mostly studied within the field of communications) and literacy (mostly studied within the field of education). Before delving into the literacy aspect, I explain some of the background and different approaches in the field of communications. For much of the second half of the twentieth century, the dominant way of understanding communication was through the *transmission* model, where 'communication is a process of sending and receiving messages or transferring information from one mind to another' (Craig, 1999: 125). Claude Shannon (1948) and Shannon and Warren Weaver (1964) developed a mathematical model in order to understand communication, reducing a complex process down into a simple and easily graspable model, which 'is widely accepted as one of the main seeds out of which Communication Studies has grown. It is a clear example of the process school, seeing communication as the transmission of messages' (Fiske, 1990: 6). The transmission model is the basis of information theory and has been a building block for a general understanding of the flow of information and communication.

The transmission model (see Fig. 2.1) consists of the producer of the message (information source); the transmitter that encodes the message; the conduit or channel through which the message is sent; the receiver that decodes the message; and the destination where the message arrives. In the process, there is also *noise,* which interferes with the clarity of the message. A common example of this model is a telephone call. The person initiating the call is the information source; their phone encodes the message; the telephone line or wireless network is the conduit; the person's phone receiving the call is the receiver that decodes the message; and the destination is the person who hears the message. The noise is any interference: static on the line or network, noises in the background, etc.

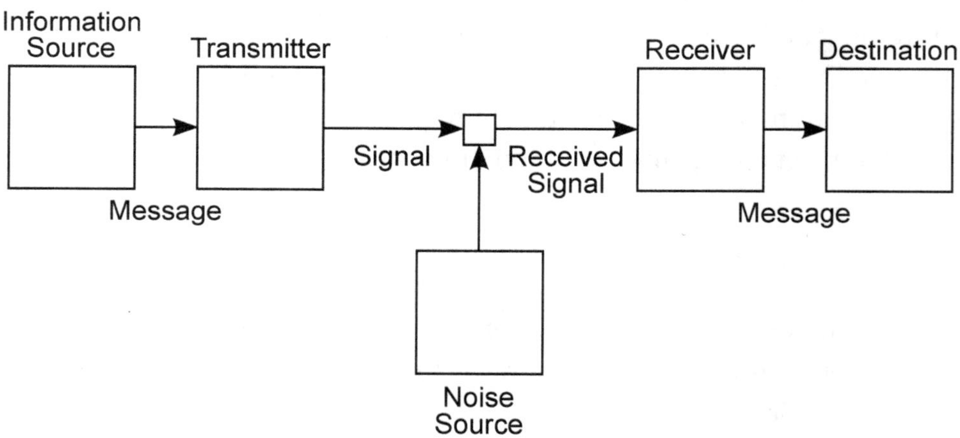

Fig. 2.1 *Transmission model of communication.* Adapted from Shannon & Weaver (1964: 34). Image by Wanderingstan (2007).

While the transmission model is still frequently used in information and computer sciences, it has drawn criticism from social sciences (Carey, 2008; Deetz, 1994; Pearce, 1989) as well as from media ecology for being too reductive and for approaching communication as something that occurs between autonomous—already fully established—entities rather than between relational beings. Robert Craig (1999) states that there has been much discussion around need and desire for the transmission model being 'supplemented, if not entirely supplanted, by a model that conceptualizes communication as a constitutive process that produces and reproduces shared meaning' (125). In other words, there is more to communication theory than a one-way transmission of a message from one source to another. There is shared meaning-making occurring. Craig advocates for the creation of a meta-model (called the constitutive model) that allows a space for many different models to exist, each being useful for a particular purpose (127).

James Carey (2008) also argues against the transmission model, saying that it is important to retain the connection to community and culture. He advocates for more of a ritual or cultural view of communication. Stuart Adam (2008) describes Carey's approach as portraying a more 'developed understanding of communication [involving] both a ritual and a transmission view' (xviii), both of which are needed for a modern society to exist. Antonio López (2014: 47–48) builds upon Carey's view (with somewhat more criticism) and cautions against the transmission model:

> In terms of media literacy, using mechanistic models of cognition and communication will reinforce the paradigm of industrialism, remaining stuck in a system of 'bad ideas'; the essential bad idea being the assumption that communication is a matter of autonomous beings transporting ideas between each other as messages, and that such communication is disembodied from the thinking system that comprises our cultural patterns and embeddedness within living systems.

López continues by describing an ecological intelligence where a person is 'not simply an autonomous self but is part of an interconnected thinking system that not only includes socially constructed knowledge but knowledge that is co-produced with the living environment' (48). This moves from an approach where people construct their own knowledge of the world to an approach that understands the co-constitution that occurs during communication.

Marshall McLuhan (as cited in Eric McLuhan, 2008) calls Shannon and Weaver's communication model a theory of transportation, not communication. He defines communication as something that transforms or changes the recipient. Without this transformation, it is not communication. Marshall McLuhan, as his son Eric McLuhan (2008: 30–31) summarizes, believes that:

> Communication means change. If something is communicated the recipient has changed in some manner or degree. Our 'common sense' idea of communication is merely one of transporting messages from point to point. Shannon and Weaver laid the foundation of all Western 'theories of communication' with their model. [...] But this only is a transportation theory, not a theory of communication. They are concerned merely with getting a bundle of goodies from one place to another, while keeping dreaded Noise to a minimum.

The constitutive model of communication, where the action of communication changes the recipient, as well as the person communicating, is how I conceive of communication in this book. The act of communication is a relational act that co-constitutes (transforms) the people involved in the communication. This co-constituting relationality is an integral concept in the development of the posthuman developed in this book.

Media Literacy Overview

The term 'literacy' in media literacy reflects the underlying echo of reading or print literacy. However, media literacy focuses on a person's competence and knowledge of media. And, with the swift speed of change in current media trends, it is becoming more and more difficult to keep abreast of the many new developments. As Lev Manovich (2013) points out, the world 'is now defined not by heavy industrial machines that change infrequently, but by software that is always in flux' (1–2). The need for media literacy has never been so important. I begin by discussing the importance of education and its impact on agency, after which I offer several definitions of media literacy from key organizations. Then, the core concepts and competencies of media literacy are discussed, concluding with an overview of the approaches currently found in media literacy.

Education, Literacy, and Agency

One of media literacy's core aspects is education (e.g., Alvermann et al., 2018; Hobbs & Jensen, 2009; Kellner & Share, 2019; Livingstone & Van der Graaf, 2008; Potter, 2018; and the journal *Teaching Media Quarterly*). This focus on education pragmatically elevates the importance of the user and helps to ground the theoretical concepts concerning media. While *literacy* is not a neutral term and comes with its own contradictions (Luke, 1989; Livingstone, 2004), it also stresses the focus on the user of media, whether as one whom consumes, produces, or simply uses it. This general educational aspect is, as John Dewey (1997) posits, critical for a healthy democracy. McLuhan (1969) says, somewhat hyperbolically, 'If we understand the revolutionary transformations caused by new media, we can anticipate and control them; but if we continue in our self-induced subliminal trance, we will be their slaves' (n.p.).

Media literacy's focus on education is key for developing awareness and thus agency. Since this educational component is not as heavily stressed in the other fields of inquiry that I analyze (specifically postphenomenology and philosophical posthumanism), I draw inspiration from media literacy in order to create an approach that is pragmatic and useful as an instrument for education.

The term *literacy* in education has its own socio-cultural baggage and should not be thought of as a neutral term. Carmen Luke (1989) points out that the basis of public schooling standardized 'what and how all children should be taught; it would provide all children with basic literacy skills and simultaneously facilitate the mass transmission of centrally selected and controlled knowledge' (5). Sonia Livingstone (2004) summarizes Luke's (1989) points by saying, literacy 'masks a complex history of contestation over the power and authority to access, interpret, and produce printed texts' (4). In other words, who gets to define and judge the qualities and knowledges that equate with literacy? And, as the primary medium of print gives way to a diversity of media, Jay Lemke (2006) suggests, 'We need a broader definition of literacy itself, one that includes all literate practices, regardless of medium' (3).

At the start of the chapter, I referred to a quote by Eric McLuhan (2009) which points out that there are many variations of literacy. Two variations that are close to (and can be considered part of) media literacy are *digital literacy* (Buckingham, 2006; Gilster, 1997; Van Dijk & Van Deursen, 2014), and *social media literacy* (Ahn, 2013; Burnett & Merchant, 2011; Livingstone, 2014; Vanwynsberghe, 2014). Livingstone (2004: 5) states,

> [P]eople now engage with a media environment which integrates print, audiovisual, telephony, and computer media. Hence, we need a conceptual framework that spans these media. Literacy seems to do the work required here: It is pan-media in that it covers the interpretation of all complex, mediated symbolic texts broadcast or published on electronic communications networks; at the same time.

Some of the most recent literacies are artificial intelligence literacy (or related literacies such as those concerning machine learning or neural networks) and algorithmic literacy. Petar Jandrić (2019) makes the case for expanding critical media literacy to encompass artificial intelligence (AI) and the postdigital context. Jussi Okkonen and Sirkku Kotilainen (2019) describe the potential effects that AI has on youth (and their parents) and the implications this has for media literacy. Jialei Jiang and Matthew Vetter (2020) make the case for becoming more literate concerning the effects of algorithms, specifically analyzing algorithmic writing bots on Wikipedia. These postdigital challenges point to future directions that are emerging in media literacy.

Education can increase a person's awareness, which in turn facilitates the ability for them to regain agency. An entire issue of the *Journal of Media Literacy* (Andersen & Arcus, 2017) is devoted to the concept of agency in media literacy. In it, Neil Andersen and Carol Arcus write, 'Agency is knowledge in action. In media literacy, agency is the exercising of awareness through critical thinking skills to effect change personally, locally and/or globally' (3). While agency of technology is discussed in more depth in Chapter 3, it is important in media literacy to understand that there is a shared agency as we interact with media, and by increasing our awareness (through education) we can increase our own agency. Tsjalling Swierstra and Katinka Waelbers (2012) say, 'Technologies affect our actions not just by altering the course of action (like billiard balls act upon each other) but by mediating *our reasons* or motives to act in a particular way' (160).

In support of media users having agency, Douglas Kellner and Jeff Share (2007) focus on audience theory to point out 'the moment of reception [is] a contested terrain of cultural struggle where critical thinking skills offer potential for the audience to negotiate different readings and openly struggle with dominant discourses' (13). Additionally, McLuhan scholar Robert Logan (2013) explains McLuhan's aphorism—the user is the content—means that 'each reader or viewer brings his or her own experience and understanding to a medium and transforms the content according to his or her own need and abilities' (76). Logan further explains, 'information does not have an intrinsic meaning independent of the user' (77). Media literacy plays a key role in helping educate people with regards to their media-rich lives, facilitating their awareness and thus increasing their own agency.

Defining Media Literacy

Bringing media and literacy together has created its own field of study. However, moving from the single-medium of print to the plurality of media-types and technologies makes it difficult to reduce *media literacy* to a single description. As Tibor Koltay (2011) states, 'media literacy is an umbrella concept. It is characterized by a diversity of perspectives and a multitude of definitions' (212).

It is Len Masterman's (1989, 2010) focus on representation that helps media literacy emerge from media studies. Masterman, from the United Kingdom, and Barry Duncan (2010), from Canada are often considered the founders of media literacy (Jolls & Wilson, 2014). According to Masterman (1989), 'The central unifying concept of Media Education is that of representation. The media mediate. They do not reflect but re-present the world. The media [...] are symbolic sign systems that must be decoded' (see Principle 2). This approach emphasizes the encoding and decoding of media representations and reflects the content-focused and transportation approach that has been dominant in media literacy.

As the U.S.-based National Association for Media Literacy (NAMLE) states, 'Media literacy is the ability to encode and decode the symbols transmitted via media and the ability to synthesize, analyze and produce mediated messages' (NAMLE, 2019). This definition is rooted in how the transmission concept of communication re-presents the sociocultural world. Masterman (2010: 5) differentiates content from representation:

> What we were actually studying was television and not its different subject contents. That is, we were not actually studying sport or music or news or documentary. We were studying representations of these things. We were studying the ways in which these subjects were being represented and symbolized and packaged by the medium.

While Masterman (1989) is making the case against a simple content-centered approach, the conceptual framework he advocates for is still directed at reading and analyzing (decoding) media content and does not, for example, include the influence of the specific technological medium.

Another definition that comes from the Center for Media Literacy (CML) (2019) in the U.S., builds upon Masterman's (1980, 1989) concepts and contributes a more extended definition of media literacy, stating that it provides,

> [A] framework to access, analyze, evaluate, create and participate with messages in a variety of forms—from print to video to the Internet. Media literacy builds an understanding of the role of media in society as well as essential skills of inquiry and self-expression necessary for citizens of a democracy. (2nd expanded definition)

This definition covers many of the standard concepts and approaches (cf. below) used by many organizations involved with media literacy—from government agencies to educational organizations. Arguably, more important than defining media literacy is how organizations have put into practice the development and implementation of competencies, core concepts, and questions.

Competencies, Concepts, and Questions

Several people and organizations have created lists of competencies in order to better articulate how a person might judge their own media literacy. This moves media literacy from being defined to being implemented, focusing on the abilities of a media literate person. Renee Hobbs[1] (2010: 19) describes five essential competencies of digital and media literacy as:

---

1 Founder and director of the Media Education Lab: https://mediaeducationlab.com/

1. Access: Finding and using media and technology tools skillfully and sharing appropriate and relevant information with others.
2. Analyze & Evaluate: Comprehending messages and using critical thinking to analyze message quality, veracity, credibility, and point of view, while considering potential effects or consequences of messages.
3. Create: Composing or generating content using creativity and confidence in self-expression, with awareness of purpose, audience, and composition techniques
4. Reflect: Applying social responsibility and ethical principles to one's own identity and lived experience, communication behavior and conduct.
5. Act: Working individually and collaboratively to share knowledge and solve problems in the family, the workplace and the community, and participating as a member of a community at local, regional, national and international levels.

Similarly, Ben Bachmair and Cary Bazalgette (2007: 84) describe the claim from the European Charter for Media Literacy that a media literate person should be able to:

- Use media technologies effectively to access, store, retrieve and share content to meet their individual and community needs and interests;
- Gain access to, and make informed choices about, a wide range of media forms and content from different cultural and institutional sources;
- Understand how and why media content is produced;
- Analyze critically the techniques, languages and conventions used by the media, and the messages they convey;
- Use media creatively to express and communicate ideas, information and opinions;
- Identify, and avoid or challenge, media content and services that may be unsolicited, offensive or harmful;

- Make effective use of media in the exercise of their democratic rights and civic responsibilities.

These core competencies are additionally reflected in the CML's handout (see Fig. 2.2), which is an effective example of bringing the concepts for media literacy into one useful document. In addition to the five core concepts, CML also has created questions for students to ask themselves since the core concepts can be somewhat theoretical. The questions can help guide students in their investigations into specific media. The document also helpfully differentiates between consumers and producers of media.

The development of media literacy questions has also been implemented by organizations such as the Association of Media Literacy (AML) in Canada and NAMLE (namle.net) in the U.S. In addition to the development of various definitions, competencies, and concepts—all of which help to pragmatically implement media literacy skills—there have also been different approaches to media literacy identified. These approaches are a helpful way of narrowing the 'umbrella concept' (Koltay, 2011) of media literacy.

Four Approaches

Kellner and Share (2005, 2007) identify four differing approaches to media literacy. These different models focus on developing skills for the media literate person. They articulate the four approaches as: media arts-based, a media literacy movement, protectionist, and critical media literacy.

Media Arts-Based

In a *media arts-based* approach to media literacy, the focus is on developing the ability and skills to use new forms of media, often for creative self-expression. The primary focus is on the individual's ability to learn the skills in order to help find and creatively express their own voice through the media (Kellner & Share, 2007). While this contributes towards the literacy and empowerment of the individual, the approach tends to view the media in an instrumental or neutral manner—as a tool

MediaLit KIT™

CML's FIVE KEY QUESTIONS AND CORE CONCEPTS (Q/TIPS) FOR CONSUMERS AND PRODUCERS

Media Deconstruction/Construction Framework

#	Key Words	Deconstruction: CML's 5 Key Questions (Consumer)	CML's 5 Core Concepts	Construction: CML's 5 Key Questions (Producer)
1	**Authorship**	Who created this message?	All media messages are constructed.	What am I **authoring**?
2	**Format**	What creative techniques are used to attract my attention?	Media messages are constructed using a creative language with its own rules.	Does my message reflect understanding in **format**, creativity and technology?
3	**Audience**	How might different people understand this message differently?	Different people experience the same media message differently.	Is my message engaging and compelling for my target **audience**?
4	**Content**	What values, lifestyles and points of view are represented in or omitted from this message?	Media have embedded values and points of view.	Have I clearly and consistently framed values, lifestyles and points of view in my **content**?
5	**Purpose**	Why is this message being sent?	Most media messages are organized to gain profit and/or power.	Have I communicated my **purpose** effectively?

CML © 2009 Center for Media Literacy / www.medialit.org

Mission: Media Literacy

Fig. 2.2 *The Center for Media Literacy's core concepts and key questions handout.* Used with Permission.

to learn in order to accomplish something. These programs can range in their level of emphasis on criticism, the danger being that if they only teach self-expression without also including a critical component, the students might be prone to 'reproduce hegemonic representations or express their voice without the awareness of ideological implications or any type of social critique' (7). Teaching the skills of working with the media technologies is very important, but it is important to teach the concept that the mediums worked with are not neutral, as well as the importance of critical analysis.

Media Literacy Movement

For the second approach, Kellner and Share (2005) situate a *media literacy movement* within broader literacies, building upon the tradition of print literacy. They primarily focus on the relatively young media literacy movement in the U.S. Here, the approach is to 'teach students to read, analyze, and decode media texts in a fashion parallel to the advancement of print literacy' (372). In the current landscape of fake news (cf. Jolls & Johnsen, 2017; Livingstone, 2018), the ability to decode and analyze what is being portrayed in the media is an important skill, critical for educating the population. As Livingstone (2018: para. 5, italics in original) warns,

> The more that the media mediate everything in society—work, education, information, civic participation, social relationships and more—the more vital it is that people are informed about and critically able to judge what's useful or misleading, how they are regulated, when media can be trusted, and what commercial or political interests are at stake. In short, media literacy is needed not only to engage *with the media* but to engage with society *through the media*.

Media literacy can often become an umbrella term for more specific literacies such as: digital literacy, internet literacy, computer literacy, and even potentially AI literacy. While Kellner and Share (2007) commend the media literacy movement, they believe that too often media educators 'express the myth that education can and should be politically neutral, and that their job is to objectively expose students to media content without questioning ideology and issues of power' (8). Literacy has its own socio-cultural baggage and should not be thought of as a neutral term. Citing Luke (1989), Livingstone (2004) states that literacy 'masks a complex history of contestation over the power and authority to access, interpret, and produce printed texts' (4). These last points are addressed by the fourth approach (cf. below).

Protectionist

A third approach in media literacy is the *protectionist* approach. This investigates the ways media can be harmful—especially for young people—with repercussions like reducing attention spans, inciting violence, or promoting capitalist propaganda, particularly in advertising (Francis, 2016; Giroux, 2002; Kellner & Share, 2007). Friedrich Kittler (1999) begins one of his books by stating, 'Media determine our situation' (xxxix). This determinist view is often foundational for the protectionists, who posit that certain media technologies are inherently harmful or destructive to human flourishing. Neil Postman (2006) and Lance Strate (2014) detail the drawbacks of electronic media like television, especially compared with print media. Kellner and Share (2007) point out that 'Some conservatives blame the media for causing teen pregnancies and the destruction of family values while some on the left criticize the media for rampant consumerism and making children materialistic' (6).

Some researchers within this approach also address the ways newer digital media are inferior for supporting a well-read society in comparison to traditional print media (Postman, 2006; Strate, 2014). This focus raises the issue of the effects of a particular medium on society. For example, Sherry Turkle (2011) warns that new information and communication technologies are driving us apart while giving us the semblance of being together through virtual communication. Kellner and Share (2007) describe this as a fear of media with an aim to 'protect or inoculate people against the dangers of media manipulation and addiction. This protectionist approach posits media audiences as somewhat passive victims and values traditional print culture over media culture' (6).

Stuart Hall (1980) challenges the view of audiences being passive victims through his work in encoding/decoding of media messages. Hall articulates that audiences are more than passive receivers of media texts and they have the ability to read the messages produced outside of a dominant-hegemonic position—preferred by the producers—in negotiated or even oppositional ways (1980). This raises the question of the role of agency. Though there is a wide variety of focus within the protectionist approach, it tends toward technological determinism, which is the opposite of the skills-based (instrumentalist) approach. The protectionist approach is inclined to consider media and technology as something harmful to humans. In general, the first two approaches tend to consider the technological medium as neutral, not focusing on any influence that the medium may have. For the protectionist approach, the content and medium become more determining, potentially endangering the user and suppressing much of the user's agency.

Critical Media Literacy

The fourth approach is called *critical media literacy* and builds on the previous three approaches. It then adds the analysis of 'media culture as products of social production and struggle [...] teaching students to be critical of media representations and discourses, but also stressing the importance of learning to use the media as modes of self-expression and social activism' (Kellner & Share, 2005: 372). According to Kellner and Share (2007: 8–9),

> Critical media literacy thus constitutes a critique of mainstream approaches to literacy and a political project for democratic social change. This involves a multiperspectival critical inquiry of media culture and the cultural industries that address issues of class, race, gender, sexuality, and power and also promotes the production of alternative counter-hegemonic media. Media and information communication technology can be tools for empowerment when people who are most often marginalized or misrepresented in the mainstream media receive the opportunity to use these tools to tell their stories and express their concerns.

Critical media literacy strives to understand the underlying cultural influences and meanings that are embedded within media messages and how they often negatively affect already marginalized people. Kellner and Share (2007) state 'The analysis of different models of representation of women or people of color makes clear the constructedness of gender and race representations and that dominant negative representations further subordination and make it look natural' (13). They summarize by saying, 'critical media literacy offers the tools and framework to help students become subjects in the process of deconstructing injustices, expressing their own voices, and struggling to create a better society' (2005: 382). This reflects how media literacy can be used to regain user agency while navigating a mediated world. Lemke (2006) states, 'More than ever we need a critical multimedia literacy to engage intelligently with their potential effects on our social attitudes and beliefs' (4).

Supporting critical media literacy, John Hartley (2002) states, 'Literacy is not and never has been a personal attribute or ideologically inert "skill" simply to be "acquired" by individual persons' (135). Hartley continues by saying, 'It is ideologically and politically charged—it can be used as a means of social control or regulation, but also as a progressive weapon in the struggle for emancipation' (136). This reflects the non-neutrality of media and emphasizes the importance of learning how media affects our lives. While these four approaches cover much of the current state of media literacy, I believe that there is still more that should be covered by the field.

Expanding Media Literacy

With the ubiquity of ICTs and the speed with which they evolve and change, it is critical for media literacy to help us learn how to quickly situate and guide our own investigation into understanding the media we not only invite into our lives, but the inescapable media that surrounds us daily as well. Joshua Meyrowitz (1994: 50, italics added) provides an apt summary of media literacy:

> Most of the questions that engage media researchers and popular observers of the media focus only on one dimension of our media environment: the content of media messages. Typical concerns centre on how people (often children) react to what they are exposed to through various media; how institutional, economic, and political factors influence what is and is not conveyed through media; whether media messages accurately reflect various dimensions of reality; how different audiences interpret the same content differently; and so on. *These are all very significant concerns, but content issues do not exhaust the universe of questions that could, and should, be asked about the media.*

While carving out an important niche for itself, media literacy has become an established area of study with its own supporting literature. However, in the process it has lost some of its original interdisciplinarity (cf. Moores, 2012; Morley, 2009), focusing mainly on issues of representation, skill development, analysis, and social construction through media content. As Tessa Jolls and Carolyn Wilson (2014) point out, 'the pioneering work of communications expert Marshall McLuhan [...] created a foundation upon which many of our current ideas about media literacy are built' (69). That said, McLuhan's focus on the effects of the medium has largely dropped off the radar for most iterations of media literacy.[2]

While media literacy brings several pedagogical tools that help people better understand not only how to use media effectively but also how to understand it critically (cf. Van Dijck & Van Deursen, 2014), there are those who believe it should not be too narrowly focused. Moores (2012) says, 'I have a longstanding interest in studying everyday media uses [...], yet I firmly believe that these uses are best investigated in context, alongside other everyday practices and within wider social processes' (11). While critical media literacy is one of the steps in expanding media literacy in order to include critically analyzing the social context of biased representations, there is room to expand it further.

I use a two-step approach that focuses on the context. The first step is to include a focus on the technological medium being used. The second is similar to the call of Moores (2016) and Morley (2007; see also Krajina et al., 2014) for a non-media-centric media literacy that goes beyond a focus on representation and skills. Morley suggest de-centering media from media studies so we can 'understand better the ways in which media processes and everyday life are interwoven with each other' (200). Investigating the aspect of the medium itself is a first step that moves beyond a focus on media representation and skills. Following this, I create an approach using fields outside of media literacy in order to bring together concepts that help situate media literacy in a broader context, which I call a posthuman approach, and can be considered a fifth approach to media literacy.

2 Canada's AML (aml.ca) being one of the few exceptions that still retain some focus on the medium.

The Medium as Non-neutral Environment

The first step in enhancing media literacy is to extend beyond the primary concern with media content to begin exploring how the content is entangled with the specific medium itself. Currently, when a medium is discussed, the discussion generally focuses on ways to categorize the content mediated by that particular medium. For instance, in Figure 2.2 the second concept is format. The core concept states, '*Media messages are constructed using a creative language with its own rules*', the emphasis being on language rather than the medium itself. This reflects media literacy's primary focus on representation and its lack of attention on the medium. Not only is it beneficial to focus on the content and social context of media messages (i.e., critical media literacy), but we should also pay attention to the effects of the actual technology itself.

Marshall McLuhan's focus on the medium can be credited for drawing a focus to and interest in media education. Jolls and Wilson (2014: 69) write,

> In Canada, the pioneering work of communications expert Marshall McLuhan in the 1940s through the 1960s created a foundation upon which many of our current ideas about media literacy are built. McLuhan was aware of the profound impact of communications technologies on our lives, our societies and our future. His famous idea, that the 'medium is the message' taught us to recognize that the form through which a message is conveyed is as important as the content of the message. [...] McLuhan's theory was based on the idea that each medium has its own technological 'grammar' or bias that shapes and creates a message in a unique way. Different media may report the same event, but each medium will create different impressions and convey different messages.

One of the few media literacy organizations that does include a focus on the medium is Canada's AML. Their Eight Key Concepts of media literacy[3] includes three where the medium is pointed out (bold was added):

1. Media construct reality
2. **Media construct versions of reality** (biases of medium and creator)

3 Canada's Association of Media Literacy (https://aml.ca/resources/essential-framework/)

3. Audiences negotiate meaning
4. Media have economic implications
5. Media communicate values messages
6. Media communicate political and social messages
7. **Form and content are closely related in each medium**
8. **Each medium has a unique aesthetic form**

However, the aspect of the medium is not mentioned in their *Triangled Questions* document,[4] which they describe as a tool for teaching media literacy. This misses an opportunity to include a focus on the medium, which—at least implicitly—tends to view the objects of ICTs in an instrumental manner, as neutral carriers (Mason, 2016).

The issue of neutrality brings up how media has been judged in the past. Often, there is a binary approach, where media is perceived as either neutral (it has no effect) or determining (it has great effect). This way of perceiving media can be used to analyze both the content of the media or the medium itself. The protectionist approach and critical media literacy approach (cf. above) are generally concerned with the determining aspects of the media, while the media arts-based education and media literacy movement are more neutral.

One way to move beyond the binary approach of either neutral or determining is through the idea of non-neutrality. This stance acknowledges media's effect on human subjects (and can be applied to both content and medium), but refrains from an absolute determining stance. According to Melvin Kranzberg (1986), 'Technology is neither good nor bad; nor is it neutral' (545). However, the non-neutrality acknowledged by Kellner and Share (2007) focuses on the content rather than the material technology: 'Media are thus not neutral disseminators of information because the nature of the construction and interpretation processes entails bias and social influence' (12).

One of the gaps in media literacy that I am addressing is the non-neutrality of the material technology: the medium. Two media-related fields of study that I include in order to demonstrate this are media ecology and the philosophical approach of postphenomenology.

4 https://aml.ca/wp-content/uploads/2019/09/triangleq.pdf

Researchers in these fields are not the only advocates supporting a non-neutral view of technology (cf. Feenberg, 1999, 2017; Latour, 1999; Puech, 2016; Williams, 2004), but they provide two approaches that help to create an inclusive understanding of the non-neutrality of media technologies. My stance is that a balanced approach, combining content analysis and technological mediation, can help media literacy be more effective.

One way to help keep this balanced approach in mind is through the analogy McLuhan often used, that of figure and ground (McLuhan et al., 1977). 'Simply stated, figure is what one notices within an environment, whereas ground consists of the things one ignores' (Mason, 2019: 4). In the case of Masterman's (1980) work on television, it is the content or message that is the figure. However, the medium of the television is the ground for the content. The medium plays an important role in shaping the content, and it should be one of the foci of media literacy, along with the content. McLuhan (McLuhan et al., 1977) uses the figure/ground analogy in order to help us retrain our perception so that we become aware of the effects that the 'ground' has on us.

At one point McLuhan (McLuhan et al., 1977) explains that, '[...] in your own experience, you are always the figure, as long as you are conscious. The ground is always the setting in which you exist and act. The ground is never static; it is always changing. The interplay between you and this changing ground changes you' (10). Being conscious and aware of media's effects are in accord with the goals of media literacy. Lance Mason (2016) states, 'because McLuhan more fully conceptualizes the non-neutrality of technologies, he provides a broader conceptualization of user agency that transcends media messages and also considers media as form or environments for engagement' (93). Mason continues (2016: 93–94):

> While critical media literacy advocates are right to insist that audiences are active appropriators of media content, ignoring the structuring role of media technologies leads them to ignore or discount the insight that the medium influences the environmental conditions within which a user transacts with the world. [...] From this perspective, McLuhan's conception of media agency could bolster the conception of critical media literacy by affording a consideration of the material environments that mediate experiences for students in particular contexts.

The technological medium contributes to the shaping of media messages and deserves to be included in a broader approach to media literacy. Lars Qvortrup (2006) states that successful communication is not a 'natural' but a highly improbable phenomenon, and 'the effect of communication [medium] is to limit the improbability of communication success, and the qualities of media can be measured by their impact on communication success' (351). McLuhan (1994) described the medium as an environment, and this environment makes up part of the context that contains media messages.

Adding Context via Domestication Theory

While domestication theory[5] is outside the realm of media literacy—as it has a sociological and ethnographic focus rather than one on educating people to become media literate—it demonstrates how media studies in general can broaden its scope to include both object and context. This highlights the importance of understanding the context of where the media object exists, how it is used, and how it changes the behaviors of people who adapt to it. This example reflects what I wish to bring to media literacy through the development of an inclusive approach that situates ICTs in our everyday world in order for media users to understand the complexity of interrelations of content, technological medium, and context.

Domestication theory examines media as it is used within its environment. Silverstone (2006) created this theory—further developing it with David Morley (Morley & Silverstone, 1990), Leslie Haddon (2007), and others—through investigating how television was assimilated into homes in the U.K. The process focuses on the context, or environment, where the media is used and how that environment plays a role in understanding media. Edgar Morin (2007) describes, 'The need for contextualization is extremely important. I would even say that it is a principle of knowledge' (15; see also Engel, 1999). Yoni Van Den Eede (2015b) also makes the case for context saying, 'No thing is ever perceived in isolation. One may focus on it, but it is always there

5 For clarity, I will only use the term domestication theory. However, there has also been research in describing double (cf. Livingstone, 2007) and triple (cf. Courtois et al., 2012, 2013; Hartmann, 2006) articulation that is usually included in domestication theory discussions.

in relation to a ground or field. We can, however, try to get that broader context in view' (145).

Maren Hartmann (2006) describes how domestication theory began by analyzing the consumption of media, specifically television, and critiqued existing television research that was not 'accounting for the complexity of culture and the social' (83). Hartmann continues (2006: 84) by describing how, in domestication theory,

> both the material and the symbolic values present in media use are researched. The most general framework was thus the contextualized processes of the integration of technologies into everyday life. This context is both complex and contingent—and this context was also still meant to include content.

Morley and Silverstone (1990) write, 'our main objective is to recontextualize the study of television in a broader framework' (31), with an approach that 'defines television as an essentially domestic medium, to be understood both within the context of household and family, and within the wider context of social, political and economic realities' (32). They conclude by stating, 'within this formulation television's *meanings*, that is the meanings of both texts and technologies, have to be understood as emergent properties of contextualized audience practices' (31, italics in original).

Domestication stresses the attention on the everyday aspect of media and how it becomes integrated into our daily routines. Merete Lie and Knut Sørensen (1996) broaden the scope of domestication by investigating media outside of the home. They find that everywhere we go, we 'consume technologies—or, more precisely, technical artefacts—by integrating and using them. We are also consumed by the artefacts when they gain our attention and have us react to them and become occupied by their abilities, functions, and forms' (8).

How domestication theory engages with complexity is also an important concept, one that is expanded upon in Chapter 4. Thomas Berker et al. (2006: 1) describe what happens when we study media relations in context:

> The emergence of the domestication concept represented a shift away from models which assumed the adoption of new innovations to be rational, linear, monocausal and technologically determined. Rather, it presented a theoretical framework and research approach, which

> considered the complexity of everyday life and technology's place within its dynamics, rituals, rules, routines and patterns.

This complexity has created problems for domestication theory. While it has been well developed as a theory, Hartmann (2006) notes that it 'was then lost in the "application" of the domestication concept in actual research' (81). According to Hartmann, the 'question that keeps reappearing and that has not yet been solved is how to adequately research the complexity of the combination of media content and media context to paint a picture of the overall whole' (89). What is needed is a way to situate and contextualize the complexity of our media-saturated, everyday lives.

Concluding Thoughts

Today, much of media literacy focuses on fake news and the challenge this trend presents to democracy (cf. Jolls & Johnsen, 2017; Livingstone, 2018). People are mediated by technologies of all sorts,[6] one of the most prevalent being the smartphone. The news is not only mediated; it is re-mediated into smaller and smaller bits, which are typically cut and re-cut, decontextualized and then re-contextualized with different meanings (cf. Chouliaraki, 2013, 2017). The many different mediums disseminate these bits in their own unique way. Ubiquitous ICTs have transformed the way most people live, especially in the developed Western world. However, people are not only mediated by ICTs in general, but also by cultural relations through power structures, social norms, language, gender, race, and many other groupings of relations. This is where critical media literacy comes into play and where there is much overlap with critical posthumanism (cf. Chapter 4).

I am not the only researcher calling for expanding the field of media literacy. There has been a push from within the field for broadening its scope, returning to a more interdisciplinary approach. Morley (2009) writes of the need to 'develop a model for the integrated analysis of communications, which places current technological changes in

6 Livingstone (2009) writes on the mediation of everything, stating, 'distinct aspects of the concept of mediation invite communication scholars to attend to the specific empirical, historical and political implication of the claim that "everything is mediated"' (1).

historical perspective' (114). To do so means avoiding the simplified and 'overdrawn binary divides between the worlds of the "old" and the "new" media' (115). It is critical for media literacy to develop a framework in order to keep an overarching perspective on the constant onslaught of new ICTs. In the words of Eric McLuhan (2009: 12),

> When change is relatively slow, the need for training awareness is not so pressing. But when major new media appear every three or four years, the need becomes a matter of survival. Each new medium is a new culture and each demands a new spin on identity; each takes root in one or another group in society, and as these flow in and out of each other the abrasive interfaces generate much violence. It is urgent that we begin to study all of the forms of knowing, now called literacies.

My approach follows several amodern—not modern but not postmodern—philosophies (postphenomenology, philosophical posthumanism, complexity theory, etc.). I balance the binaries of technological determinism and technological neutrality. One of the most effective ways to reduce technological determinism—following Michel Foucault (1988), Michel Puech (2016), and others—is to become aware of the systems that have influence on us, and this is where media literacy can excel. John Culkin (1967: 51) stresses the importance of being media literate:

> The environments set up by different media are not just containers for people; they are processes which shape people. Such influence is deterministic only if it is ignored. There is no inevitability as long as there is a willingness to contemplate what is happening.

As critical media literacy helps to fill the critical social theory gap within media literacy, my aim is to create an approach that can be used by media literacy in order to situate the wider range of effects of media that a mediate literate person should be aware of: content, medium, and context. As Lemke (2006) states, 'We need conceptual frameworks to help us cope with the complexity and the novelty of these new multimedia constellations' (5).

The first step towards an expansion of media literacy is developing an understanding of the co-constituting effects of technological relations, especially embodied relations, which I investigate in the next chapter. Both media ecology and postphenomenology help us keep in mind the way media and technologies enable and constrain our abilities, allowing us to have more realistic expectations for complex media environments. This aspect of co-constitution is the focus of the next two chapters. First, I look at the medium/technology side (Chapter 3) and then focus on which subject we are discussing that is being constituted by media relations (Chapter 4). This is not the subject of the transmission model of communication, but the subject of the constitutive model (Craig, 1999) and the transformation model (McLuhan, 2008). We are not standalone entities simply transporting discreet messages back and forth through various media; rather, we are being constituted within a complexity of mediated relations.

3

The Technological Medium and its Impact

Human subjects are inundated with new mediums of technology, both of the hardware variety (smartphones, smartwatches, digital home assistants) and software infrastructures (Facebook, Twitter, Instagram, Snapchat). What elements go into our decisions to invite any of the plethora of choices we have into our lives? How can we go beyond the promised benefits of the technologies and become more aware of the possible downsides—the constraints—that these technologies always bring with them?

In order to begin developing a more inclusive and situating approach for media literacy, the first step is to better understand the effects that the technological medium plays in the constitution of not only media messages but also the constitution of the human subject. To be clear, my intent is to complement media literacy, not to replace what media literacy already does so well (cf. the four approaches in the previous chapter). Media literacy should continue with its varied approaches towards media messages and skills-based media literacy. However, attending to the effects of the medium can help make media literacy a more robust and effective field of inquiry.

In this chapter I explore the effects of the technological medium through two aspects. The first uses postphenomenology to better understand technological mediation—how our specific relations with technologies transform not only the media messages, but our own selves. The second uses media ecology to understand the technological medium as an environment of complex relations. The first aspect is a micro approach and the second a macro approach. Concepts from each of the two fields are brought together to help create a way to understand the posthuman subject that is developed later in Chapter 4. This chapter is not meant to be an extensive review of either postphenomenology or media ecology, as there are many excellent resources that do this already.[1] Rather, I extract concepts from them to begin a holistic investigation of the technological medium, which is not sufficiently developed in media literacy.

In Medias Res[2]

To better understand the human subject that is transformed by media relations, it is beneficial to begin by explaining the relations with technologies that contribute to the subject's constitution. I therefore begin in the middle, *in medias res*. This is apropos when discussing the in-between of mediation—how media technologies constitute our selves by being in between the world and us. However, in order to refrain from falling into a Cartesian subject/object duality, the relation is not something that comes in between two already established entities (cf. Lemmens, 2017; Smith, 2015; Van Den Eede, 2012; Verbeek, 2005), but rather the relation and entities are constituted *through the act of relating*. The subject is not the standalone humanist subject from the Enlightenment and modernity but a posthuman subject (cf. Chapter 4) that experiences ongoing constitution through its ever-changing relations. It is this constituting relationality that is the foundational building block for the approach I develop. These relations mediate and co-constitute the world and our selves, and as Sonia Livingstone (2009) posited, 'everything is mediated' (4).

1 A good starting point for media ecology is: Anton, 2016; McLuhan, 1994; Postman 1974, 2006; Strate 2014, 2017. And, for postphenomenology, see: Ihde, 1990, 2002, 2009, 2012; Rosenberger & Verbeek, 2015; Verbeek, 2005.

2 Latin for 'in the middle of things'. It is also the name of the Media Ecology Association's newsletter.

Micro and Macro Approaches

The focus of this chapter is on understanding the mediums[3] of media technologies. While not all mediums of media communications are technological,[4] the focus of my research is directed toward the ones that are, especially the digitally networked variety that are currently so prevalent. In order to understand these technological mediums, it is helpful to have a firm grasp of the concept of perception. According to Maurice Merleau-Ponty (2002: 373),

> The thing is inseparable from a person perceiving it, and can never be actually in itself because its articulations are those of our very existence, and because it stands at the other end of our gaze or at the terminus of a sensory exploration which invests it with humanity.

Perception is never passive; rather, it is active and constructive. It is an embodied process, as Merleau-Ponty (2002) describes: 'a theory of the body is already a theory of perception' (235). It is not the body alone, but the entanglement of our bodily sense with our sociocultural situatedness, what Don Ihde (1990, 2002) calls macroperception. Ihde (1990) devotes the second half of his seminal work, *Technology and the Lifeworld*, to this concept of macroperception, which he also refers to as cultural hermeneutics. He further develops the concept of cultural hermeneutics in *Bodies in Technology* (2002) through the concept of 'body two'. This idea is similar to Michel Foucault's (1995) concept of

---

3 While the plural of medium is media, I am using media to refer mainly to the content-focused media studies definition of media. When I want to indicate the specific media technology that is the 'channel' (in the traditional language of communication) I will attempt to use the singular medium. However, this tends to become a bit challenging when trying to discuss the many types of mediums, so I will use the plural mediums.

4 John Peters (2015) wrote an excellent book on *Elemental Media* that is directed at some of the non-technical mediums—water and air primarily—and how they also influence how humans and non-humans communicate. For instance, air is the medium for oral communication (see Innis, 2008; Ong, 2012). Its properties greatly contribute to how far our voices travel, limiting how far apart we can communicate without technologies to extend our range. At the same time, air allows us to see quite far. Peters makes the case that more of our brains are consumed with visual rather than auditory perception because of this. Water, on the other hand, allows sound to travel quite far and sight to be more limited. This has likely been a factor in the development of whale and dolphin brains to devote more area to auditory rather than to visual perception (Peters, 2015: ch. 2).

a culturally constructed body, as opposed to 'body one', which is 'the located, perceiving active body' (Ihde, 2002: xviii). Ihde continues by saying, 'Traversing both body one and body two is a third dimension, the dimension of the technological' (xi). Researchers within the field of postphenomenology investigate how technologies mediate and constitute bodies one and two.

Body two—or the macroperceptual—is used to understand how cultural relations influence our technological relations. For instance, different cultures have different approaches towards time. The clock in China was invented (circa 1077), 'not for telling hours but for setting the astrological calendar for an Imperial need' (Ihde, 1990: 130). Ihde explains (1990: 29),

> There is no microperception (sensory-bodily) without its location within a field of macroperception and no macroperception without its microperceptual foci. The relation between micro- and macroperception is not one of derivation; rather, it is more like that of figure-to-ground in that microperception occurs within its hermeneutic-cultural context; but all such contexts find their fulfillment only within the range of microperceptual possibility.

While postphenomenology does discuss macroperception, it most often stays grounded in an embedded and embodied perspective, analyzing the enabling and constraining aspects of mediating technologies. Unlike media ecology, postphenomenology generally stays clear of making sweeping statements concerning the effects and biases of technologies. For the most part, researchers in the field avoid criticizing technologies, which has caused some to criticize or challenge postphenomenology to be more critical (cf. Borgmann, 2015; Feenberg, 1999; Lemmens, 2017; Michelfelder, 2015; Scharff, 2006; Smith, 2015). Technologies are viewed as being *multistable*, meaning they are never just one thing; they are always able to be used in multiple ways, which is why postphenomenology usually keeps to describing technological relations instead of judging them.

Media ecology, on the other hand, most often looks with a macro lens at the broad influences that the mediums of media have on individuals and cultures. Lynn Clark (2009) describes how 'the role of media in social change is a primary concern in media ecology' (12). Media ecologists tend not to shy away from making sweeping statements concerning the effects and biases of a medium's influence on individuals and cultures. This does not mean that researchers in media ecology do not pay attention to the micro level, especially when they focus on media education. Marshall McLuhan et al. (1977) demonstrate this micro approach in *City as Classroom*. However, on the whole media ecology is an effective field of study for looking broadly at the effects of media technologies. While there has not been much interaction between the media ecology and postphenomenology (Van Den Eede, 2016), there has recently been a tentative bridge developing between the two (Irwin, 2016; Ralón, 2016; Van Den Eede, 2016), where scholars are exploring their conceptual commonalities.

Ihde (1990) points out that the micro and macro are not discrete or exclusively binary positions. They can both be used in order to contribute important ways of considering the effects of media technology. Looking into specific technologies, such as speed bumps, hammers, smartphones, or typewriters, we should keep both micro and macro perspectives in mind. A smartphone is multistable, with various—but not infinite—possible ways of being used in particular situations. At the same time, we can look through a macro lens and see how the smartphone, widely speaking, has transformed both individuals and cultures. Both perspectives together offer an inclusive understanding of the impact of media technologies. I begin by discussing concepts from postphenomenology and then discuss concepts from media ecology.

Postphenomenology and the Technological Relation

> Postphenomenology is the practical study of the relations between humans and technologies, from which human subjectivities emerge, as well as meaningful worlds. As a result of this practical and material orientation, postphenomenology always takes the study of human-technology relations as its starting point. (Rosenberger & Verbeek, 2015: 12–13)

Like much of media literacy, postphenomenology is pragmatic and often grounded (embedded and embodied) in the user's experience. Arising from philosophy of technology, postphenomenology uses several concepts that can be beneficially applied to media literacy, specifically: 1) non-neutral technological mediation; 2) sedimentation; and 3) multistability. I first situate postphenomenology and its concept of the non-neutral, co-constituting technological relation. As the co-constituting relation is the foundational component from which I formulate the posthuman approach, I discuss it in detail. I then introduce the concept of sedimentation and how it relates to time and transparency. Finally, I discuss the concept of multistability, which is a key concept that pushes back against an essentialist approach to understanding technology.

Situating Non-neutral Human-Technology Relations

Postphenomenology has grown out of the empirical turn, which shifts 'away from' transcendental and reifying approaches to technology[5] and moves instead toward an empirical approach (see Achterhuis, 2001; Kroes & Meijers, 2001; Smith, 2015, 2018). In order to create postphenomenology, founder Ihde (1990, 2012) builds on the concept of phenomenology and adds pragmatism, which helps to empirically ground research on technology and avoid making sweeping claims (mostly negative) in an essentialist manner. This is in contrast to Martin Heidegger (1977), Jacques Ellul (1964), and others, who have tended to approach technology in a more reified and deterministic way. Postphenomenologists[6] often explore the specific constituting relations that occur between subjects and technological objects, such as ICTs, helping to dissolve a strict duality between the two and working to describe how technologies co-constitute both subjects and the world.

Neutrality, Determination, and Agency

> [I]n each set of human technology relations, the model is that of an interrelational ontology. This style of ontology carries with it a number

5 However, Smith (2018) writes, 'there is no reason why this turning towards the empirical has to occur at the price of a turning away from "transcendental" concerns regarding conditions' (78). Smith advocates for keeping both transcendental and empirical.

6 For some examples, see: Boltin, 2017; Ihde, 1990, 2002, 2012; Ihde & Selinger, 2003; Irwin 2014, 2017; Kiran, 2012, 2015; Lewis, 2018; Rosenberger, 2012, 2014, 2017; Rosenberger & Verbeek, 2015; Selinger, 2012; Smith, 2015; Van Den Eede, 2011, 2016; Van Den Eede et al., 2017a; Verbeek, 2005, 2008, 2011; Wellner, 2016, 2017a, 2017b.

> of implications, including the one that there is a co-constitution of humans and their technologies. Technologies transform our experience of the world and our perceptions and interpretations of our world, and we in turn become transformed in this process. Transformations are non-neutral. (Ihde, 2009: 44)

This quote from Ihde (2009) refers to an interrelational ontology, meaning that humans are relational; we are always being constituted through our relations. Furthermore, these relations are non-neutral; they influence us and contribute to constituting our subjectivity, although they are not completely determining. Because our relations constitute us, when our relations change, we change. This change is always non-neutral, meaning it transforms the way we perceive and interact with the world (cf. Lewis, 2020). Both Bruno Latour (1999) and Ihde (2003) describe this concept by referencing the gun debate in the U.S. and the attitude reflected by the slogan of the National Rifle Association (NRA), *guns don't kill people, people kill people*. This slogan represents a neutral view of technology, one where the technology does not affect any change in the individual subject. The complete opposite (deterministic) view places all the blame on the guns.

The non-neutral approach suggests the understanding that once I have a gun, I am transformed. Neither I, nor the world around me, are the same. The gun does not completely determine my actions (as technological determinists might contend) nor is the gun a completely neutral object (as the NRA might contend). This holds true for ICTs such as a smartphone. I am a different traveler if I have a networked smartphone than if I travel without one. My actions are not determined by the smartphone, but they are influenced.

One way of understanding the non-neutrality of technologies is through the concept of shared agency. In a neutral view of technology, the user has complete agency. In a determined understanding of technology, the user has little to no agency. The non-neutral approach to technology represents the middle ground of a shared agency between humans and technologies (Ihde, 1990; Latour, 1999; Pickering, 1995; Puech, 2016; Verbeek, 2005). As Robert Rosenberger and Peter-Paul Verbeek (2015) offer, 'Agency, then, is not an exclusively human property anymore: it takes shape in complicated interactions between human and nonhuman entities' (20). Andrew Pickering (1995, 2005) refers to this as the dance of agency.

One of the strengths of postphenomenology is how its approach helps researchers to analyze relations with specific technological objects and describe what is enabled and what is constrained (cf. Ihde, 1990; Kiran, 2015; Rosenberger, 2012; Van Den Eede, 2012; Verbeek 2005; Wellner, 2016). Postphenomenology helps to shed light on effects that might be hidden or have become transparent through habitual use of technologies and to understand how we, and our lifeworlds, are transformed by those technologies. As Ihde (1990) notes, 'There is no "thing-in-itself". There are only things in contexts, and contexts are multiple' (69). In other words, objects are always situated objects-in-relation.

The Relation as Building Block

In order to create an approach to help media literacy become more effective, I begin with a foundational component: the relation. In this chapter I will specifically focus on the technological relation. There are three interconnected aspects that comprise a relation. In Chapter 5 I will expand this to include five other groupings of relations beyond the technological. Though I discuss them one at a time, it is important to note that they *become* part of a whole as the relation occurs. This is similar to Karen Barad's (2007) use of the concept of phenomena: '*phenomena* are the *ontological* inseparability of agentially intra-acting components [... which are] basic units of reality' (33). In other words, the basic unit of the phenomenon is comprised of (at least) two things in relation, which are intra-acting (or co-constituting in postphenomenological terms). Barad points out, 'the "distinct" agencies are only distinct in a relational, not an absolute, sense, that is, *agencies are only distinct in relation to their mutual entanglement; they don't exist as individual elements*' (33, italics in original).

Because this co-constituting relation is the core concept upon which I design the approach, I have designed a symbol to demonstrate, in one holistic view, the significant components (see Fig. 3.1). This loosely builds on the idea of entangled particles and waves that are explored in quantum mechanics (Barad, 2007). I equate the 'particles' with the human and technology, and I equate the 'wave' with relationality that connects and (at least in part) constitutes the two. The Deltas (the triangles), used in mathematics to represent change, represent the change that occurs for both the subject and technological object, as a specific relation (represented by the wave) between them is enacted.

Fig. 3.1 *Symbolizing the Co-constituting Relation.* Image by author (2021), CC BY 4.0.

While postphenomenology uses a hyphen to signify the relation between the human and technology (human-technology), this leaves more chance to potentially misinterpret the relation as a subject-object duality, especially from outside of the field. The relation demonstrated in Figure 3.1 is the actual irreducible building block from which our lifeworlds and our selves are constructed. From this relation we can begin investigating the mediating relations.

Technological Mediation: Four Types

In postphenomenology the fundamental concept of technological mediation is represented by the formula, *I-technology-world* (Ihde, 1990; Rosenberger & Verbeek, 2015). While the term 'mediation' highlights the in-between role that technology performs between a person and the world (Van Den Eede, 2011), several postphenomenologists point out that the term can erroneously imply that the person and the world are already independently established before the mediation takes place. Instead, it is more appropriate to understand that both subject and world (as well as the specific technology) are constituted through the mediating role of the technology (cf. Fig. 3.2). There is a transformation of subject and world that takes place when relation occurs, what Barad (2007) calls intra-action. As Peter-Paul Verbeek (2005) states, 'When analyzing the mediating role of artifacts, therefore, this mediation cannot be regarded as a mediation "between" subject and object. Mediation consists in a mutual constitution of subject and object' (130). This constituting role of technological mediation is how I define the word mediation throughout this book.

Fig. 3.2 *Symbolizing the Co-constitution of Technological Mediation.* Image by author (2021), CC BY 4.0.

With the building block of the relation explained, I will now discuss the types of relations described by postphenomenology. Ihde (1990) specifies four types of technological relations (embodied, hermeneutic, alterity, and background) in order to more specifically describe the general I-technology-world formula.

Embodied Relation. The first relation, embodied, describes the mediating relation where we perceive, or interact with, the world *through* the technology. The classic example is a pair of eyeglasses. Our focus is not on the glasses (unless there is something wrong with them), but the view through them. By wearing glasses, our perception of the world is mediated and transformed, both in an enabling way (things become clearer) and a constraining way (they are a weight on our face; we need to take care of them and keep them clean; and they are breakable). In this relation, the technology has the tendency of becoming transparent (cf. below), as our intention moves through the technology towards something else. This relation is revisited in chapter five, as it is a key component of the framework developed.

Hermeneutic Relation. The second relation is a hermeneutic relation. This is where we *read* the technology in order to get a new understanding of the world. Robert Rosenberger and Verbeek (2015) describe how 'the user experiences a transformed encounter with the world via the direct experience and interpretation of the technology itself' (17). The common example for the hermeneutic relation is the thermometer. We read the technology in order to gain an understanding of the world (how cold or warm it is). The thermometer mediates our understanding of the world and we gain insight without necessarily feeling or sensing the temperature directly.

Alterity Relation. The third type of relation is called alterity, where the technology becomes a quasi-other. Evan Selinger (2012: 6) describes alterity relations as,

> when we enter into practices with artifacts that display the feature of 'otherness' (i.e., an evocative quality that transcends mere objecthood but resonates with less animateness than actual living beings such as people or animals). Unlike embodiment relations and hermeneutic relations, alterity relations focus attention upon the technology itself.

Examples of this relation include video games and ATM machines. This is the one relation where the intentional focus is on the technology itself.

Background Relation. The final relation is described as background relations. These are relations that affect us but we are mostly unaware of them, such as the heating and cooling system in our house. We set the thermostat, and as long as the system operates properly, we do not pay much attention to it. These are the four traditional types of relations described in postphenomenology. Occasionally, researchers suggest new relations, such as Verbeek's (2008) *cyborg* relation or Galit Wellner's (2017a) *writing* relation. Verbeek (2015) also describes *immersion* relations which describe smart interactive background technologies and *augmentation* relations which cover augmented reality, such as Google Glass.

Sedimentation and Multistability

There are two concepts that are important for the development of the posthuman approach: sedimentation and multistability, both of which concern perception. Sedimentation brings in an aspect of time, referring to how our past experiences with technologies affect the way we interact with those technologies. This often leads towards a type of transparency that occurs, where we simply use the technologies without needing to focus on them. Multistability refers to the way technologies are never simply one thing; they can be used and perceived in multiple stable ways.

Sedimentation's Impact on Transparency

The concept of sedimentation comes from phenomenology. Sedimentation is the idea that our past experiences with a phenomenon influence our current experiences of the same phenomenon (Husserl,

1973; Merleau-Ponty, 2002). Merleau-Ponty (2002: 149–50) states that our previous experiences offer,

> a 'world of thoughts', or a sediment left by our mental processes, which enables us to rely on our concepts and acquired judgments as we might on the things there in front of us [...] without there being any need for us to resynthesize them. [...] But the word 'sediment' should not lead us astray: this acquired knowledge is not an inert mass in the depths of our consciousness.

Rosenberger (2012) uses sedimentation 'to refer to the particular level of habit, the particular degree to which the past provides meaning to the present, in a given human–technological relation' (85). Sedimentation also 'provides the pre-perceptive context that enables our current perceptions to occur with immediate meaningfulness' (Rosenberger & Verbeek, 2015: 25). Sedimentation brings into the conversation the concept of time and how our past experiences contribute to the way mediating technologies currently constitute us. This temporal component is developed in more detail in chapter five.

Our experiences with technologies become sedimented within us the more we use them, eventually causing a technological object that we are using to recede into the background, becoming at least partially transparent. Transparency[7] is a term used in philosophy of technology to describe,

> the degree to which a device (or an aspect of that device) fades into the background of a user's awareness as it is used. As a user grows accustomed to the embodiment of a device, [...] the device itself takes on a degree of transparency. (Rosenberger & Verbeek, 2015: 14)

Merleau-Ponty (2002), along with several other scholars (Dreyfus & Dreyfus, 1986; Heidegger, 2010; Ihde, 1990; Van Den Eede, 2011; Verbeek, 2012), use various examples to describe the different ways technologies can become transparent. Merleau-Ponty describes the blind man's stick and how it is not an object that is perceived by the blind person using it; rather, the person uses it as an extension of their self. The stick becomes ever more transparent as an object as it is used to sense the world.

7 For a more thorough discussion into various approaches to transparency, see Van Den Eede (2011).

Heidegger (2010) refers to this transparency when he describes the hammer as being ready-to-hand (*zuhanden*), where a person simply uses it for their purpose and does not attend to the tool itself. For Heidegger, 'the tool or equipment in use becomes the *means*, not the object, of the experience' (Ihde, 1990: 32). This changes only if the tool is broken or in some way disrupts a person's use of it, thereby changing to a presence-at-hand (*vorhanden*).

While Ihde (1990) concurs with Heidegger's assessment, he believes that there are more nuanced ways of describing our technological relations. His four relations (cf. above) back this up. His embodied and hermeneutic relations can be considered similarly to Heidegger's *zuhanden*, where a person engages with the world through the technology and the technology is mostly transparent. However, Ihde describes alterity relations with technology as a way of engaging with technology itself, even when it isn't broken.

A common example of sedimentation and transparency is the first time we drive a car; our concentration is almost completely focused on the car as we attempt to operate it. However, as we become more and more habituated through experience, the car begins to become 'transparent', receding into the background of our awareness and transforming into an extension of our selves while we use it to move from one place to another (Dreyfus & Dreyfus, 1986; Merleau-Ponty, 2002; Verbeek, 2012). This transparency contributes to the difficulty of being aware of the effects of how media technologies affect us.

Multistability of Technology

Perception is the cornerstone to phenomenology (cf. Merleau-Ponty's, 2002) as well as postphenomenology (cf. Ihde, 1990, 2002). Ihde (1990) uses the Necker cube (see Figure 3.3) to begin his explanation of the multistability of perception, which leads to his concept of the multistability of technology.

As Ihde (1990: 145) explains,

> The Necker cube is an ambiguous perceptual object, essentially bi-stable, in which (a) the uppermost part of the figure is seen as the far corner of its top face; but, through a 'spontaneous' gestalt switch, (b) the uppermost part is seen as the near corner of its top face, with a second

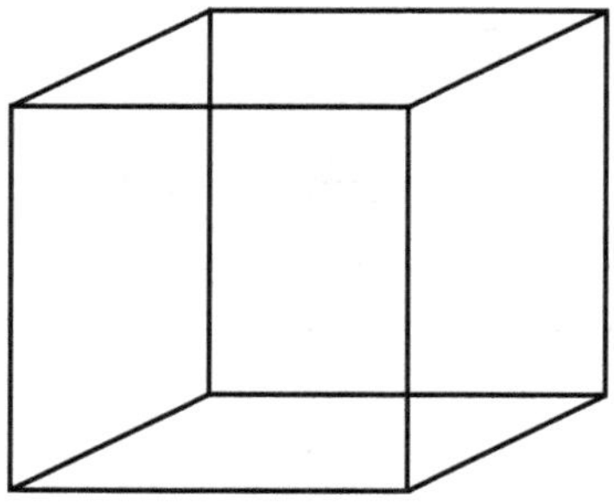

Fig. 3.3 *Necker cube.* Named after Louis Albert Necker. Image by BenFrantzDale (2007).

> three-dimensional stability. These two variations may switch with each other in the viewer's gaze, in a set of alternations distinct from one another, exclusive but related as three-dimensional appearances of a cube.

Ihde continues to go beyond the two variations of perception (bi-stability) that are the most common to the Necker cube and describes a way of perceiving the cube as an insect as well as two variations of a weirdly cut gem (145–46).

Ihde's point is that we have the ability to perceive things—specifically, technologies—in multiple stable ways. We can perceive something in a stable way, but then we can change our perception and see it in a different stable way. Multistability is a core concept in postphenomenology and the main idea that is used to counter essentialist or normative claims concerning technologies. Ihde (2002) states, 'No technology is one thing, nor is it incapable of belonging to multiple contexts' (106). Ihde makes a point of the gestalt switch of perception[8] when it comes to multistability. We get used to perceiving technology in one or two ways, but it can be transformed into something completely different through a 'simple' gestalt switch in our own perception.

While the object's physical attributes influence how they are perceived in multistable ways, objects do not *have* multistabilities; this is not an 'essential' quality of the object itself. Rather, through the object's affordances and material attributes, a subject can *perceive* an object in

8 McLuhan et al. (1977) also point this out in their explanation of figure and ground.

multistable ways. According to Ihde (2002), all structures and patterns 'display multistable sets of limited possibilities' (33). This view counters essentialist ideas of technologies, which can lead toward normative values being placed on technologies. Technological objects have multiple, though not infinite, stabilities. A hammer can be perceived as a tool used to pound and pull nails, but it can also be used as a paperweight, a doorstop, or even as a weapon.

Summary of Postphenomenology

Any new technology mediates our relation with the world and is transformative. Postphenomenology does not perceive technology as neutral or completely determining, nor does it attempt to describe an essence of technology. Rather, a postphenomenological approach views mediating technologies as *non-neutral*, which are able to become transparent through *sedimentation* and are *multistable*. I incorporate these three postphenomenological concepts later into the posthuman approach in order to better understand how technological relations co-constitute the subject, technology, and the world.

Media Ecology

The field of media ecology has a particular way of approaching media studies. This section investigates the effects of media technologies through the lens of media ecology, which views media as environments. These environments play a role in shaping message, sender, and receiver.

Corey Anton (2016) describes how, 'The particular expression, "media ecology" grew out of a conversation in 1967 between Neil Postman, Marshall McLuhan and Eric McLuhan, and, within a year, Postman was using it in public talks' (126). Anton continues by describing Walter Ong, Marshall McLuhan, and Postman, the primary thinkers (along with several others, such as Harold Innis) who laid the foundation for what would become known as media ecology (127). Lance Mason (2016: 86) describes how,

> To McLuhan, a medium is an environment that structures interactions among and between humans and the rest of the world. This can be

contrasted with the traditional understanding of media as a conduit for information transfer, which I identify as a neutral conception of media employed by those that emphasize media content analysis, while ignoring media forms as objects of study.

I explore these ideas in order to demonstrate the importance of how media technologies and ICTs affect not only individuals but cultures and societies. Media ecology's concept of media as environments complements postphenomenology's emphasis on the embodied microperception and media literacy's focus on the message. This complementarity demonstrates the benefit of using an interdisciplinary approach to build an inclusive method for studying media.

Background

Media ecology approaches media in a very broad and medium-focused manner. Researchers within the field often do not shy away from making sweeping statements concerning the effects of specific mediums, even broadening their scope to analyze the larger paradigms of communication and how they affect individuals and society; an example being Ong's (2012) seminal work, *Orality and Literacy*. One of the tenets of media ecology is that media environments are mostly invisible to us. We exist within them and are affected by them, but we often do not realize the effects they have on us. Only by becoming aware of them can we begin to retain some agency. This is further discussed in the 'Figure/Ground' section below.

Media ecology takes a systems—or complexity—approach towards understanding media and communications in order to understand the differences each medium affords (Logan, 2015). Anthony Giddens (1990) says that the mechanized 'technologies of communication have dramatically influenced all aspects of globalization since the first introduction of mechanical printing into Europe' (77). Media ecology investigates and probes these influences of specific mediums in order to understand how each are different, uniquely enabling and constraining individuals, societies, and cultures.

Media Ecology as a Field of Inquiry

Media ecology is better conceived of as a field of inquiry rather than an established discipline or subject (Postman, 1970; Strate, 2017). Lance Strate (2017), a student of Postman and one of the key voices in media ecology, contrasts the field of inquiry concept to the disciplines found in contemporary academics. Disciplines are considered well-established subjects with 'a widely accepted cannon, introductory curriculum, theories, methods, etc.' (10). However, an established body of knowledge does not usually define a field. Instead, a field is held together through a mutual interest in a particular topic and is generally interdisciplinary in nature. Strate continues by indicating 'media ecology may be described as interdisciplinary, drawing upon not only all of the social sciences and humanities, but the fine arts and hard sciences as well' (10).

Media ecology contrasts with media literacy in that it is less interested in the content of each medium and more interested in the unique effects of each medium. Postman (1974: 76–77) describes media ecologists as researchers who,

> want to know what kind of environment we enter when we talk on the telephone or watch television or read a book. We want to know the answers to such questions as, at what level of abstraction does a medium operate? What aspects of reality does it isolate and amplify? What aspects of reality does it exclude? What is the nature of the information it gives? What are its spatial biases? Its temporal biases? What does a particular medium require us to do with our bodies and our senses? In what directions does it encourage us to think? And how do such biases determine our relations with others and ourselves?

Media ecology is a loose group of interdisciplinary scholars who approach studying the effects of media technologies through various avenues. In the following sections, I explain their approach to understanding media and how specific media have specific biases. While this leads some to make claims that media ecologists are technological determinists, I counter that accusation. Finally, I use the concept of the Gutenberg Parenthesis (Pettitt, 2007) to demonstrate how media ecologists can use a macro view to investigate the effects and biases of broad communication paradigms, specifically focusing on a comparison of print photographs and digital images.

Defining Media as Environments

The cornerstone of media ecology's contribution to media literacy is in how the field defines the term *media*. Rather than narrowly defining the term, media ecology expands the term and equates it with the idea of environments. John Naughton (2012: § *After Gutenberg, What Next?*) defines the term as follows:

> The word 'media' is the plural of 'medium' [...] The conventional—journalistic—interpretation holds that a medium is a carrier of something. But in science, the word has another, more interesting, connotation. To a biologist, for example, a medium is a mixture of nutrients needed for cell growth [...and which] are used to grow tissue cultures—living organisms. [...] It seems to me that this is a useful metaphor for thinking about human society; it portrays our social system as a living organism that depends on a media environment for the nutrients it needs to survive and develop. Any change in the environment—in the media that support social and cultural life—will have corresponding effects on the organism. Some things will wither; others may grow; new, unexpected species may appear. The key point of the metaphor is simple: change the environment, and you change the organism; change the media environment and you change society.

This definition of the medium as an environment emphasizes that the media environment is *primary*, the thing through which our culture grows. This contrasts with a media literacy view 'where media are situated *within* culture, and are seen as a product of a culture' (Strate, 2017: 26, italics added). Since media are approached as environments, we are able to try to understand how each specific media can,

> affect human perception, understanding, feelings, and value [...]. In the case of media environments (e.g., books, radio, film, television, etc.), the specifications are more often implicit and informal, half concealed by our assumption that what we are dealing with is not an environment, but merely a machine. Media ecology tries to make these specifications explicit. It tries to find out what roles media force us to play, how media structure what we are seeing, why media make us feel and act as we do. (Postman, 1970: 161)

Though complexity is dealt with more fully in the next chapter, it is worth a brief mention here since it is a commonly acknowledged component of ecology and environmental studies (cf. Hirsch et al., 2011). Therefore, when viewing media as environments, it is not surprising that there is also an element of complexity, and this element is a useful way of understanding the effects a medium-as-environment has. Complexity helps to manage expectations when we interact with such systems. Edgar Morin (2007) discusses an ecology of action, suggesting that once any action enters an environment, it leaves the control and intention of whoever or whatever created the action. It 'enters a set of interactions and multiple feedbacks and then it will find itself derived from its finalities, and sometimes to even go in the opposite sense' (21). These complex environments behave in non-linear ways, where simple cause and effect can no longer be counted on.

Figure/Ground

Marshall McLuhan (in McLuhan et al., 1977) points out that a quality of one's environment is that it is usually not in the foreground of our awareness. McLuhan uses the idea of figure/ground to describe this. He credits Edgar Rubin for introducing this concept in 1915. 'Rubin adopted the terms *figure* and *ground* to assist the study of structure in visible phenomena' (9). For McLuhan, 'figure and ground are not categories: they are tools that will help you discover the structure and properties of situations' (31). And, as a tool, it can be leveraged in media literacy. For example, McLuhan et al. (1977) discuss how it can provide 'a useful method of finding meaning in advertising' (27).

In describing how environments tend to be invisible, McLuhan (1970) was fond of saying, 'Fish don't know water exists till beached' (191). The water, in this case, is the environment or ground for the fish, which is so immersed within the environment that it has no perspective to perceive the water. McLuhan (McLuhan et al., 1977) points out that it is the media messages that are the figure and capture our attention, and the medium is the environment or ground that people rarely focus on. However, it is the medium that exerts a significant influence on the creation of the messages, the messages themselves, and the receivers of the message.

While the technology fades from our focus—moving from figure to ground—it continues to transform our abilities, a transformation we typically do not pay attention to. Strate (2017) explains that anything can become routine and taken for granted, causing it to recede from our awareness and effectively become invisible to us. At this point it can be considered environmental. Often, the only times we actually perceive mediums on their own terms is when a medium is new to us, when it breaks down, when we exert an active control over its operation, or when people use it creatively or artistically.

This is an important concept in the everyday aspect of media literacy. Our focus tends to steer away from the medium that is being used to communicate the message. However, Strate continues, 'an older medium may serve as what McLuhan [...] termed an anti-environment or counter-environment, an alternate environment that, by its unfamiliarity, brings our current environment into conscious awareness and visibility' (112–13). For example, I recently have been collecting old manual typewriters. When I type on them, I experience a counter-environment to using a word processing program on my laptop, allowing me insights to how each technology enables and constrains differently. The danger of media receding into the background (such as using word processing programs to write with) is that we become less likely to notice its effect on us or on our culture. This is where the concept of media bias can be leveraged. By becoming aware of media bias, we have the potential to regain some agency in our engagement with media.

Media Bias

I now look into how these environments have a bias that affects individuals and cultures, which often is not explicitly recognized by the users of the medium. While identifying a bias of communication mediums has caused some to accuse McLuhan and media ecology of technological determinism (cf. Moores, 2012; Smith & Marx, 1994; Williams, 2004), I explain why I believe claims of determinism are in error. Finally, I use the example of the Gutenberg Parenthesis (Pettitt, 2007, 2012) to demonstrate how the communication eras of orality, print, and digital can be understood through the different affordances of print photography and digital images.

Harold Innis (2008) describes cultures as having a certain bias due to the dominant communication medium. He discusses the effects of heavy media (such as stone) and light media (such as papyrus or the air for speech or radio waves) (33):

> A medium of communication has an important influence on the dissemination of knowledge over space and time and it becomes necessary to study its characteristics in order to appraise its influence in its cultural setting. According to its characteristics it may be better suited to the dissemination of knowledge over time than over space, particularly if the medium is heavy and durable and not suited to transportation, or to the dissemination of knowledge over space than over time, particularly if the medium is light and easily transported. The relative emphasis on time or space will imply a bias of significance to the culture in which it is embedded.

Looking at what is afforded by each broad paradigm of communication is a way to understand the fundamental influences that each can have on a culture. For instance, oral traditions rely on and value memory. A person's memory is then likely to be more developed in an oral culture than a print culture, where print acts as an extended memory (Ong, 2012).

When writing was being developed, there were people who were skeptical of this new medium. In *Phaedrus,* Plato lamented that writing would give us the semblance of knowledge without the knowledge itself (*Phaedrus*, 274–77). While people would have the written word, Plato questioned how much actual meaning and knowledge would be transmitted by the words alone, especially if the written words traveled far from the author and were read by people who might not be ready for them. The initial use of writing was as an external memory device. For example, early religious texts did not have punctuation or spaces as they were simply meant to jog the reader's memory in order to be read out loud. The performance was up to the reader and experienced orally by the audience (Martin & Cochrane, 1994).

Writing and print still contain aspects of orality. As McLuhan (1994) states, 'the "content" of any medium is always another medium' (8). Robert Logan (2000) points out that Innis and McLuhan often speak of three ages, or eras, of communication: oral, written, and electric. It is acknowledged that not every culture goes through, or has gone through, all of these ages—let alone at the same time. However, by looking at the macro perspective concerning the paradigms of human communication and the effect each has on individuals, societies, and cultures, we can gain insight into how these specific communication media have influenced us.

Technological Determinism and Agency

The focus of media ecology on the way media technologies affect individuals and cultures is often criticized—mostly from those outside the field—as being technological determinist. In other words, media ecologists are criticized for believing that technology determines people's actions, taking away most, if not all, human agency. Raymond Williams (2004) responds to McLuhan's approach by saying, 'For if the medium—whether print or television—is the cause, all other causes, all that men ordinarily see as history, are at once reduced to effects' (130).

Claims of technological determinism are sometimes well founded. For example, consider the words of Edmund Carpenter (1973), who worked with Marshall McLuhan:

> I think media are so powerful they swallow cultures. I think of them as invisible environments which surround and destroy old environments. Sensitivity to problems of culture conflict and conquest becomes meaningless here, for media play no favorites: they conquer all cultures. One may pretend that media preserve and present the old by recording it on film and tape, but that is mere distraction, a sleight-of-hand possible when people keep their eyes focused on content. (191)

This statement, that media 'conquer all cultures', comes across as quite deterministic. It also represents a pattern in media ecology, likely influenced by McLuhan himself, who was known for possessing a rather dramatic style of writing. Clark (2009) mentions, 'Metaphorical allusions, poetic flourishes, and theories on a grand scale have remained some of the hallmarks of style within the field of media ecology itself' (11). It may be that McLuhan writes this way in order to effectively shock society's attention into noticing the influence of the medium that is all but invisible, even to many academics. In addition, because media ecology is a varied field with many voices, it is natural to have some scholars who might lean more towards technological determinism than others.

Ong (1977) defends his own work against being perceived as deterministic by saying that his analysis of orality, print, and digital mediums of communication do not explain everything about culture and human consciousness. Instead, he claims that there is a relation between the major developments in culture and human consciousness and the evolution of the word from a primarily oral state to its present state. However, the relationships are 'varied and complex, with cause and effect often difficult to distinguish' (10).

Strate (2017) claims that technological determinism is, for the most part, 'a label applied by critics, rather than a term used, let alone embraced, within the field' (34) of media ecology. He explains, 'A bias does not represent absolute command over us, however, but rather a path of least resistance. [...] The concern within the field of media ecology, then, is the degree to which we cede control to the biases of technology' (36). This is similar to postphenomenology's concept of the non-neutrality of technology. Just because a technology is not neutral does not mean that it is completely determining.

To guard against the determining aspects of the technological medium, education can help bring about awareness of these effects. Developing this awareness is invaluable, allowing us greater agency, without which we risk living as beings determined by the technologies in our lives. Michel Puech (2016) explains, 'The lack of awareness implies here the absence of self-construction: living as an object in commercial and societal networks, not as a self' (173). This is where media literacy has a role to play. Education is a key way of helping people pay attention to the effects of media (McLuhan et al., 1977). By bringing the effects of a specific medium to a person's awareness, that person then has a better chance of retaining some of their agency in their relationship with the medium. Rather than a binary between neutral and determining views of technology there is a continuum; where one is on that continuum at any moment depends in part upon our awareness of the multiplicity of relations that are influencing us at any moment.

Media Ecology in Action: The Gutenberg Parenthesis

In sum, we can understand media bias by looking at how the dominant medium of communication for an age has specific effects on individuals, cultures, and societies. By understanding the current media environment through a broad historical context, we can bring more awareness to the affordances of specific media. In this section, I explore the print and digital mediums through the concept of the Gutenberg Parenthesis, using it to compare the different media biases between a print photograph and a digital image.

Thomas Pettitt (2007, 2012) explores three different communication paradigms: 1) the pre-print age before Gutenberg's printing press allowed for the dissemination of easily acquired printed materials; 2) the age of print dominance, where the primary way of communicating was through the printed word; and 3) the current age of digital and electronic media. Pettitt (2007: 3) describes this middle age, where print was the dominant means of communication, as the Gutenberg Parenthesis:

> Since the Renaissance, the communication of Western culture has been dominated and in many ways determined by mechanically mass-produced texts, symbolized by (but not restricted to) the printed book, but this is now discernible as merely a phase, discernibly coming to an end under the pressure of developments in relation to the electronic media, the internet and digital technology.

When Gutenberg's printing press popularized the ability to make copies of texts, print-based literacy became democratized, moving reading and writing out of the hands of the elite, and into the lives of the masses. This was a major disruption, at least in the Western world, especially for the Christian church and in politics (Postman, 2006). It was estimated that 'between 1640 and 1700, the literacy rate for (white) men in Massachusetts and Connecticut was somewhere between 89 percent and 95 percent' (Postman, 2006: 31). As one example of the socio-cultural impact, this literacy rate, combined with the printed news stories, was integral for the United States' revolution against Great Britain (Humphrey, 2013).

Western culture is now just emerging from the print-dominated era, but our mindset is still heavily influenced by the print paradigm. Ong (2012) provides an in-depth study on the differences that orality and print have on societies and cultures. While orality is heavily reliant on, and limited by, memory, the shift to print allows for externalized memory. Books become repositories for knowledge and information.

We are now entering an age dominated by a digital medium. While it might be assumed that as we move forward, we have more in common with the recent past than the distant pass, this is not always true. By looking at the affordances of an oral, print, and digital communication paradigm, we begin to notice, somewhat surprisingly, that digital communication has a lot in common with oral tradition, often more so than with the era of print communication. This is why Pettitt (2012) refers to the age of print as a *parenthesis*. According to Pettitt, the inception of a parenthesis in a sentence 'interrupts an earlier phase, which resumes when it concludes, if inevitably with modifications resulting from what has happened in the meantime' (96). In other words, the era of print communication has interrupted and changed our oral means of communication. Ong (2012) describes this new digital/ electronic age as a *secondary orality* that, 'has striking resemblances to the old in its participatory mystique, its fostering of a communal sense, its concentration on the present moment, and even its use of formulas' (133–34). As we move fully into the digital age it will not be surprising to find specifically print-based affordances like copyright being challenged by the affordances of the new digital medium.

Investigating Print Affordances

How exactly did the era of print as a dominant communication paradigm change individuals and culture? Ong (1977) posits, 'The tendency to closure had to do with a state of mind encouraged by print and its way of suggesting that knowledge, and thus indirectly actuality itself, could somehow be packaged' (330). In other words, print packaged ideas into a beginning, middle, and end, and this influenced the thinking process for print-based cultures. Print is static and materially bound. As Pettitt (2012) describes, 'A work in a book is self-contained, and resists any textual intrusion or extraction that would compromise this integrity. The technology places not merely physical but psychological boundaries around the text' (102). The print medium adds a sense of stability, a static nature to knowledge, even lending a sense of permanence.

Writing enables us to externalize our thoughts, which helps us develop more complicated ideas. Writing functions as an extended mind (Clark & Chalmers, 1998), helping to advance not only science and technology but also critical thought and social theory. By writing down what we know and turning this information into an object, the words are lent an air of objective truth, which has both benefits and drawbacks. This process allows knowledge to become an externalized *thing*; a thing that can be copyrighted and owned. The *thingness* of print is quite important, affording different abilities than the ephemerality of oral communication. Text is also linear, a straight path through time and space. It is read in one direction and is meant to be read in a sequential order, one word following another. And finally, there is a sense of authorship, of ownership, which leads to copyright and the ownership of knowledge, something that is not found in oral traditions.[9]

However, the externalized, static print model can be understood as an anomaly in how we have historically communicated. As Pettitt (2007) explains, 'the post-parenthetical period after and the pre-parenthetical period before may have more in common with each other than either has with the parenthetical phase that came in between' (3) Since we are directly evolving out of an age dominated by print, much of our media literacy is still greatly influenced by print. In order to exemplify this, I look next at the differences between print and digital photography.

Print Photographs and Digital Images

Since the investigation I use to develop an instrument in chapter six involves a specific digital image of a museum selfie, I use an example of the Gutenberg Parenthesis in order to explore the differences in medium-affordances between print photographs and digital images. Building upon Pettitt's (2007) original language,[10] I have updated the terminology—which I will explain—in order to compare the traits in

9 However, oral traditions will often have certain people whose role is to be a keeper of knowledge.

10 The table below illustrates Pettitt's (2007: 2) original terminology:

Pre-Parenthetical	Gutenberg Parenthesis	Post-Parenthetical
re-creative	original	sampling
collective	individual	remixing
con-textual	autonomous	borrowing
unstable	stable	reshaping
traditional	canonical	appropriating
Performance	composition	recontextualizing

terms of ICTs (see Fig. 3.4). These are considered on a meta level; they have a general influence on the society as a whole but are not meant to be prescriptive for every individual case in every situation. This is what media ecology describes as the bias of the medium, which then leads to cultural biases (Innis, 2008). Again, these biases have influence on us, but through media literacy education we have the ability to regain some of our agency.

Gutenberg Parenthesis

Orality	Print (~1500 – ~2000)	Digital
Unstable	Stable	Temporary
Memory	External	Networked
Improvisation	Linear text	Hypertext
Performance	Artifact	Performance
Anonymous	Authored	Appropriating
Subjective truth	Objective truth	Post-truth

Fig. 3.4 *Modified Gutenberg Parenthesis.* Image by author (2018), CC BY 4.0.

Photography battles with the fantasy that it captures a neutral view of reality without modifying it. Susan Sontag (1973) refers to a judiciary use of the printed photograph that 'passes for incontrovertible proof that a given thing happened' (3). However, she states her opinion that 'photographs are as much an interpretation of the world as paintings and drawings' (4). Additionally, the art of dodging and burning[11] during the transfer from negative to print was well established before Photoshop and digital photography. Ansel Adams is known for spending many hours in the darkroom developing a single print and said, 'dodging and burning are steps to take care of mistakes God made in establishing tonal relationships' (as cited in Li et al., 2015: 131). However, digital images tend to be one more step removed from reality. While the negative in print photography is still an image, the file of a digital image

11 Dodging and burning are used to lighten or darken specific parts of the rendered print photograph.

is comprised of bits—computerized 1's and 0's—that are not an image until interpreted and displayed by a combination of software and an electronic display device.

Additionally, a print photograph is a tangible artifact, a physical object with unique qualities. Though it is possible to replicate photographs, a photographer can have a reasonable amount of control[12] over how many copies are produced and how they are printed (size and quality, as well as original framing). The print photograph is not necessarily one specific thing or another, but it is rather as a vehicle, a medium, which can portray and achieve various designations (art, document, snapshot, mnemonic device, etc.). Joanna Zylinska (2017) describes the act of photography as 'cutting reality into small pieces [...where] we enact separation and relationality as the two dominant aspects of material locatedness in time' (43). The materiality of the photograph adds concreteness and limits its spatial existence. Using the qualities in Figure 3.4 under 'print' and 'digital' we can compare a print photograph with a digital image. I italicize the words from this figure that I am referring to when making the comparisons.

Print Photographs. The affordances of the print photograph are that it is a *stable* medium; it is light, transportable, and somewhat fragile, but under the right conditions can be still quite recognizable after 50–100 years. Print is an *external memory* device, able to invoke memories, especially of the people immediately concerned with the subject of the photograph. It is *linear*, a snapshot in time, occurring after some events and before others. It is an *artifact*, a material object. It is *authored*. Someone took the photograph, and they are the creators of the object, legally acknowledged (unless they work for a company or a government agency that is paying them to take the photo) as the copyright owners. Finally, being a material object that re-presents an image of reality, there is a semblance of *objective truth*. This is reflected in the ability to use photographs in court as evidence.

Digital Images. In comparison with print photographs, a digital image is *temporary*. It is a computer file, represented by 0's and 1's, which is only able to be displayed (performed) through its contextualizing metadata. It can be saved onto many different types of physical mediums (e.g., thumb drives, hard drives, and DVD/CDs).

12 They had more control before the invention of high-definition color copiers.

While saving something to 'the cloud' sounds immaterial, the actual file is stored on at least one material server/storage device. If it is not rewritten after a period of time (around 10–15 years, depending upon the specific medium), there are several issues that can threaten the integrity of the stored information:[13]

1. The deterioration of the medium itself (DVD's have a 15–20-year lifespan or up to 50 years for the archival variety).
2. The file format can become unreadable as software programs and formats continue to advance. Twenty-five years ago, WordStar was a very popular word processing program, but trying to get a computer to display a WordStar file now would be quite difficult. Eventually, the file format needs to be 'saved as' a newer version.
3. The memory storage device eventually becomes unsupported due to the physical structure. 5 ¼ inch disks gave way to 3 ½ inch disks, which gave way to CD-ROMs, then DVDs then USB drives, etc.

The digital image also has a *networked memory*, meaning that it affords the ability to be accessed in a networked manner. This allows many people simultaneous access to the same file, unlimited by proximity if the digital image is connected to the internet (where a print photograph is more limited by proximity and space). This also relates to *hypertext*, where the image can be linked non-linearly. With a shared link, the image can be embedded into most digital documents, accessible either by being embedded or by clicking on a link.

The digital image is greatly affected by what is *performing* the image (the printed photograph is also a performance of the negative but has

13 While it is true that some of these possible futures can be remedied through automated processes, there is a parallel between traits from an oral tradition and the need for each generation to decide what information is 'saved' in order to be transmitted to future generations. Decisions of what to transmit and what not to transmit are important as knowledge is passed down through generations. Inherently, information will be lost. It is also not possible to know what information and knowledge will be relevant or significant for future generations with shifts in culture, language, lifestyle, relationship with technology, etc. Even with the intention of transmitting something, the most proven medium devised with the longest and most successful means of archiving is still microfilm. Its estimated longevity is 500 years and can be read with a strong magnifying glass.

more fixity and materiality than the digital image). The type of screen and software interpreting and performing the digital bits has an impact on how the image looks. The exact same file can be a grainy thumbnail displayed on an old cellphone, or it can be viewed on a very large high-definition widescreen display. While a print photograph is 'performed' in an analog process using chemicals, light, and special paper, a digital image is performed by both hardware and software that mediate its appearance, whether on a smartphone, a website, a laptop, or a large screen television display. A single digital file of an image depends upon the technological mediation of the software and hardware to display the file. However, as Figure 3.5 demonstrates, the actual image is built upon code—binary bits and bytes—which are then interpreted and performed through many technological steps.

0xA1	0x2E	0xBB	0x01	0x23	0x1F	0x3E	0x41	0x04	0xBC	0xB2
0xB9	0x72	0xA5	0x9F	0x60	0x7D	0x71	0xF6	0x40	0xDE	0x92
0xA1	0xD0	0xFA	0xA2	0xE0	0xCA	0xB3	0x12	0xC1	0x29	0x50
0x78	0xDF	0x97	0xE5	0x94	0xBD	0xB3	0x6D	0xF5	0x05	0xD7
0x2E	0xC2	0xFF	0xB5	0x30	0xF2	0xA7	0x91	0x1C	0xDA	0x5A
0x9C	0xAC	0xDB	0x6C	0xFB	0xD2	0xCA	0xF0	0x2D	0x10	0x70
0xED	0xD8	0x3B	0xAE	0x7C	0xED	0x8F	0x5D	0x68	0x45	0xFD

Fig. 3.5 *Partial Display of a Digital Image File as Performed in Hexadecimal.* Image by author (2021), CC BY 4.0.

Much more so than a static object, the authorship of a digital image is open to *appropriation*. It is very easy to take a screenshot of somebody's digital image, potentially modifying it, and portraying it as your own. Due to the ease of copying or pirating digital content, there has been much effort to create digital rights management policies in order to protect original authors. However, it is the ease of the digital format that creates this need, as it both enables and constrains.

Coming to the final word in Figure 3.4, the digital image lends itself to *post-truth* rather than the semblance of objective truth of print photographs. This is because of the ease of modifying the original photo, making the 'reality' of its original capture appear quite different yet still realistic. Software such as Adobe Photoshop can dramatically alter the original image in a way that is very hard to detect (Hanson, 2004; Manovich, 2013). For instance, the ability to remove or add people from the image is quite simple. Because this is possible, digital images need to be (or at least should be) professionally analyzed to detect any modification if they are going to be used as evidence in court cases. Mark Hansen (2004) writes, 'Following its digitization, the image can no longer be understood as a fixed and objective viewpoint on "reality" [...] since it is now defined precisely through its almost complete flexibility and addressibility [*sic*], its numerical basis, and its constitutive "virtuality"' (7–8). He continues by describing the digital image as no longer being 'restricted to the level of surface appearance, but must be extended to encompass the entire process by which information is made perceivable through embodied experience' (10). The digital image, therefore, needs to be understood not only by how it looks, but also through interpretation by software and hardware.

These examples demonstrate the need for unlearning the previous construct of the print photograph as we are now primarily dealing with digital images. By deterritorializing (Deleuze & Guattari, 1987) the photograph from the print paradigm and reterritorializing it within the affordances of the digital, we can let go of our previous concepts of 'the print photograph' and develop more realistic expectations afforded by digital images. The communication paradigms—orality, print, and digital—are transformative, enabling some things while constraining others. Becoming aware of these details can allow us to modify both our own expectations and help us to decide what is important (or not) to fight for once something we value becomes constrained.

Copyright issues are a useful example of the affordances of specific communication mediums. Copyright does not exist in a strictly oral society. It only comes about with the externalization of knowledge into an object—the written word. This allows for the ability of ownership, of authorship. What should we do now that the digital paradigm makes it much easier to break copyright laws? Do we still value copyright and believe it should be retained? If so, what are the policies and technological developments that need to happen to continue enabling and respecting copyright? Investigating this further is beyond the scope of my research (cf. Chen, 2017, for further discussion on copyright and the link to print), but this brief overview demonstrates the importance of understanding the broader communication paradigms, and these issues warrant further study and discussion.

Concluding Thoughts

While there have traditionally been two sides of the 'media coin', the message and the medium, this book focuses on changing this binary to an assemblage of medium, content, and context. I have approached understanding the effects of the medium through a micro and a macro lens. Postphenomenology and media ecology help improve our awareness of the impact of technology on the constitution of the subject, understanding that the subject is constituted through technological relations.

Postphenomenology contributes to our understanding of the non-neutrality of technological mediation. It helps us become aware of how media technologies can become sedimented through our experiences, causing them to fade from our awareness and become transparent. Postphenomenology also adds the concept of multistability of media technologies, keeping us from falling into essentializing claims. Media ecology can help us understand media as complex environments that have unique biases, which influence us. Media ecology also emphasizes the use of a figure/ground approach, a tool that can help us identify the media biases that are often backgrounded and not part of our awareness. Both of these fields of study can be used to construct an inclusive, holistic approach to enhance media literacy.

While we now have a solid foundation in understanding technological mediation, the focus until now has been directed *toward* the media technologies themselves. These technologies can be understood as having a shared agency with human subjects, as we relate to the media in our daily lives. However, as some of the agency moves away from the subject and into technological objects, Tamar Sharon (2014) points out that disciplines such as postphenomenology seem to focus more on 'breathing life into objects [...] than delving into the implications of having breathed life out of subjects' (9). She proposes that we take a closer look at what is going on with the subject. In the next chapter, I take on Sharon's challenge in order to understand the transformational effects of technologies that occur within the subject. I also explore what is meant by the posthuman subject.

4

Human-Technology Relations and the Location of the Subject

> I take the posthuman predicament as an opportunity to empower the pursuit of alternative schemes of thought, knowledge and self-representation. The posthuman condition urges us to think critically and creatively about who and what we are actually in the process of becoming. (Braidotti, 2013: 12)

After focusing on the technological relations in the previous chapter, I now bring the discussion to the human side of the human-technology relation, trying to better understand what makes up the human subject under discussion. I first give a brief historical account of the humanist subject, consider the transhumanist subject, and discuss how they each are involved with the human enhancement debate. I then make the case for a philosophical posthuman subject that is complex and emergent. Through a contemporary approach to the human, I use complexity to understand our selves not as standalone individuals but as complex and interrelational beings who are always becoming through the relations in our lives. This chapter will finalize the background and theoretical underpinnings for the framework developed in Chapter 5.

It is difficult, if not impossible, to fully comprehend the effect of information and communication technologies (ICTs) without first having an accurate understanding of the human subject. While we have made great advances in developing technologies, it is surprising how challenging it remains to answer the question, *what are we?* While it may be simple to ask the question, contriving an answer is much more complicated. Finding the answer to this question has been one of the primary concerns of philosophers (and humankind) throughout recorded history.

In order to understand how the technological relation discussed in chapter three constitutes us, it is helpful to understand what is this 'us' we are talking about. While understanding the human subject has changed throughout history, it is further complicated by the wide range of cultures with radically different ways of interpreting the human. My main focus remains on the contemporary, Westernized world. This is not to discount other cultures that have beneficial contributions and perspectives, but simply to limit the scope and stay embedded within my own situated knowledge so as to avoid 'appropriating the vision of the less powerful while claiming to see from their positions' (Haraway, 1988: 584).

Humanists and Transhumanists Debating Enhancement

As ICTs encroach more and more into our lives, questions of the convergence of humans and technology are raised. The majority of people in the developed world now have a constant connection with the digital world through smartphones—roughly 72%—and the undeveloped world has reached almost half who have a constant connection (Poushter et al., 2018: 4). This connection provides instant information retrieval via a browser search (often Google) and an ever-present network of friends via social media. At one's fingertips are answers to almost any question, from restaurant reviews, to directions, to definitions. Translation apps can use augmented reality by using the phone's camera to change an image's words into one's preferred language (Fragoso et al., 2011). Wearable technology is taking advantage of being located on one's body and provides a person with health-related information and insights (Van Den Eede, 2015b). Technologies are indeed 'moving towards us, into us' (Van Den Eede, 2017: xxv).

Recent advances in nano, biological, and information technologies, along with cognitive sciences (collectively referred to as NBIC technologies), have sparked a passionate 'human enhancement' debate concerning what it means to be human (Roco & Bainbridge, 2003). On one side are transhumanists, who cite our long history of using technology to survive and improve our lives; from fire, to shelter, to cross-breeding plants for better agricultural yields. In the transhumanist view, gene splicing and nano technologies are simply next steps in this long history. On the other side of the spectrum are the bioconservatives, or traditional humanists, who believe that human enhancement can lead to the potential loss of something essentially human.

First, there is no one humanism or one transhumanism. Both have evolved over time, and both are comprised of many people with differing opinions. My ultimate goal is not to disprove either of these approaches, but to create a contemporary understanding of the human subject in order to more fully realize how relations with technologies contribute towards constituting the human subject. I attempt to limit making sweeping statements. I also restrain from spending too much time defining myself against other approaches, saving the bulk of my argument for an *affirmative* building of my position.

Convergence of Humans and Technologies

As ICTs come ever more entangled with our lives, one question might be raised concerning how much longer it will be before we move from wearable to wide spread *embedded* technology? This brings about the question of NBIC technologies and human-technology convergence. Already there are advances to neural interfaces, where the goal is to 'seamlessly integrate the interface between neurobiology and engineered technology to record from and modulate neurons' (Wellman et al., 2018: 1; cf. Neely et al., 2018). Brain-to-machine interfaces are being developed for assistive technologies (Donati et al., 2016) but also more generally for 'interaction between a person and a machine via thought' (Sargent et al., 2017: 1). There are now even brain-to-brain interfaces being developed (Zhang et al., 2019).

In addition to this convergence between humans and technological artifacts, the door is now open to inexpensive manipulation of the human genetic code; for example, through CRISPR-Cas9 process (Doudna & Sternberg, 2017; Ran et al., 2013), which makes it relatively easy and inexpensive to cut out unwanted genes and replace them with different genes, even genes from non-humans. Technologies and humans are converging on many different fronts. Possibilities that a few years ago seemed like science fiction appear to have credible potential in the near future. The situation has caused a polarized debate concerning human enhancement. On one side of the debate are the exciting possibilities of eradicating chronic diseases and improving the quality and longevity of human lives. On the other side, there are concerns over losing something essentially *human* (Fukuyama, 2004) through the convergence with technology.

There is also concern over equity and the increasing division between the haves and have-nots. It is possible that the more affluent will be able to give their children improvements with enhanced minds and bodies while the less affluent remain 'behind'. This could even lead to some humans becoming so enhanced that they become *post*-humans, taking an evolutionary step beyond what we consider as *Homo sapiens*. This situation highlights the need to address how we define 'human' in relation to converging technologies. We now are starting to possess the technological ability to be able to play a more active role in the evolution of humanity, causing some to question our ability to understand the long- and short-term ramifications of playing the role of *Homo deus* (Harari, 2016). This leads to questions like: What is the most helpful approach to understanding the convergence of technology and the human? How can the human be separate from technology at the same time it is converging with it? Is there a more relevant representation of the human individual than the centuries old humanist ideal as captured by Da Vinci's *Vitruvian Man*?

Humanism and the Enlightenment: An Old Foundation

Today, the humanist mantel is interpreted differently by bioconservatives (or conservative humanists) on one side (e.g., Fukuyama, 2002, 2004; Habermas, 2003; McKibben, 2004) and transhumanists on the other (e.g., Bostrom, 2005, 2013; Kurzweil, 2005; Moravec, 1988; More, 2013). However, both sides of the debate have foundations in humanism and the Enlightenment. Because the foundation of the human enhancement debate rests on rational humanism and the Enlightenment, I begin with an overview.

As Sharon (2014) points out, both bioconservatives and transhumanists are founded upon humanist ideals. The rational humanist subject, stemming from the seventeenth and eighteenth centuries and closely connected to the Enlightenment, is an empowered subject, able to think for itself and not necessarily depend upon religion for answers. Rationalism and the age of reason led European society (and beyond) toward great advances, including the industrial revolution. The autonomous individual became the norm. Beatrice Han-Pile (2010) states that in the English-speaking world humanism is:

> often associated with an optimistic and secular view of the world which asserts the privilege of human beings over non-organic (or organic but nonhuman) entities, defending the rights of human beings to happiness and to the development of their individual potential (118).

Humanism helped move humanity out of the 'Dark Ages' and into an age of reason and control, elevating and empowering the human individual. While humanism and modernism have contributed to reducing famine, plagues, and deaths due to wars (Harari, 2016), it has also led to humanity consuming the Earth's resources[1] at an alarming rate. This has contributed to bringing us into the sixth mass extinction (Cafaro, 2015) at the same time as the fourth industrial (technological) revolution (Schwab, 2017).

Humanism was not always so singularly (and narrowly) defined (Braidotti, 2013; Han-Pile, 2010; Hayles, 2008; and additionally,[2] Hughes, 2010a). However, with the backlash against positivism and the outcry from the French poststructuralists and postmodernists, humanism has been shaped into a discipline that has lost some of its previous diversity and is now seen in a more singular manner; as valuing the rational, autonomous, and exceptional self, where the natural world is a Heideggerian (1977) reserve of resources available for our use and

1 Humanism's merger with capitalism has teamed up to provide us with an industrialized and global economy that churns out profits and supplies us with a seemingly unlimited number of gadgets. While we have never been so entertained, with access to so much fantastical variety of fetishes, fantasies, and spectacle, the question remains: at what price and *what happened to the promised enlightenment*?

2 In relation to divisions within the Enlightenment.

exploitation. And yet, the embrace of 'the human' obscures those who remain un-embraced; marginalized groups who are too slowly being accepted as equal or even included, and who are still far from counting as fully human in the eyes of too many (Latour, 1993). As Braidotti (2013: 1) points out,

> Not all of us can say, with any degree of certainty, that we have always been human, or that we are only that. Some of us are not even considered fully human now, let alone at previous moments of Western social, political and scientific history. Not if by 'human' we mean that creature familiar to us from the Enlightenment [...]. And yet the term enjoys widespread consensus and it maintains the re-assuring familiarity of common sense. We assert our attachment to the species as if it were a matter of fact, a given. So much so that we construct a fundamental notion of Rights around the Human. But is it so?

A very troubling aspect of humanism is the shift toward eugenics and the genocide of Jews, LGBTQs, people with abilities that were perceived outside of a socially-constructed norm, and various marginalized groups in the name of perfecting the human 'race'. Even now, women are not paid a wage equal to men in nearly all places around the globe, LGBTQ rights are not accepted worldwide, and racism[3] continues to be widespread. While the humanist concept of the human has helped some become empowered, it has left other humans outside of what is accepted, or desired. Another part of the criticism of humanists is that they adopt an anthropocentric perspective, considering the human as exceptional and placing people above any other species in the world.

Transhumanism: Reasonable or Extreme?

Rather than focusing on the humanist past, transhumanists tend to be futurists. For instance, one of the main voices in the transhumanist movement is Nick Bostrom, who is the founding director of the Future for Humanity Institute in Oxford. In this section, I consider two types of approaches that transhumanists concern themselves with. The first is the near future and the idea of making incremental improvements

3 As I write this in June 2020, there are massive global protests in support of the Black Lives Matter movement, sparked by continual killings of mostly black men by police in the U.S.

to humans. I then consider the more distant future ideas such as mind uploading, which I believe distract more than help the transhumanist cause. However, the most troublesome aspect of much of transhumanism is the foundational idea of the standalone individual that is rooted in the Enlightenment. While I believe this critical flaw needs to be remedied, there are also positive aspects of transhumanism.

My intention here is to not provide a sweeping criticism of transhumanism per se, but to critically engage with some of its fundamental concepts and attempt to tease apart concepts and ideas that can be beneficial from others that I believe are flawed. Rather than focusing on its strong libertarian past, I am encouraged by the increased focus on social democratic ideals from James Hughes (2010a, 2010b, 2012). While I don't believe all of the problem issues have completely disappeared from transhumanist dialogues, I do believe there is an increased focus on social equity and the acknowledgement of the complexity of human consciousness and cognition. For example, Max More (2013: 10) writes,

> The search for absolute foundations for reason, for instance, has given way to a more sophisticated, uncertain, and self-critical form of critical rationalism. The simple, unified self has been replaced by the far more complex and puzzling self revealed by the neurosciences. The utterly unique status of human beings has been superseded by an understanding that we are part of a spectrum of biological organisms and possible non-biological species of the future.

A common idea within the transhumanist field is, 'within certain limits, [...] it is desirable to use emerging technologies to enhance human physical and cognitive capacities and to make other beneficial alterations to human traits' (Blackford, 2011). Stephen Sorgner (2019) explains, 'expanding the human health span is a central goal of most transhumanists' (17). More (2013: 5) coined the term *extropy*, which concerns

> perpetual progress, self-transformation, practical optimism, intelligent technology, open society, self-direction, and rational thinking. Perpetual progress is a strong statement of the transhumanist commitment to seek 'more intelligence, wisdom, and effectiveness, an open-ended lifespan, and the removal of political, cultural, biological, and psychological limits to continuing development. Perpetually overcoming constraints on

> our progress and possibilities as individuals, as organizations, and as a species.' [...] The implementation of transhumanism [is] a continual process and not about seeking a state of perfection.[4]

More's statement refutes the claim that transhumanists are utopians striving to become perfect. The immediate goal of transhumanism is not necessarily a complete convergence with technology; rather, it is to improve the lives of humans, primarily through the use of technology.

While the transhumanist movement began in the 1980s (Lewis, 2018) with a fair amount of unabashed exuberance, it has since matured and looks more closely at, for instance, the risks[5] involved with new technologies. For example, Bostrom's Future of Humanity Institute in Oxford (and others) has begun focusing on existential risks (Bostrom, 2013). Additionally, there has been more attention to the societal issues, expanding beyond the focus on the individual (Hughes, 2004, 2012; Wood, 2017). Hughes (2012) states, 'Much transhumanist politics has been shaped by the libertarian leanings of its affluent, educated, male, and American base. But in the last decade transhumanists have become far more culturally and politically diverse' (758), moving more toward a liberal democratic focus.

Looking over the Transhumanist Declaration (More & Vita-More, 2013) and the recommitment to the Technoprogressive Declaration (Wood, 2017), I have attempted to distill a vision statement in order to capture the fundamental goals of transhumanism and to make sure that the changes to the philosophical foundations that I later suggest will only further support, and not take away from, this vision. This vision disconnects any necessary link to Enlightenment ideals. The vision of transhumanism I propose is as follows: *To reduce suffering, inequality, and premature death—or more positively: to increase access to health, happiness, and longevity of all humans and their environment—through the strategic use (including non-use) of technology.* I include the 'environment' as an extension to some of the more anthropocentric leanings of the declarations since, without an environment there will be no human flourishing. I do not claim that this vision would be unanimously agreeable to transhumanists, but I do believe it captures much of the current positive intention behind the field.

4 More is citing the 2003 version of the Principles of Extropy (https://hpluspedia.org/wiki/Extropian_principles).

5 See also Coeckelbergh (2013).

Transhumanist discussions concerning near-term goals of improving the human condition through technology can still be understood by many outside the movement as being potentially beneficial. However, there are also transhumanist discussions concerning more fantastical scenarios, such as whole brain emulation, also referred to as mind uploading (Bostrom 2014; Kurzweil 2005, 2012; Moravec, 1988; Sandberg, 2013). This is the concept that the brain could possibly be digitized, replacing the biological neurons that are in an on or off state with a computerized/mechanical replacement. The idea is that this process could possibly capture the 'mind' and consciousness of a person, making them no longer reliant on a biological body. This potentially would allow their consciousness to live almost indefinitely, or at least greatly enhance their lifespan, and would qualify—at least in the minds of many—as a *post*-human. This also ties into allowing for easier interstellar travel, allowing for humanity (or post-humanity) to more easily move beyond the confines of the Earth and reducing the existential risk for humans (Bostrom, 2013).

There are others—like myself—who believe that there is no way to separate the brain and the body; the mind exists in both entities (Hayles, 1999; Varela et al., 1992). This concept of mind challenges the transhumanists' desire to upload our minds into machines by scanning our brains, and at the very least, would indicate the need to upload more than just the brain (maybe a full body upload?). While there are other extreme potentialities entertained by transhumanists, such as variations on a singularity due to super intelligence that may or may not include humans (Kurzweil, 2005), I keep my focus on the more practical near-term goals and the relevancy to understanding the human subject.

Reactions to Transhumanism

As Francis Fukuyama says, 'It is tempting to dismiss transhumanists as some sort of odd cult, nothing more than science fiction taken too seriously' (2004: 42). I, myself, have found it difficult at times not to paint transhumanists in a reductive manner, one based more on the early beginnings of transhumanism than on some of the current, more reflective, dialogues that are taking place within the discipline. And yet, as Fukuyama asks,[6] 'is the fundamental tenet of transhumanism—that we will someday use biotechnology to make ourselves stronger, smarter, less prone to violence, and longer-lived—really so outlandish?' (42).

Transhumanists often claim to have to defend themselves against *strawman*[7] attacks. One can see this in various articles and rebuttals throughout Gregory Hansell and William Grassie's (2011) book on transhumanism and its critics. I myself have struggled with reactionary tendencies while listening to some exuberant self-described transhumanist discuss their—in my opinion—nearly religious belief in the virtues of technological possibilities for human enhancement. However, I have also had the pleasure of having dialogues with transhumanists such as James Hughes, who I find to be intelligent and articulate. In my opinion, Hughes gives many very reasonable arguments for transhumanism, and he, too, has pointed out internal conflicts within transhumanism connected with its ties to the Enlightenment (2010a; 2010b).

I believe that there are several reasons why people react against or misunderstand ideas from transhumanists. Transhumanism's exuberance towards technology and willingness to embrace long-term possibilities like whole brain emulation can get in the way of some of its more feasible goals and objectives. For some, the focus on mind uploading is a distraction or red herring[8] (Sorgner, 2019), and they believe the focus should stay on the immediate future, working towards improving human health, both mental and physical, and extending human lifespans.

Another aspect that I believe works against transhumanism is the tendency to present technology in a glossy, high-tech, marketing manner[9] rather than grounded and situated, demonstrating both benefits and constraints and highlighting the complexity involved with manipulating living systems. Additionally, there is a tendency to be too focused on the individual, which might be the most difficult to overcome. This focus on

---

6 Fukuyama's response to transhumanism was resoundingly negative, claiming the goals fundamentally threaten our human essence.

7 Philosophical *strawmen* arguments are arguments where the person criticizing a concept first defines the concept without providing all of the context or nuances, allowing them to easily identify flaws.

8 Red herrings are dried and smoked herrings (the processing turns their coloring reddish) and were, at least anecdotally, used for their smell in order to throw off pursuing dogs or wolves by confusing the scent trail.

9 Doing a simple web search for images relating to 'transhumanist' reveals this.

the exceptional individual has led some to indicate that transhumanism is really 'ultra-humanist' (Onishi, 2011: 103).

Ihde (1990: 75–76) describes the concept of 'technofantasy', where:

> I want the transformation that the technology allows, but I want it in such a way that I am basically unaware of its presence. I want it in such a way that it becomes me. Such a desire both secretly rejects what technologies are and overlooks the transformational effects, which are necessarily tied to human-technology relations.

Don Ihde (2011) links transhumanists with technofantasy and equates the technofantasy to magic in the sense that new human enhancing technologies are often portrayed without 'ambiguous or unintended or contingent consequences' (57). He also worries about the unpredictability of these consequences 'and the introduction of disruptions into an ever-growing and more complex system' (60). Ihde's point is that we cannot simply add technology to our lives without experiencing a transformative change—one that enables and constrains (cf. Lewis, 2018). However, I believe that the most fundamental flaw with certain transhumanists is the focus on, and the near sanctity of, the standalone individual.

A New Foundation for Transhumanism

Since the Enlightenment and rational humanism, the de facto basic building block of our existence in the Western world has been the individual, which literally means indivisible (OED online, 4th edition). One way for transhumanists to 'win' the human enhancement debate against the bioconservatives is to stop trying to fit into the humanist ideology. In a way, the human enhancement debate is a red herring, as both sides come from a humanist standpoint. There is a need to deterritorialize the human from the standalone individual humanist subject. Figure 4.1 represents the move from a humanist view of the autonomous individual to the relational foundation developed in chapter three. In the humanist representation, Da Vinci's *Vitruvian Man* is inside a bold circle, anchoring it to the Enlightenment view of the subject who is self-sufficient, exceptional, and able to achieve enlightenment or self-sustainability purely by 'his' own abilities. Instead, my proposed approach builds upon the idea of the subject as constituted through relations.

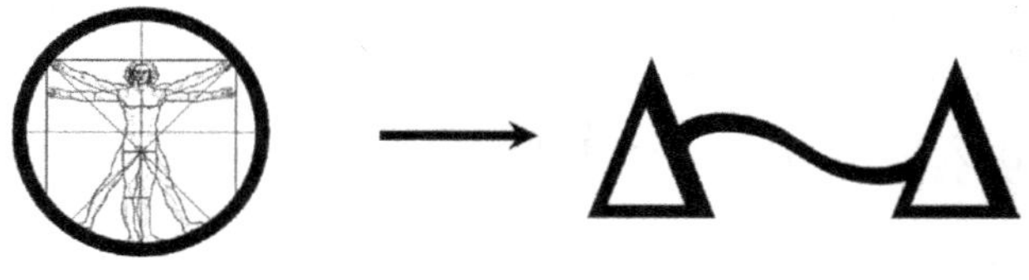

Fig. 4.1 *The Humanist Individual to the Co-constituted Relational Subject.* Image by author (2021), CC BY 4.0.

The underlying issue is that, while transhumanism is a forward-looking discipline, it is still tied to and hampered by its foundation in rational humanist and Enlightenment concepts, dating back to the seventeenth and eighteenth centuries (Hughes, 2010a; More, 2013). While its goals center on improving the human condition through contemporary and future technologies, transhumanism would benefit by taking a critical look into the philosophy it is built upon. As a discipline, it generally views the world and the human condition as complicated but solvable, allowing for an engineering approach to solve many of humanity's issues (cf. Allenby & Sarewitz, 2011). While transhumanists have had a more liberal (Sharon, 2014) attitude when it comes to using technology to enhance our biological selves, they have still based their approach on the sanctity of the individual. As Hughes (2010b) points out, 'transhumanists need to understand how the ideological conflicts within transhumanism today are the product of these 300-year-old conflicts within the Enlightenment' (para. 4).

Transhumanism's best chance at improving the human population globally is to move away from traditional humanism and begin to embrace the complex posthumanist subject, which is based on the contemporary amodern philosophies of philosophical posthumanism, postphenomenology, and complexity theory. As Barad (2007: ix) states,

> To be entangled is not simply to be intertwined with another, as in the joining of separate entities, but to lack an independent, self-contained existence. Existence is not an individual affair. Individuals do not preexist their interactions; rather, individuals emerge through and as part of their entangled intra-relating.

Transhumanists represent the desire to go beyond any conservative view of the human, to challenge who we are and explore avenues of becoming something better. Transhumanism can leave humanism to the bioconservatives and embrace more contemporary disciplines that are better positioned to help fulfill transhumanist's goals. As Hughes (2010a) points out, 'Most transhumanists argue the Enlightenment case for Reason without awareness of its self-undermining nature' (624). Transhumanists would be better served by evolving their thinking, adapting ideas from philosophical posthumanism, complexity, and postphenomenology, moving from technological exuberance to a reflexive and critical (though still affirmative) view on improving humanity through the intentional and critical use of technologies.

According to Samantha Frost (2016: 1),

> The characteristics, qualities, and capacities that heretofore have been taken to define and distinguish a human, humanity—the human—have been so profoundly discredited through historical, social, and scientific analysis that the notion itself seems to be bankrupt, with very little left to recommend it.

At the same time that we find it difficult to find a concise definition of the human, we are also noting the effects humans have made on the planet. We are, amongst other things, a force of nature as we are beginning to take note, as indicated by naming our current geologic age the Anthropocene (Lewis, 2018; Steffen et al., 2007, 2011).

For transhumanists, the *post*-human is an evolutionary development that will occur as we, through the use of technology, evolve into a species that essentially is no longer human. This is radically different from what the field of philosophical posthumanism defines it as. I use *posthuman* to refer to a way of defining our selves as we are now (and as we have been). It is an attempt to undermine the prevalent use of the term 'human' that is tenaciously linked to the Enlightenment and rational humanist thinking: the concept of the human as a standalone, exceptional individual. The time has come to decisively turn our backs on the idealization of a perfect human speci-*man* and make the move for inclusivity, diversity, and plurality. It is a posthumanist approach that I will use in developing a way for understanding the effects of new media technologies.

The Posthuman Subject

In this section, I describe the posthuman subject, one that is interrelational, emergent, and complex. This is the co-constituted subject from Chapter 3, and it is the foundational concept upon which the framework in Chapter 5 is constructed. The exploration of the posthuman subject has involved many thinkers (cf. Adams & Thompson, 2016; Badmington, 2011; Barad, 2007; Braidotti, 2002, 2011, 2013, 2016a, 2016b; Ferrando, 2019; Gergen, 2009; Haraway, 1985, 2016; Hayles, 1999; Puech, 2016; Roden, 2014; Wolfe, 2010), not all of whom use, or are comfortable using, the term 'posthuman'. While the previous section focused on what the human subject is *not* (countering a humanist version), this section examines what the posthuman *is,* and affirmatively embraces the concept as a way to reterritorialize the human subject. Braidotti (2013) summarizes the need for this new imagining of the subject by saying 'we need to devise new social, ethical and discursive schemes of subject formation to match the profound transformation we are undergoing' (12).

Historically Situating and Defining Posthumanism

In *Cyborg Manifesto*, Donna Haraway (1985) challenges the boundaries of separation (animal/human, machine/human, male/female) and instead petitions for hybridity by using the concept of the cyborg. This is one of the foundational texts for posthumanism. Another significant contribution to the field is N. Katherine Hayles (1999), *How We Became Posthuman*. In this book, Hayles specifically takes on transhumanism's desire of mind uploading and traces the movement back through to its cybernetic roots, explaining how the disembodiment of information has led transhumanists to believe that a separation of the mind and body is possible. Karen Barad (2007: 136) explains posthumanism in opposition to the traditional humanist approach:

> Posthumanism, as I intend it here, is not calibrated to the human; on the contrary, it is about taking issue with human exceptionalism while being accountable for the role we play in the differential constitution and differential positioning of the human among other creatures (both living and nonliving). [...] Posthumanism eschews both humanist and structuralist accounts of the subject that position the human as either pure cause or pure effect, and the body as the natural and fixed dividing line

> between interiority and exteriority. Posthumanism doesn't presume the separateness of any-'thing,' let alone the alleged spatial, ontological, and epistemological distinction that sets humans apart. The posthumanist subject eschews binaries such as human/nature, nature/culture. It also resists the concept of an exceptional and essential self.

Rosi Braidotti (2002, 2011, 2013) has been highly influential in the field of posthumanism with her *Metamorphoses*, *Nomadic Theory*, and what is now the classic text of posthumanism, *The Posthuman*. Braidotti (2013) states, 'I find [posthuman] useful as a term to explore ways of engaging affirmatively with the present, accounting for some of its features in a manner that is empirically grounded without being reductive and remains critical while avoiding negativity' (5). This affirmative criticism, one that does not fall into postmodernism or nihilism, looks for positive ways of becoming. 'The strength of posthuman critical thought [...] is in providing a frame for affirmative ethics and politics' (Braidotti, 2016a: 23). Michel Foucault's (1970) 'death of man'[10] (373) offers the opportunity for a new approach for human becomings and is seen as an opportunity rather than a loss.

Employing an affirmative critical outlook allows one to acknowledge the very real current inequities and problems and then to implement creative and positive potential responses. 'The selection of the affective forces that propel the process of becoming posthuman is regulated by an ethics of joy and affirmation that functions through the transformation of negative into positive passions' (Braidotti, 2016a: 26). Francis Ferrando (2019: 187) neatly summarizes posthumanism as,

> the philosophy of our age. The posthumanization of society is happening. Even if anthropocentric and dichotomic tendencies are still regarded as the norm, a growing number of beings are becoming aware for the need of a paradigm shift, and are thus revisiting old concepts and new values from a different perspective, bringing together post-humanist, post-anthropocentric, and post-dualistic insights.

Postphenomenology and posthumanism have many similarities. They are anti-essentialist and relational, concentrating on situated and embodied beings-in-the-world. Both are amodern, avoiding Cartesian dualism and the idea of an autonomous and independent individual.

10 See also Han-Pile (2010).

The subject is perceived not as static but a process, constantly being constituted through its relations. And in general, while both conceive of the entanglement and co-constitutionality of subjects and objects, postphenomenology directs its focus primarily on technologies while posthumanism concentrates more on understanding the subject. As many amodern—neither modern nor postmodern—schools of thought[11] believe, the individual is never an autonomous, standalone entity, but one that is always in, and being constituted by, relations. Kenneth Gergen (2009) states, 'there is no isolated self or fully private experience. Rather, we exist in a world of co-constitution' (xv).

Braidotti (2016a) writes about the 'posthuman turn' in philosophy and describes 'an explosion of scholarship on nonhuman, inhuman and posthuman issues' (13). Ferrando (2013) identifies various types of posthumanism: critical, cultural, and philosophical.[12] Recently, Ferrando discusses philosophical posthumanism (2019), which is the posthuman area most attuned with my focus. While there is no agreement on a single definition for the term 'posthuman', I follow Ferrando's (2019) description for philosophical posthumanism, which is post-humanist, post-anthropocentric, and post-dualist. According to Ferrando, 'these three aspects should be addressed in conjunction, which means an account based on a philosophical posthumanist approach shall have a posthumanist sensitivity as well as a post-anthropocentric and a post-dualistic one' (54). This inclusive definition with the three aspects is how I use the terms posthuman or posthumanism throughout the book.

Looking more closely at the three aspects, a post-humanist approach (one that is beyond or after a humanist approach) should be fairly clear after covering the humanist ideas in the previous section. The second aspect, a post-anthropocentric approach, discusses the human as removed from the center of all things and the exceptionalism that

11 For example: complexity theory, actor-network theory, or postphenomenology.

12 Ferrando (2013) states, '(T)he posthuman turn was fully enacted by feminist theorists in the Nineties, within the field of literary criticism—what will later be defined as critical posthumanism. Simultaneously, cultural studies also embraced it, producing a specific take which has been referred to as cultural posthumanism. By the end of the 1990s (critical and cultural) posthumanism developed into a more philosophically focused inquiry (now referred to as philosophical posthumanism), in a comprehensive attempt to re-access each field of philosophical investigation through a newly gained awareness of the limits of previous anthropocentric and humanistic assumptions' (29).

has surrounded this idea since the Enlightenment. There is some irony in discussing the human in a post-anthropocentric way when we so recently have claimed to be now in a new geologic age called the Anthropocene (Lewis, 2018). However, the Anthropocene focuses on the effects we have had on the planet, not our place in it.

And the third aspect, post-binary, refutes a modernist, mechanistic, reductivist, or positivist worldview, which often approach the world in terms of dualisms or binaries: nature/culture, humans/others, agency/determinism, mind/body, etc. Instead of an either/or mentality, Braidotti (2016b) describes using 'and ... and' as a more inclusive choice (31). Ferrando (2019) further explains, 'The posthuman destabilizes the limits and symbolic borders posed by the notion of the human. Dualisms such as human/animal, human/machine, and more in general, human/nonhuman are re-investigated through a perception which does not work on oppositional schemata' (5; cf. Haraway, 1985).

Braidotti's (2013) research is strongly connected with Gilles Deleuze and Félix Guattari (1988) and builds upon feminist and post-colonialist work, specifically focusing on the interrelatedness of all life—including the human—within a vast living network. Posthumanism calls for a move away from the reductive, atomistic, rational-science mentality that attempts to understand the whole by breaking things down to its parts, and towards a *productive and generative* philosophy, which includes building relations and interdependencies that actually reflect the complexities of life.

In general, posthumanists are affirmative of life, believe in the importance of de-centering the human, and approach the world with a holistic and interrelated perspective. We are situated and embodied beings, taking ownership by acknowledging our own background and being honestly open to others. This involves the larger situatedness of being a part of the sixth mass extinction on the planet (Cafaro, 2015) and understanding that it is in our own best interest to attempt to have a positive effect on this situation. We are also situated in the fourth industrial revolution (Schwab, 2017), where technologies for most, but not all, of the humans in the world have a dramatically increased role to play. And while not all of us may be directly affected by this technological revolution, we are all affected by the current mass extinction that is happening.

The Dance of Agency

Reconceptualizing the individual involves reconceptualizing agency. As discussed in Chapter 3, postphenomenology[13] makes the case that our relations with technological objects are non-neutral and share in a portion of agency. Even before any physical convergence of technology and human, relational disciplines within philosophy of technology have been describing how agency, which primarily remained in the domain of the modern humanist subject, is actually shared with technological objects. The most elegant phrasing I found for the concept of shared agency—which is similar to postphenomenology's concept of non-neutrality—is Andrew Pickering's (2005) *dance of agency*. Pickering describes how there is a '*temporal emergence*' (35, italics in original), where the posthuman object,

> does not display the atemporal regularities that physics, ecology or sociology like to look for [...]. This shift exposes a genuine posthuman object which lies [...] along at least two axes: it is a unity that spans what are usually held apart — the human and the non-human—and this unity is essentially temporal: the coupling of the human and the non-human is situated in time, in the dance of agency.

Posthumanism attempts to unlearn the gestalt of the individual. However, an either/or mentality might assume that if we are not individuals, then we may lose our free will, potentially becoming Borg-like,[14] determined beings (Liberati, 2018). Throughout this book I attempt to avoid the binary choice of either/or, preferring to use an 'and ... and' approach (cf. Braidotti, 2016b: 31), which allows us to be positioned between determinism and agency (cf. Fig. 4.2). The fictional 'Borg' are interrelational, but—for the 'drones'—with little to no agency. We our selves are made up of thousands upon thousands of relations, yet we still retain some agency. Relations are dynamic, coming into existence as we move through both space and time and increase or decrease in influence, depending upon the interplay of other relations (cf. Chapter 5).

---

13 Others also make this case, for example, Bruno Latour (1987) and actor-network theorists.

14 The Borg are a fictional alien race—from the Star Trek series—where all the 'drones' are connected to the collective mind and have no individual agency (Consalvo, 2004).

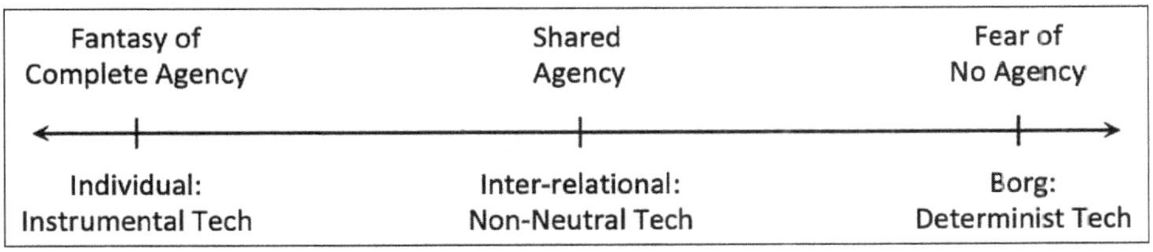

Fig. 4.2 *The Middle Path of Agency*. Image by author (2020), CC BY 4.0.

As Gergen (2009) notes, 'The attempt in this case is to reconfigure agency in such a way that we [...] bring relationship into the center of our concerns. By viewing agency as an action within relationship, we move in exactly this direction' (82). Through awareness we can increase our agency and affect the different relations we are in.[15] As Foucault (Foucault et al., 1987) points out, 'these relationships of power are changeable relations, i.e., they can modify themselves, they are not given once and for all' (123). We cannot choose *not* to be in certain relations, such as the power of discipline in society (Foucault, 1995), but we do have a certain amount of agency in how we interact with that power. And, the more we are aware of the relationships that affect us, the more likely it is to increase our agency. Christian Ehret and Daniella D'Amico (2019) sum this up nicely stating, 'Agency is therefore not a matter of human power *over* the world, but of nonhuman and human bodies' emergent capacities to affect and to be affected as becoming *part of* the world' (148).

Individual to Interdividual to Human Becomings

While the idea of being an individual is compelling and, for some, self-evident, this view is becoming more problematic. Bruno Latour (1993) makes the case that we have never been a modern standalone person and, 'So long as humanism is constructed through contrast with the object that has been abandoned to epistemology, neither the human nor the nonhuman can be understood' (136). Here Latour is deriding the practice of perceiving objects as only epistemological 'things' that do not play an agential role. Instead, Latour (1987, 1993) seeks to understand

15 See Chapter 2, section 'Education, Literacy, Agency' and Chapter 3, section 'Technological Determinism and Agency'.

the human in a symmetrical way with the other non-human 'actants' in the world all possessing a certain degree of agency.

What is needed is a gestalt change in our conception of our selves as individuals. Braidotti (2013) states, 'Individualism is not an intrinsic part of "human nature", as liberal thinkers are prone to believe, but rather a historically and culturally specific discursive formation, one which, moreover, is becoming increasingly problematic' (24). The specific language we use is important in how the understanding of the human subject is conceived. Terms such as 'human' and 'individual' carry a historicity that is entangled with hundreds, if not thousands, of years (Han-Pile, 2010).

One approach is to use new terms or neologisms in order to bypass this issue, though this also is not ideal, especially if the new term is not easily understood and resists adoption into the lexicon of the society it aims to improve. For instance, René Girard (1978) uses the term 'interdividual'. We are not individuals with various relations, but rather it is the relations that constitute us as 'interdividuals'. Chris Fleming (2004), describes Girard's concept of the interdividual as being 'constituted, at base, by its interactions with others. "Individuality" then, strictly speaking, doesn't exist — it is always already "interdividuality"' (36). However, so far there is not much widespread usage of the term.

The dance of agency and co-constitution of the subject through its relations can be brought together in what Pickering (2010) calls an 'ontology of becoming'[16] (30). Describing our selves thus moves away from the static implication of a 'human being', and some researchers are now using the term 'human becomings' (cf. Ingold, 2013; Zylinska, 2009) in order to enact a gestalt shift on how we perceive our selves. For Braidotti (2002), 'the point is not to know who we are, but rather what, at last, we want to become, how to represent mutations, changes and transformations, rather than Being in its classical modes' (2).

Braidotti's (2011) concept of nomadic subjectivity also pushes against the concept of an essential and static subject. In her *Nomadic Theory*, Braidotti investigates the structure of subjectivity (2011: 66), exploring ideas such as becoming animal, becoming earth, or becoming machine. We are always emergent, changing, a process of continual becoming.

---

16 Ihde (2009: 44) similarly discusses an interrelational ontology where humans and their technologies are co-constituted.

Our relations are never static and vary highly in their influence upon us, each changing as we our selves change.

Barad (2007: 139, italics in original) approaches the idea of becoming through her concept of intra-action:

> The notion of *intra-action* (in contrast to the usual 'interaction,' which presumes the prior existence of independent entities or relata) represents a profound conceptual shift. It is through specific agential intra-actions that the boundaries and properties of the components of phenomena become determinate and that particular concepts (that is, particular material articulations of the world) become meaningful... rather, *phenomena are the ontological inseparability/entanglement of intra-acting 'agencies'*.

In other words, subjects and objects emerge—become—through their relation as discussed in Chapter 3 (see Fig. 3.1).

Continuing in the interdisciplinary[17] spirit, certain researchers in contemporary anthropology have also begun using the concept of becoming; specifically, Tim Ingold and Gísli Pálsson's (2013) book on *Biosocial Becomings*. In that book, Ingold (2013: 20) writes that we need to

> think of humanity not as a fixed and given condition but as a relational achievement. It requires us to think of evolution not as change along lines of descent but as the developmental unfolding of the entire matrix of relations within which forms of life (human and non-human) emerge and are held in place. And it requires us to think of these forms as neither genetically nor culturally configured but as emergent outcomes of the dynamic self-organization of developmental systems.

In summary, 'there is the shift away from an epistemological theory or representation to an ontology of becoming' (Braidotti, 2011: 214). Another way of framing this is by using the concept of multistability

17 Other philosophers have also stressed the aspect of becoming, as can be understood through Henri Bergson's (1965) understanding of time as duration (flow) rather than a fixity or instant. It also is similar to Heidegger's (as cited in Sheehan, 2014) notion of thrown-openness of ex-sistence, 'the always-already-operative "unfolding" (*Zeitigung*)' or emergence of being (266). And, 'The characteristic property of a duration is termed "unison of becoming"' (Whitehead, 1978: 126). Stengers (2008) explains, 'What Whitehead calls a subject is the very process of the becoming together, of becoming one and being enjoyed as one, of a many that are initially given as stemming from elsewhere' (103). This continual process of becoming for the subject fits within posthumanism's concept of exploring an *ethics of becoming* (Braidotti, 2013).

from postphenomenology. However, rather than the multistability of an object, we can use it to conceptualize the multistability of the subject. This fits nicely into the idea that we are not one stable *thing*. On the contrary, we are always becoming, changing moment to moment. We nurture a way of perceiving the self in multiple ways, moving beyond any single understanding. By undermining the idea of a stable subject, we open up space, allowing the posthuman subject room to become.

Complexity: The Key to Understanding Human Becomings

The key to reterritorializing the human subject to the posthuman subject is through the concept of complexity. Complexity is an inclusive approach that focuses on a system's interrelationality rather than trying to understand a system by reducing it to its components. The section in Chapter 3 on media ecology briefly introduced complexity. In this section I discuss complexity in more depth, highlighting concepts that are fundamental to creating the framework in Chapter 5, thereby helping to situate the complex interrelationality of media.

There are various overlapping terms that describe or use complexity theory, some of which include: chaos theory, cybernetics, non-linear dynamics, general systems theory, quantum mechanics, and non-linear (or complex) adaptive systems. The approach to complexity that I use is a continental approach, similar to Ilya Prigogine and Isabelle Stengers' works (1984, 1997), rather than the more analytic approach of the Santa Fe Institute (Mitchell, 2009)—or what Edgar Morin (2007) calls *restricted complexity*. The continental view approaches complexity more critically. 'This view argues that complexity theory does not provide us with exact tools to solve our complex problems, but shows us (in a rigorous way) exactly why these problems are so difficult' (Cilliers, 2005: 257).

Posthumanist researchers often bring up issues of complexity. Braidotti (2013) states, 'Nomadic subjectivity is the social branch of complexity theory' (87). Her concept of the nomadic subject equates with the posthuman subject, one that is not constrained by geographies (physical or mental), but rather is constantly becoming and interrelated with the world. This interrelation with the world is at the forefront of the question Hayles (1995) poses: 'What happens if we begin from the premise not that we know reality because we are separate from it (traditional objectivity), but that we can know the world because we are connected with it?' (48). Complexity theory describes open systems that are fluid and autopoietic (self-organizing and generative). They are in a state of tension between chaos and stasis, described as being in non-linear equilibrium. They do not always respond in a linear cause and effect manner, which makes future states of being almost impossible to predict. However, in complex systems, the more diverse relations there are in the system, the more resilient the system often is.

Situating Complexity

Complexity is a critical shift in comprehending the nature of interrelationality and opposes some of the main assumptions of modernity. While complexity is a common thread that runs through media ecology and posthumanism, it is generally not articulated specifically in a way that foregrounds its traits (some exceptions in media ecology are Logan, 2015; Qvortrup, 2006; and in posthumanism Barad, 2007; Hayles, 1999; Roden, 2014). Complexity has roots in quantum mechanics, directly challenging the classical Newtonian mechanics, which focused on objective truth, linear causality, and clear divisions between humans and their world.

Hayles (1990, 1991) has written about chaos and complexity. Hayles (2014: 204–5) uses complexity with regard to human subjectivity in the following:

> The same faculty that makes us aware of ourselves as selves also partially blinds us to the complexity of the biological, social, and technological systems in which we are embedded, tending to make us think we are the most important actors and that we can control the consequences of our actions and those of other agents.

Braidotti (2002: 8) employs complexity in the concept of nomadic becomings, where she has sought 'a style of thinking that adequately reflects the complexities of the process itself'. And Barad (2007) suggests that complexity fundamentally alters our perception from being autonomous, humanist subjects to beings constituted in our intra-relations. According to Barad, 'Intentionality might better be understood as attributable to a complex network of human and nonhuman agents, including historically specific sets of material conditions that exceed the traditional notion of the individual' (23).

Complex or Complicated?

The social sciences are now occasionally using complexity in order to analyze societies and social relations (Byrne & Callaghan, 2014; Turner & Baker, 2019; Urry, 2003, 2005a, 2005b, 2007). While in some research there is a very rigorous definition of complexity that is adhered to, in others the term 'complexity' is used in a manner that leaves it ambiguous and loosely defined (if it is defined at all). Sometimes it is used in a way that would better be served by the adjective 'complicated'.

For example, in postphenomenology Ihde (1990) uses complexity as it is meant in complexity theory when he states 'multistability also may be seen in human-technology relations and even more strongly in the complexities of technology-culture gestalts' (146). However, in the same book, *Technology and the Lifeworld*, he occasionally uses complex when referring to complicated technologies. For instance, he refers to kidney dialysis machines as 'large, complex, very expensive to operate, and of limited quantity' (178).

Roberto Poli (2013: 142) succinctly describes the difference between complicated and complex systems thus:

> Complicated problems originate from causes that can be individually distinguished; they can be addressed piece by piece; for each input to the system there is a proportionate output; the relevant systems can be controlled and the problems they present admit permanent solutions. On the other hand, complex problems and systems result from networks of multiple interacting causes that cannot be individually distinguished; must be addressed as entire systems, that is they cannot be addressed in a piecemeal way; they are such that small inputs may result in disproportionate effects; the problems they present cannot be solved once and for ever, but require to be systematically managed and typically any intervention merges into new problems as a result of the interventions dealing with them; and the relevant systems cannot be controlled.

To put this another way, complicated systems are closed systems that can be engineered and (mostly) controlled in situations where there is a good possibility of accurately predicting causal outcomes. Sending a rover to Mars is an example of a complicated system that responds very well to controlled engineering. However, living systems, such as the human subject, are complex systems, which are open systems comprised of interrelating and constituting parts that are in a state of non-linear equilibrium, causing constant and irreversible emergence while nested within—and nesting their own—complex systems. While we have a significant amount of control in complicated systems, we have far less ability to control complex systems. Ecological and biological sciences now often embrace complexity in how they model living systems (Smith & Jenks, 2006).

Connections, not Divisions

Complexity focuses on connections rather than divisions. Morin (2007) points out, 'Since we have been domesticated by our education which taught us much more to separate than to connect, our aptitude for connecting is underdeveloped and our aptitude for separating is overdeveloped' (21). The concept of complexity helps provide a posthuman lens for media literacy, where constituting media relations are situated within the complexity of interrelations in our lives. Complexity aids our ability to focus on both the whole system and the parts that make up the system, without losing sight of either. Rather than approaching situations by reducing and dividing in order to gain understanding, Barad (2007) argues for using a *diffractive* approach, one that is, 'attuned to the entanglement of the apparatuses of production, one that enables genealogical analyses of how boundaries are produced rather than presuming sets of well-worn binaries in advance' (29–30; see also Mazzei, 2014).

Understanding complexity helps realign assumptions concerning both what we can know and how things are. This brings together both ontology and epistemology. Barad (2007) supports this combining, saying:

> We don't obtain knowledge by standing outside the world; we know because we are of the world. We are part of the world in its differential becoming. The separation of epistemology from ontology is a reverberation of a metaphysics that assumes an inherent difference between human and nonhuman, subject and object, mind and body, matter and discourse. *Onto-epistem-ology*—the study of practices of knowing in being—is probably a better way to think about the kind of

> understandings that we need to come to terms with how specific intra-actions matter. (185)

Rather than using complexity as a theory, I am using it as an onto-epistemological (practice of knowing in being) foundation in order to create the posthuman approach. Using complexity is a way of perceiving the interconnections of things, rather than a separating or reducing systems down in order to find invariants or essences. It is about seeking the constituting linkages of relationality instead of reducing in order to identify. This helps gather the constitutive relations of the human subject into a useful framework that allows us to situate, illuminate, and reflect upon our human becoming-ness, primarily with regard to media technology relations.

Complex Concepts for Framework

Complexity itself is difficult to reduce down into clear and separate concepts, as the various aspects of complexity interact and affect each other. However, I identify three main interconnected concepts from complexity theory that are used to reframe the human subject: open systems, non-linearity, and emergence. These three concepts are useful for understanding the framework I develop.

Open and Nested Systems

Understanding complexity is facilitated through the understanding of two types of systems: open and closed. Open systems are complex and closed systems are complicated (or simple). Fritjof Capra (2002) explains, 'At all scales of nature, we find living systems nesting within other living systems—networks within networks' (231). These complex open systems are nested within larger complex environments, where they exchange matter and energy. While complex systems are bounded in some manner, their boundaries are permeable, and they 'are not boundaries of separation but boundaries of identity. All living systems communicate with one another and share resources across their boundaries' (Capra, 2002: 231).

Understanding that complex systems can be nested within other complex systems helps to provide context. According to Capra (1996: 37),

> The properties of the parts are not intrinsic properties but can be understood only within the context of the larger whole. Thus systems thinking is 'contextual' thinking; and since explaining things in terms of their context means explaining them in terms of their environment, we can also say that all systems thinking is environmental thinking.

This is similar to the aspect of domestication theory I discussed in Chapter 2, where Maren Hartmann (2006) points out how the complex context makes the actual application of the domestication theory very difficult. I develop the framework in order to specifically help in this regard.

Non-Linear Equilibrium

One of the founding voices in complexity theory, Nobel Laureate Ilya Prigogine (Prigogine & Stengers, 1984, 1997), calls complex systems 'dissipative structures'. The traits of these structures are the irreversibility of time (complex systems change and can never be returned to an original condition) and probability (unpredictability). The irreversibility of time counters the classical Newtonian model that upholds the idea that time is reversible.

This notion counters the classic linear cause and effect idea stemming from Newtonian mechanics (Barad, 2007; Hayles, 1991). Rather than rational causality (cause and effect being relatively equal), complexity places relations in non-linear equilibrium where predictability no longer applies, replaced by probabilities. Non-linear equilibrium enables the possibility of small changes having large effects.[18] Yet, the reverse is also true: large changes can have very little effect on a system. Complexity is not unstructured chaos where no relations exist, but rather a tremendous number of relations all interrelating.

Complex systems are in a state of non-linear equilibrium, kept there through the input of energy and material from outside the system, as well as 'waste' that leaves the system. Capra (2005) states, 'A living organism is an open system that maintains itself in a state far from equilibrium, and yet is stable: the same overall structure is maintained in spite of an

18 This is often referred to as the butterfly effect, where under specific initial conditions, the air movement from a butterfly's wing can potentially cause a tornado a great distance away (Lorenz, 1972).

ongoing flow and change of components' (37). This interrelational non-linearity leads systems to be self-generating.

Emergence, Resilience, and Sympoiesis

Because these open systems are in an interrelational state of non-linear equilibrium, they self-organize without a guiding organizer. This is most commonly known as *autopoiesis*, which is a quality of all living complex systems (Capra, 1996). Citing Humberto Maturana and Francisco Varela's (1972) essay that first defined autopoiesis, Capra (1996) explains that *auto* 'means "self" and refers to the autonomy of self-organizing systems; and *poiesis*—which shares the same Greek root as the word "poetry"—means "making." So *autopoiesis* means "self-making"' (97). Melanie Mitchell (2009) describes 'systems in which organized behavior arises without an internal or external controller or leader are sometimes called self-organizing. Since simple rules produce complex behavior in hard-to-predict ways, the macroscopic behavior of such systems is sometimes called emergent' (13). Other ways to describe this aspect that have been used are 'generative' and 'adaptable'.

Haraway (2016), however, prefers using the term 'sympoiesis' rather than autopoiesis. According to Haraway, 'Sympoiesis is a simple word; it means "making-with." Nothing makes itself; nothing is really autopoietic or self-organizing. [...] Sympoiesis enfolds autopoiesis and generatively unfurls and extends it' (58). Ferrando (2019) concurs, saying of autopoiesis that it 'does not seem to take enough into account [of] all the necessary relations and exchanges that occur between the organism and the environment' (141).

While complex systems are not organized from outside the system (being self-organized), they do respond to outside influences. The resilience of a system is how it is able to adapt to these outside disturbances and still retain its identity. In complex ecosystems, it has been shown that the more diversity that a complex system has, the more likely it is to be able to be resilient in the face of perturbations (Folke, 2006; Levin, 1998). Discussing the principles of ecology, Capra (2002) states, 'Ecosystems achieve stability and resilience through the richness and complexity of their ecological webs. The greater their biodiversity, the more resilient they will be' (231).

Paul Cilliers (2005) explains, 'Complex systems are not balanced on a knife's edge between chaos and order. They have mostly robust structures, which change over time and enable the system to respond to different circumstances' (264). These important concepts of open and non-linear emergent systems are part of the foundation for creating the framework in Chapter 5. However, before moving to the actual framework there are a couple aspects to note concerning technology and complexity.

Complexity and Technology

There are two aspects of technology that intersect with complexity. The first aspect is that traditional technologies can be primarily perceived as closed systems, which can be complicated but do not often count as being complex. These are technological artifacts, bounded and engineered. But once these technologies are nested or merged within complex systems—such as embedding a technology within the human body—we lose an aspect of control, reducing predictability to probability as to the effects those technologies cause. For example, the printing press itself is a closed technological system. However, when implementing it within sociocultural environments, it affects them in complex ways.

The second aspect is that there are some types of technologies that are moving away from being closed, complicated systems and qualifying as new complex systems (see Fig. 4.3). AI (artificial intelligence) and machine learning exemplify this idea; we no longer control and write specific code but rather let machine learning do it sympoietically. We are developing true black box technology, where in some cases we can no longer pinpoint how a specific decision or answer is reached. This goes in the opposite direction of the transhumanists who want to upload their consciousness into machines. Their desire can be understood as a desire to have more control over the complexities of biological living systems by housing a person's consciousness in a more controllable 'closed' mechanical system (see Fig. 4.3).

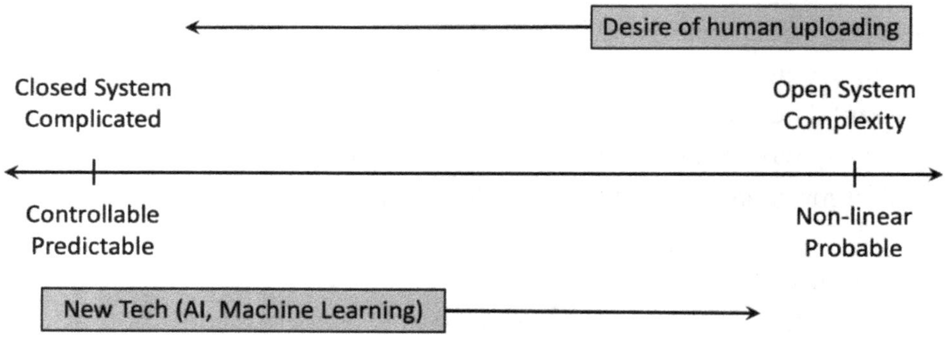

Fig. 4.3 *Technology and Complexity*. Image by author (2019), CC BY 4.0.

Quantum computing is also another move away from complicated closed systems and into the realm of complex open systems. The standard computer 'bit' is replaced in quantum computing with quantum bits—or 'qubits', which 'can assume multiple states simultaneously, rather than simply representing a 0 or 1, as bits do in classical computing' (Castelvecchi, 2017: 59). Google recently claimed to have reached 'quantum supremacy' using a quantum computer with 53 qubits (Arute et al., 2019). Frank Arute et al. ran an experiment that complete a calculation in 200 seconds, where a 'state-of-the-art classical supercomputer would take approximately 10,000 years' (505). At the time of writing, quantum computing has not fully arrived, but it appears to be just over the horizon (Gyongyosi & Imre, 2019).

Summarizing the Complex Posthuman Subject

As Braidotti (2013) notes, humanist ideas are tenacious and not easily moved away from (cf. 26–30). The concept of the ideal, exceptional, autonomous individual human is deeply rooted in the minds of many individuals in the Western world. Even if we ontologically understand how we are relational beings, entangled and co-constituted by the things and the world around us, we still inherently have a sense of our individuality or separateness from the world of things (Van Den Eede, 2015a).

Hayles (1991) explains that the greatest implication of understanding complexity is 'not in how the world actually is [...] but how it is seen' (8). This change in perception helps to re-envision the human subject from an autonomous individual to a continually becoming interrelational being through co-constituting relations (cf. Fig. 4.3). The idea of complexity as a foundation for how we exist in the world undermines the modern mindset of an individual *being* living in a linearly causal world, replacing it with the concept of a complex and interrelated *becoming*. As Pickering (2011) states, 'The self, as revealed here, turns out to be inexhaustibly emergent, just like the world—the antithesis of the given human essence of the Enlightenment and cybernetic immortality' (86).

The concept of complexity shifts the gestalt from the individual subject to the complex and multistable posthuman subject. We are always and already in relation, not only with other humans but also with technologies and the world. My mind does not solely exist in isolation in my body; my mind is in relation with the world around me. These relations are complex, situated, dynamic, and emergent. How these relations influence me continually changes. Even the ability to bring my awareness to a particular relation can affect the amount of influence the relation has on me.

Concluding Thoughts

Posthumanism, complexity theory, and postphenomenology all focus on the interrelatedness of existence, the notion that there is no standalone individual. This is a powerful concept that helps steer our understanding away from reductionist thinking toward thinking in terms of inclusive and interrelated systems. This mindset is not only helpful when thinking about using technologies to improve or 'fix' something, including our selves, but also when we invite new types of media into our lives. According to Sharon (2014: 135),

> The human being is conceptualized here not as an independent and autonomous entity with clear cut boundaries but as a heterogeneous subject whose self-definition is continuously shifting, and that exists in a complex network of human and non-human agents and the technologies that mediate between them.

A common issue in research is a too-narrow focus on a limited number of influencing relations. Instead, we exist within a complexity of relations, most of which exist in the background of our awareness (where they still have an effect upon us). Rather than one or two determining factors in our lives there is a complexity of influencing relations: social, technological, temporal, and spatial. This network of relations is a living web in that it is dynamic and ever changing. Each relation increasing or decreasing its influence depends upon a multitude of factors, not least, our own awareness of the relation. While we are mostly, but not always, in a stable equilibrium, this equilibrium is not static, but is constantly evolving as we move through time.

We are complex systems (ecosystems), greater than the sum of our parts. We exist, or are nested, within greater complex systems, not discreetly, but as entangled and co-constituting. This chapter has moved the focus from media and technology towards the concept of the human subject, and in order to understand how media and technology affect 'us', we need an understanding of who and what the 'us' actually is.

The approach for most transhumanists is to perceive technology—and our selves—as complicated but understandable and 'engineerable'. Their primary desire is to use technology to enhance and improve the human condition, pushing back against old age and disease, in order to bootstrap the individual into an enhanced version of their idealized self. Their desire is for the human-technology convergence to bring the understandability and controllability into the realm of life itself. Unfortunately, we are not complicated, but *complex* beings. And, to quote an acute insight from businessman Dave Gray (2009), 'When you make the complicated simple, you make it better. When you make the complex simple, you make it wrong' (n.p.). In order to create a more accurate understanding of how technology and living systems relate, we need to reframe the foundation of the human subject from the standalone autonomous individual to an inter-related and complex post-humanist subject.

The term of 'technofantasy', as defined by Ihde (2011), refers to the idea that we want the benefits of technology without being changed. This ignores the non-neutral aspect of technologies, which bring both benefits and drawbacks. Since we are fundamentally relational, we change any time one of our relations change. By overcoming this technofantasy attitude, we become more realistic in our expectations of our relations with technologies. Every technological relation is transformative, both enabling and constraining. Invited or not, every time a technology enters our lives we are irreversibly changed. The idea of the irreversibility of time, coming from complexity theory, also helps in our understanding by removing the idea that we can undo some experiment that did not work out. While we might be able to undo some aspects of the experiment, we cannot completely return to the way we were.

The idea of the complex posthuman subject helps bring a relational and inclusive perspective rather than one that is individual and reductive; an understanding that living systems are complex systems that do not necessarily respond in a predictive manner; and a more realistic and grounded understanding of non-neutrality of technology. We can and should use technology to help improve our lives, but we should go about it in an inclusive, interrelated, and pragmatic manner. Given this post-humanist, non-dualist, non-anthropocentric, and complex human becoming, I offer a situating and comprehensive framework in the next chapter in order to understand the interrelational constitution of such a human subject. I suggest a cartography, not to prescribe or dissect the relations into separate and discrete categories, but as a way to take a particular situation—say a media-related event—and probe the various groupings of relations in order to uncover and foreground some of the complex interrelations that contribute to the human subject's becoming.

PART II

A Posthuman Perspective

5

Intrasubjective Mediating Framework and the Process of its Development

Simply put, before we can truly achieve media literacy, we need to be self-literate. This involves moving beyond the 'content' of *who* we are and becoming knowledgeable as to *what* and *how* we are as a complex system. The 'what' can be understood as the structure or cartography of relations that constitute our selves and the 'how' is the complex process of our mediated constitution. Both give rise to a system of becoming that is continually emergent and complex. Media technologies are a part of this process and are also affected by—and affect—the other constituting relations in our lives. In order to comprehensively understand and situate media literacy, I develop a two-part posthuman approach that consists of 1) an intrasubjective mediating framework developed in this chapter[1] along with 2) a pragmatic instrument that leverages the framework in Chapter 6.

This process of situating is a means of providing context, and as Anthony Wilden (1980) states, 'if there is one constantly recurring question for a critical and ecosystemic viewpoint, it is the real and material question of context' (xxix). I first describe the process of how we intra-relate with the world *through* the transformations caused by the various relations in our lives. I then create a simple structure that brings these constituting relations into six groupings: technological,

1 Parts of this chapter overlap with the chapter I wrote (Lewis, 2020) for the book *Perception and the Inhuman Gaze.*

sociocultural, mind, body, space, and time. And finally, I describe how both structure and process are involved in an interrelating dance of complexity.

The co-constituting technological relation from postphenomenology —described as I-technology-world (Ihde, 1990)—is leveraged in this chapter to also include groups of relations beyond the technological. The focus is on the continual transformation of the human subject through all of the relations that influence the subject and the subject's experiences in its lifeworld. Because the focus is on the constitution of the 'I' component, the constitution of the 'world' component of the equation is only indirectly addressed, not because it is not important, but only because a primary focus on how the world is constituted through this process is outside the scope of this book.

Discussing the complexity of structures and processes, Tim Ingold (2013; see also Grishakova, 2019; Rubin, 1988) points out that there are two different approaches. One approach is to have a complex structure and a simple process. In this scenario, the complex structure determines the process of the system, and the process simply follows the rules dictated by the structure. This creates a situation with little to no free will and follows the structuralist and determinist schools of thought. Instead, I follow Ingold's recommendation and use a simple structure that relies on complex processes, leading to the emergence of the human becoming.

We are not simply aggregates of all of our relations added together. Instead, our constituting relations interrelate in an emergent dance of complexity. These relations enable and constrain each other in unpredictable ways. By understanding our selves as these complex systems of becoming, we are better able to situate specific relations—such as with media technologies—into the broader whole.

Situating the Intrasubjective Mediating Framework

One way to position an argument in philosophy is by using difference, a negative approach showing what something *is* by illustrating how it is *not* like something else. This often follows a reductive approach that uses binary oppositions. Rather than using this negative approach, I use a positive and inclusive approach, looking for similarities to what already exists in various research fields and then bringing them together in a comprehensive and situating framework. The bringing together of many fields of research into one framework helps to leverage what has already been—and is continuing to be—studied in order to better understand the human subject.

For example, Michel Foucault's (1995) power discourse, Donna Haraway's (1985) cyborg manifesto, Michel Callon and Bruno Latour's (1981) actor-network theory, Don Ihde's (1990) postphenomenology, Rosi Braidotti's (2013) posthumanism, Martin Heidegger's (2010) being-in-the-world (*Dasein*), Karen Barad's (2007) agential realism, and so on; all of these amodern (as in not modern), relational thinkers have made profound contributions to an understanding of our selves and our place in the world. They have helped overcome much of the subject/object dichotomy and helped describe the human subject in a more relational manner. However, like the proverbial group of blind people describing an elephant by touching different places on its body, they all are correct, but in a limited way, missing a unifying perspective. By approaching the subject through an interdisciplinary lens, there is a better chance of coming to a transdisciplinary understanding of the human subject by creating an inclusive framework that can accommodate many of the ideas that come from various relational disciplines dedicated to understanding the human subject.

While the main fields I have used so far—postphenomenology, media literacy, media ecology, complexity, and posthumanism—bring certain benefits to understanding the human subject, each has certain limitations concerning the creation of a unified framework that can help maintain an inclusive perspective. For instance, postphenomenology contributes well to our pragmatic understanding of the constituting nature of technological relations, but it is technocentric and lacks an approach to leverage the concepts of a culturally constructed 'body two' (cf. Ihde, 2002) and sedimentation. Postphenomenology has also been criticized for not being critical enough on the normative and ethical issues surrounding technology (cf. Lemmens, 2017; Scharff, 2006; Thompson, 2006). As for media literacy, it has various approaches that contribute in many beneficial ways, including critical media literacy that brings the influence of critical cultural theory into the dialogue. However, media literacy lacks a focus on the impact of the technological medium.

It also lacks an effective approach for understanding the impact of the broader context that the media are used within, as domestication theory demonstrates.

Media ecology, which effectively investigates the impact of the medium itself on the human subject and society. However, media ecology is less able to provide a way to pragmatically understand specific technological relations and how sociocultural aspects such as representation, power, and gender also co-influence the effects of the technological media. And finally, philosophical posthumanism helpfully provides a focus on the complex transformations of the human subject in a non-humanist, non-dualist, and non-anthropocentric manner, but it lacks a pragmatic way of investigating specific relations, including technological, which contribute to the constitution of the human subject.

The posthuman approach I propose creates a solution for these problems without losing the valuable contributions of each field. Holistically, this provides a way to situate media literacy investigations into an all-encompassing framework. By so doing, this allows investigators to keep a broad perspective while facilitating a deep analysis into any of the specific areas.

Critical media literacy opens the field of media literacy to influencing relations beyond media technologies by including the effects of structures of power and privilege embedded within media messages (Kellner & Share, 2005, 2007). My point in this chapter is to demonstrate how media literacy can expand even further by including the effects that time and space as well as body and mind have on our selves and our media relations. Adopting a more inclusive framework for media literacy can help us understand how our media relations affect all the other relations in our lives and vice versa. We are immersed in an environment of complex relations, most of which are in the background of our awareness. The literacy aspect of my framework is the effort to foreground these relations in order for us to become aware of them so we can choose how we might engage with them.

I begin this chapter by discussing the process in which we continue to be affected by the non-neutral transformations that we experience through our relations. I then propose a structure in order to include all of the relations that contribute to our constitution. This helps bring attention beyond the technological to the other groups of relations that also contribute to our constitution. My goal is to help us become more literate about our selves, not necessarily to answer 'who' are we—as that is akin to a content question—but rather 'what' are we? This approach is similar to Marshall McLuhan's (1994) aphorism, *the medium is the message*. How does *what* we are affect *who* we are? And, how do our processes and engagement with the world—the *how* we are—affect how we exist and *become* in this world? Only by better understanding the what and how of our existence will we then be able to situate media literacy and the various relations that contribute to constituting the human subject, thus enabling the development of a comprehensive perspective. This reduces the tendency towards deterministic claims that focus on only one or two specific factors. By establishing this framework, we can become more aware of what contributes to the constitution of our selves in a holistic and encompassing manner.

Intrasubjective Mediation

To more deeply explore what it means to be constituted—or transformed—by our relations, I introduce the concept of *intrasubjective mediation*. While constitution and transformation can have slightly different meanings, I will use them both to describe the process of becoming. The concept of intrasubjective mediation helps to identify how the transformations that take place due to our relations both affect and continue to affect how we perceive and engage with the world. As Ihde (2009) points out, 'Technologies transform our experience of the world and our perceptions and interpretations of our world, and we in turn become transformed in this process. Transformations are non-neutral' (44). The first sentence in this quote describes the constituting effects of the six groups of relations, and the second sentence gets to the core of intrasubjective mediation.

I define intrasubjective mediation as *the process of how the transformations that occur in the human subject through technological, sociocultural, mind, body, time, and space relations mediate—and continue to mediate—how the subject perceives and engages with the world*. What intrasubjective mediation enables is the ability to understand how all of our relations continue to contribute to our constitution through the transformations that originally took place. How this relates to the technological relations described by postphenomenology is that every technological relation—be it embodied, hermeneutic, alterity, or background—leaves an intrasubjective transformation that we then perceive and experience the world through.

For example, a GPS enabled mapping app on our smartphone allows us to explore a new city differently than if we did not have this technology. After we become familiar with using the GPS app and have had positive experiences navigating new areas with the app, our confidence in exploring new places can increase. In addition, as we become less concerned with getting lost, we become different travelers. We are travelers transformed. Enabling and constraining still occurs, and we will likely have new concerns, such as our phone's battery level and finding cellular access spots.

We interact with every relation in our life through an assemblage of our current relations and the accumulation of our transformations caused by the relations we have already experienced. I build upon postphenomenology's embodied relation in order to conceptualize this process. Intrasubjective mediation creates a language for investigation and a method of inquiry to explore the transformations that happen within the subject due to specific constituting relations and how we continue to engage and perceive the world through these transformations. This moves our initial focus on an individual relation experienced in the present moment and expands our attention and awareness in order to perceive the current interrelating relations as well as the accumulation of all our experiences gathered together.

Why Intra?

At first, the idea of *intra*-subjective mediation may seem somewhat confusing. After all, what does it mean to be mediated by an aspect within our selves? Why use 'intra' instead of simply using 'subjective mediation?' I do so because 'subject' is often conceived of as singular, equating to the entirety of our selves. 'Intrasubjective' points to a more specific internal aspect that contributes to our overall constitution. Our subjective self is not a unified subject, but a multiplicity through which we intra-relate (Lamagna, 2011). Therefore, in order to know our selves more fully, it is helpful to understand these relations and how they contribute to our continually constituted subjectivity. Additionally, the way a subject perceives the world through the intrasubjective relations can vary, depending upon the context of the situation; how the subject is feeling: whether they are stressed or relaxed; what is currently motivating them; their particular upbringing; etc.

The intrasubjective mediating framework developed below creates a way to investigate both the current and continuing impact from relations, which in the case of media technology will help us to become more media literate by understanding the broader effects of media technologies. While my primary focus will continue to be on technological relations, I will situate them within a framework that includes five other groupings of relations. Before describing the specifics of how intrasubjective mediation works through a type of embodied relation, I will first describe all six groupings of relations that make up the framework.

The Intrasubjective Mediating Framework

In order to leverage the concept of intrasubjective mediation, I first develop a general framework before then creating a pragmatic instrument that can be used for media literacy (Chapter 6). To begin discussing the framework, I start with the foundation of our existence—one with no hard boundaries of separation that is instead interrelated and emergent. I gather all of our constituting relations into six groups, which enables us to look deeply into the particular qualities and aspects of each group while remaining cognizant of the other groups.

This chapter builds on the concept that we are multi-relational, that there is never just one relation involved with anything we do in any single moment. There is a tendency to perceive technology and media in a gestalt-like manner—all at once and often as one thing. This can erroneously translate into thinking of media technology as a single relation, instead of multiple relations happening at the same time. For example, I can analyze my relationship with my smartphone. At first, it can feel like one relation, as the object being one 'thing'. However, the smartphone is not only functionally more than one artifact—camera, phone, GPS, web browser, social media site, etc.—but it is also an assemblage of relations. It is, amongst many other things, a cultural status symbol, a way to reduce distance by creating a virtual space, and an extension of my mind, used for storing memories and information externally. The framework I develop is a way to keep this broader perspective in mind when analyzing specific media and technological relations.

The framework builds upon the I-technology-world formula used to describe technological mediation, which is very effective in analysis on a microperceptual level. However, this formula does not portray the entirety of what is happening to the subject in the constituting moment. There are more than just technological relations that are happening, and postphenomenology acknowledges this by describing a culturally constructed body two (Ihde, 2002). However, postphenomenology has made little progress in creating a method or an instrument to easily implement the sociocultural component in a similar way to the I-technology-world formula that focuses on the microperceptual, let alone investigating the effect of other groupings of relations. The following framework serves this purpose by situating all of our mediating relations into groups for the goal of identification and discovery.

Framework Caveats

George Box (1979) offers a helpful perspective to keep in mind as I begin to describe the framework: 'All models are wrong but some models are helpful' (202). Representations are not reality, but they can help provide ways for us to interact and understand reality. The framework is useful as a situating anchor, helping to keep research tethered to the overarching perspective of what comprises the human subject. And yet, there is a tension between creating an inclusive framework and striving not to be reductive. Paul Cilliers (2005) says that the limitations of a framework make 'it possible to have knowledge (in finite time and space). At the same time, having limits means something is excluded, and we cannot predict the effects of that exclusion' (264). Keeping this in mind can help us pay attention to not only how we may be enabled, but also how we might be constrained when using this framework. For instance, by portraying the framework as inclusive, I create an expectation of completeness, which ultimately is impossible. To counteract this expectation, I include the group 'unknown/unknowable' (cf. Fig. 5.1). It is also possible that there is a better way to organize or name the groups. The publication of this book captures the framework at a certain point in time, and it is quite likely that it will continue to change in the future.

An additional caveat is that the intrasubjective mediating framework (Fig. 5.1) *looks* anthropocentric. It has the mind/body at the center and is all about identifying the human subject's relations and even risks reflecting a mind-body split. However, this is absolutely not the intention behind the framework. Instead, it is a starting point to help enable us to understand our entangled interconnectedness and interrelatedness with the world. The framework demonstrates our embedded and embodied reality, our immanent beingness. We start from here in order to understand our interconnectedness and interrelatedness. This is not the view from above approach, nor a way to explore objective beingness. This is our subjectiveness with which we interrelate and are interconnected with the world. By using this framework as a starting point, we can increase our awareness of how we are constituted by the entirety of our relations. Only then will we be in a good place to critically judge the specific relations in our lives and decide how we may want to engage with them.

The Framework's Cartography

Before going into the details of each group, I explain the structural configuration of Figure 5.1. First, I identify the six groups: technological, sociocultural, mind, body, space, and time. This framework is dedicated to understanding the human subject, and places the mind and body in the middle, reflecting the central role they play. They are placed together with the co-constituting symbol to indicate the continual becoming of the human subject. Often these two groupings are considered the fundamental aspect of what we simply 'are'. The lower portion of the configuration captures time and space, which in physics are the first four dimensions of reality. This foundational pair is like the warp of a weaving, the structure upon which our reality—and the human subject itself—is constituted. The upper portion contains the technological and sociocultural relations that are human constructions.

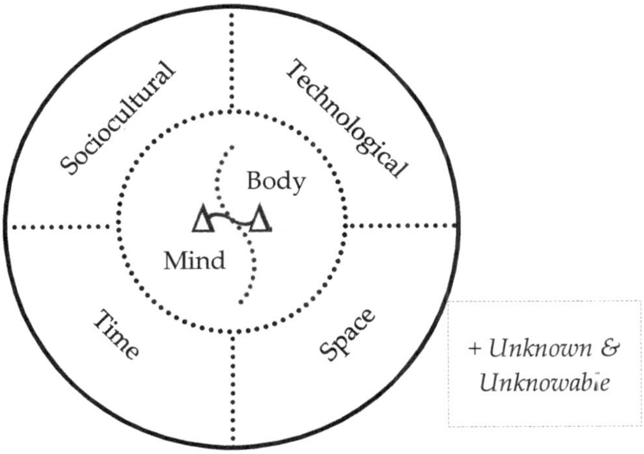

Fig. 5.1 *The Framework of Intrasubjective Mediating Relations*. Image by author (2021), CC BY 4.0.

The figure represents a way to look for and identify various groupings of relations, all of which contribute to constituting the subject. The boundaries between the groupings are porous, as the relations are entangled. These groupings simply gather relations with shared similarities. All relations within each group can interact directly or indirectly with relations from other groups. The subject is not so much constructed by these relations, but constituted through their totality in a dynamic manner; a constant *becoming*. These relations interrelate and influence each other, like waves that sometimes cancel each other and sometimes increase each other's effects. The focus for now is on the structure rather than the specific content, though I will attempt to explore examples within each group. I create a placeholder for 'unknown and unknowable' relations in order to build into the framework the idea that we do not, and cannot, know all of the relations that are affecting us. Later, in Chapter 6, I will leverage this 'simple' structure into a pragmatic instrument.

Technology and Sociocultural

I begin by grouping the relations that can arguably be called the most human-constructed: technological and sociocultural relations. I place them on the top of Fig. 5.1 since they are not too difficult to foreground. For all of the groups I frame them in the I-___-world formula in order to emphasize how each grouping of relations mediates and co-constructs our selves and the world.

Technological Relations: I-Technology-World

The concept of technological mediation from postphenomenology—the I-technology-world relation—is the primary building block for the framework. In chapter three, I described in detail the aspects of the technological relations, including the four types of relations identified in postphenomenology. Rather than restate all of the details concerning technological relations—such as non-neutrality, multistability, and sedimentation—I will add to those ideas by describing a way to group technologies into three different genres: simple, complicated, and complex. Doing so can help us understand that all technologies are not the same, that the three groups have unique qualities that differentiate them and their broader effects on society and people.

Simple and complicated technologies have been a subject of Ursula Franklin (2004), though she describes them as holistic and prescriptive respectively. Franklin focuses on the cultural aspects of technology, describing technology as a system. She states that it 'entails far more than its individual material components. Technology involves organization, procedures, symbols, new words, equations, and, most of all, a mindset' (1). Franklin discusses technologies as a practice, focusing on *how* the technological process is being done more than *what* the process is actually creating.

Holistic technologies are often 'associated with the notion of craft. Artisans, be they potters, weavers, metal-smiths, or cooks, control the process of their own work from beginning to finish' (6). In these relations, the technology is fairly simple, and the skill in creating or producing or using the technology is mostly dependent upon the user. Franklin focuses closely on the interconnection between culture and technologies, how the craft process of creating technologies influences the type of culture that develops around it.

The second type of technology uses a prescriptive process, which Franklin (2004) describes as 'based on a quite different division of labour. Here, the making or doing of something is broken down into clearly identifiable steps' (7). There is a division of labor, where different people take on specific and controlled roles. While the industrial revolution exemplifies this process, Franklin describes how the process was already being used in China in 1200 BC for casting bronze. The division of labor moves the overall control from the worker to the person in charge. The worker must follow a prescribed plan in order for the technological production to work properly. 'Prescriptive technologies constitute a major social invention. In political terms, prescriptive technologies are designs for compliance [...where] external control and internal compliance are seen as normal and necessary' (7–8).

While prescriptive technologies are exceedingly effective and efficient, they have a dramatic impact upon the culture, where 'we are ever more conditioned to accept orthodoxy as normal, and to accept that there is only one way of doing "it"' (8). This type of technology can be considered complicated, especially when compared with holistic craft technologies. This is where most contemporary ICTs can be found, though some aspects of ICTs are now moving into a third type: complex technologies.

Complex technologies can be understood as another paradigmatic shift. While prescriptive technologies move the control and responsibility from a single person in holistic technologies to an external control, complex technologies move much of that control more to the technology itself. These are technologies such as machine learning, where humans no longer control the specific inner workings of algorithms and predictability gives way to probability. The technology programs itself, and we can no longer pinpoint exactly how a specific output is reached.

Each of these subgroupings of technology brings different benefits and constraints to both individuals and cultures through their mediation. Their differences can be linked to different constituting effects on the human subject. All three retain the qualities of the technological relations discussed in Chapter 3: non-neutrality, multistability, and sedimentation. Having already covered these, I now move on to the second foregrounded group of relations: sociocultural.

Sociocultural Relations: I-Sociocultural-World

Some of the co-constituting sociocultural relations that mediate between our selves and the world have already been discussed:

postphenomenology's concept of body two; critical media literacy; and critical posthumanism. This group consists of the sociocultural relations that influence human subjects. Creating a place for these types of relations allows them to be analyzed and acknowledged as having an effect on how we are constituted moment by moment. This group is messy, wide-ranging, and very difficult to reign in to a neat tidy 'category'. However, I am not looking to categorize. My goal is to simply encourage investigation in order to reveal the sociocultural relations that have a constituting effect on us. Subgroups, such as power, gender, race, and language, that are a part of the sociocultural group tend to be entangled, and I do not believe it is necessary to fully separate them. I do not go into a great deal of specificity expanding on the many potential subgroups because I believe that the social science and cultural studies fields have already made a lot of progress in this regard. This grouping simply allows a place in the framework for these fields of study to be included. To exemplify this group briefly, I discuss postphenomenology's sociocultural concepts, as well as those from critical cultural studies.

Sociocultural Concepts in Postphenomenology. Postphenomenology has two concepts for cultural influences: macroperception and body two. However, it does not leverage these concepts into a method or instrument for exploring their influence on the human subject in a similar way to how it instrumentalizes technological relations through its I-technology-world formula. Additionally, the use of macroperception is focused on 'the ways in which cultures embed technologies' (Ihde, 1990: 124), but not on how cultures mediate human subjects microperceptively.

Microperception is focused on the embodied and embedded perspective of the human, which gives rise to the four types of I-technology-world relations in postphenomenology. However, as I have pointed out, Ihde (1990) states that there is no 'microperception (sensory-bodily) without its location within a field of macroperception and no macroperception without its microperceptual foci' (29). Ihde devotes a significant section of his *Lifeworld* book to the concept of macroperception (1990, cf. chapter 6), describing how technologies and our microperceptions are necessarily entangled within the broader sociocultural landscape. In practice, however, it is challenging to pragmatically incorporate the concept of macroperception into specific research on technologies. While microperception is tightly linked with the I-technology-world mediation theory, macroperception and body two have more often been used as general concepts.

Robert Scharff (2006) criticizes Ihde's usual separation of micro and macroperception, saying, 'from what sort of perspective does he [Ihde] make the distinction between perceptual "embodiment" and cultural "context," put their discussions in separate chapters, and often discuss one without reference to the other?' (137). Lasse Blond and Kasper Schiølin (2018) 'suggest that postphenomenology has placed too much emphasis on technology, leaving the mediated human "I" and the world in the dark' (152). The framework developed here is an attempt to include how the sociocultural relations contribute to our own constitution.

Leveraging co-constituting sociocultural relations helps us to understand the transformative effects of culture on our microperceptions. This is a solution for the criticisms just discussed from Scharff and as well Blond and Schiølin. It is a way to bring body one (the microperceptual body) and body two (the culturally constructed body) from postphenomenology together and focus on how sociocultural relations constitute the human subject in a similar manner to technological relations. In Chapter 6 I will demonstrate the constituting effects of sociocultural relations that I experienced while taking a museum selfie. This sociocultural component is a strong influencing force on the individual, one that is sedimented over a lifetime. Developing this specific relation can help us better analyze its influence on the human subject. We can modify Ihde's (1990) original technological mediating formula in order to identify these constituting sociocultural relations: I-*sociocultural*-world. Like technological relations, sociocultural relations are co-constituting and multistable. How the sociocultural relations constitute the individual is not only unique to each individual, but is changeable (multistable) within the individual.

Sociocultural Concepts in Cultural Studies. Sociocultural elements influence people's practices and experiences. Tony Bennett (1998) offers elements of a definition for cultural studies, describing how there are diverse forms of power in relation to culture that should be examined, including gender, class, race, colonialism and imperialism. According to Bennett, 'The ambition of cultural studies is to develop ways of theorizing relations of culture and power that will prove capable of being utilized by relevant social agents to bring about changes within the operation of those relations of culture and power' (28).

Building upon Bennett's (1998) work, Chris Barker and Emma Jane (2016) review some of the key concepts within cultural studies, creating a list that includes, in part, language, representation, materialism, political economy, power, subjectivity and identity, class, and race. Barker and Jane stress that cultural studies is non-reductionist, meaning situations cannot be reduced down to a single causal category or concept. Emily Grabham et al. (2009) describe one of the ways in which cultural studies leverages the concept of non-reductionism through intersectionality, which focuses on the intersection of several inequalities people experience 'that are rooted through one another, and which cannot be untangled to reveal a single cause' (1). Additionally, Leslie McCall (2009) points out that complexity, 'arises when the subject of analysis expands to include multiple dimensions of social life and categories of analysis' (49).

The framework I develop can lead to an increased awareness of this complexity and intersectionality of constituting relations. From the many potential subgroups available within sociocultural relations, I will briefly highlight normativity as an example of identifying sociocultural constituting relations. In Chapter 6, I use two other subgroups as examples in my exploration of analyzing my experience taking a museum selfie—language and politics.

Using normative relations, we can analyze how sociocultural relations influence by both enabling and constraining us. The concept of normativity can be understood by looking at two different scenarios where I would be different when taking museums selfies. In the first scenario, other people are also taking selfies and the museum itself encourages, or at least does not restrict, the taking of selfies with the museum objects. In this situation, I feel fairly comfortable taking a museum selfie. In the second scenario, nobody else is taking selfies. When I do try to take one, people in the area give me what I perceive to be unpleasant looks. Without explicitly asking if this was their intention, these reactions from the people around me are a way of communicating that taking selfies is not acceptable museum behavior. In this second scenario, I perceive my proximal social group as negatively judging me, and this has an inhibiting effect on my desire to take any further selfies.

These two scenarios demonstrate the importance of going beyond only the technological relation, as the constituting effects in the scenario have very little to do with any technological relation. I am being mediated and constituted culturally before I get to the point of the technological relation. Within these sociocultural relations, we can investigate the various ways that our culture mediates us as we relate with and through technology. This can include studying power dynamics, economics, language, ethics, and the normative values that arise when we look into sociocultural issues. I will now move on to explain Body and Mind relations.

Body and Mind

Both the body and mind can be considered core groupings of relations that comprise our human subjectivity. Often, these two groups are considered who or what we are, not necessarily as relations, but simply as 'us'. However, by considering the body and mind as part of a larger framework of constituting relations, we can analyze their relations using the mediating formula. The primary goal is not to answer the question of what the mind and body are specifically, but to create a structural approach that includes and organizes all the relations that constitute both body and mind in order to better understand the human becoming.

Body Relations: I-Body-World

We—each individual human subject—are greatly mediated by our bodies. The body provides the condition of possibility for relations by materially being-in-the-world. The materiality of our bodies—the chemistry and bodily systems—contributes to constituting our human becomingness. The physical bodily aspect—that many transhumanists would like to enhance and even one day overcome—is a major component of our subjectivity. Physical changes, such as taking psychological enhancing medication, sickness, hunger, or the loss or change of certain physical abilities, can dramatically change how we exist in our lifeworld.

To illustrate how my body can affect my relating to the world through technology, I use a simplified example of attempting to take a photograph of a bird out in nature. Under normal circumstances it is advantageous for a bird photographer to be patient and slow in their movements.

However, if my body desperately needs to empty its bladder, this biological imperative changes my ability to be patient, and my body's mediation begins to dominate and supersede the technological relation that I have with my camera and my attempt at taking a photograph. I am a much different photographer in this scenario than I am in a similar scenario where I do not need to use the bathroom.

The concept of being mediated by our bodies is not new. Mark Coeckelbergh (2019) writes 'we project ourselves towards things through the body and its movement. The moving body is a medium' (17). He continues by expanding postphenomenology's use of embodiment by stating that it 'is not just a particular human-technology relation (Ihde, 1990; Verbeek, 2005); it is the very way we exist in the world' (18). Lance Strate (2017) points out that even 'face-to-face communication is simply a differently mediated form of communication, and the body is the medium through which much of nonverbal communication takes place' (103). Strate continues discussing the mediation of the body by saying (2017: 102):

> The differences between the structure and functioning of human eyes and the ears are differences that make a difference [...]. When we include all of the senses, not just vision, hearing, touch, smell and taste, but also the bodily senses, the kinetic, vestibular, and proprioceptive, it becomes clear that the nervous system, the brain, and the body in its entirety can be included under the category of media, characterized by specific structures that impose certain constraints and provide certain affordances.

Understanding the body as a medium—as something that we are mediated by—allows us to perceive it in a relational, co-constituting manner.

We are embodied beings, and our bodies make a difference in how we think and interact with the world. Bodies are foundational when it comes to many sociocultural relations such as race, gender, and sexuality. Our bodies also make a difference in how other people engage with us (Butler, 1993). Appearance, ability, and perceptual astuteness all have dramatic effects on a subject's engagement with the world. These aspects exemplify an entanglement of bodily and sociocultural relations.

Another entanglement is the body and mind groupings. While I identify these relations as two different groups, they are only separate in order to identify and gather together specific relations. Strate (2017) countermands the traditional opposition of body and mind: 'The mind is not the body, but it emerges out of the body, is contained within the body, is dependent upon the body, but may also affect and alter the body' (114). Research and debate continue on the brain/mind/body entanglement. The physical brain has a tremendous influence on our minds, or the mind can be understood as emerging from the brain and body (Varela et al., 1992).

Mind Relations: I-Mind-World

The human subject is not an isolated, singular being, but always and already in relations, constantly being constituted by the shifting current state of all the relations that affect it. As with the sociocultural relation subgroups, the mind subgroups are not new but are groupings of already existing areas of study. My goal is not to bring new content to these groups and subgroups, but rather to include them in a cartography that can help guide our investigations into our own constituting relations, keeping a perspective of the whole subject as we do.

We 'cut' reality into a specific relation by doing and by deciding, using our mind's imagination, awareness, consciousness, and perception. The ability of our mind to mediate our experience with the lifeworld is exemplified by the well-known experiment of Daniel Simons and Christopher Chabris (1999), who conducted a study where people watched a video and were told to count how many times the team in white passed the basketball. As the team was passing around the ball, a woman in a dark gorilla suit walked between the players, turned to the camera, beat her chest, and then continued out of the screen. Only about 50% of the viewers who were concentrating on the number of passes noticed the gorilla. This demonstrates that even though our eyes receive information, our mind's attention and intention play a significant role in what we actually perceive.

Some of the subgroups of the mind that I note are imagination, awareness or consciousness, and identity. The concept of identity here, while heavily influenced by the sociocultural, focuses on our mind's role in our agency of creating our self-identity. Not all identity issues are contained within this subgroup, as the sociocultural also contains many of the identity relations. This will be further explained below (see the section 'Awareness, Agency, and Identity'). Our mind helps us choose what we focus on, and is where we interpret what our bodily senses detect. It is the mind, through awareness, that helps us regain some of the agency lost to the various other relations and structures in our lives.

The following subcategories of the mind are an attempt to show some of the nuances of this aspect of the human subject. These subcategories are not separate from each other, and even their definitions remain contested. Several areas of study are still trying to figure out exactly what constitutes the mind (fields such as cognitive science, psychology, and the philosophy of mind). However, I use 'the mind' as a general grouping that contains mind-related relations, of which I will use the concepts of imagination, awareness/consciousness, and identity as subgroups.

Imagination and Technology. Imagination is one of the relational subgroups of the mind. It is a non-neutral relation, dynamic even within an individual, influencing more at certain times and less at other times. By formulating imagination as a relation, it is possible to use the concept to understand how humans are mediated by this element of our selves, allowing us to become more aware of the enabling and constraining effects on both the individual and broader sociological levels. To demonstrate, I will explore how the imagination affects our relations with technologies.

The concept of the multistability of technology discussed in Chapter 3 is only possible through our ability to imagine. It is our imagination that allows us to perceive technologies in multiple stable ways.[2] It is also our imagination that allows us—and hundreds of other species—to both identify and create technologies in the first place. Without being able to identify technology, we would not recognize any object in a tool-based or technological manner. Therefore, whoever (or whatever) does not have an ability to imagine technology will not have or be able to perceive technologies. Through imagination, a rock can be perceived as a hammer or a weapon, and a stick can extend the body to reach something. This first aspect of imagination is the condition for the possibility of perceiving an object in such a way as to accomplish a

2 When Kyle Whyte (2015) theorizes that there are two conceptions of multistability, he names one imaginative multistability (and the other practical multistability).

desired task in a technological manner. It also enables the ability to perceive things in multistable ways.

The second aspect of imagination allows for the design and creation of new tools and technologies. Humans are not the only species that have this ability (cf. Beck, 1980). Vicki Bentley-Condit and E. O. Smith (2010) identify 284 species that have demonstrated a clear ability to *identify* tools; a portion of those species has also clearly demonstrated an ability to *create* tools. Benjamin Beck (1980) identifies four categories of how certain species actively create tools: detaching, subtracting, adding/combining, and reshaping. This goes beyond the mere identification of an object for tool use, as in picking up a stick.[3]

Imagination has its own enabling and constraining qualities. By conceiving of this concept as a relation, we can investigate what is enabled when we have a well-developed imagination. More importantly, we can consider what is constrained, since often what is constrained is backgrounded. Our imagination helps us create technological solutions. However, the danger here, as Heidegger points out (1977: 27–28) is that the enframing aspect of technology contributes to obscuring our ability for non-technological solutions to be revealed to us. Thus, our perception becomes obscured and we tend only to envision technological solutions rather than holding a space for non-technological solutions to be revealed.

For instance, in the contemporary Western world,[4] solutions for climate change are predominantly technology based (Preston, 2018). By being aware that we have a strong inclination to use our imagination for technological purposes, we can become aware of our predisposition and then actively search for possible non-technological solutions. Michel Puech (2016) points out that technology can nurture a command-and-control attitude, which is helpful for complicated and closed systems—systems that are engineerable—but not as useful for complex living systems. According to Peter Hershock (2003), 'The better we get at controlling our circumstances, the more we will find ourselves in circumstances open to and requiring control' (595). This can lead

3 For examples of using postphenomenology to discuss animal tool use, see Ihde and Malafouris (2018) and Wellner (2017b).

4 This refers to the specific macroperception of a culture. Our cultures have an influence on how much we use our technological imagination (cf. Ihde, 1990).

to a runaway use of technology, which reflects what much of Western culture seems now to be experiencing.

Awareness, Agency, and Identity. In addition to imagination, other subgroups of the mind are awareness, agency, and identity—however, these subgroups do not easily stay separate from each other. As we investigate all of these various constituting relations, we might ask if we are simply a self-emergent system reacting to both external and internal relations? If we are on 'auto pilot', we are in an autopoietic mode, mindlessly self-becoming without agential intervention from the aware 'self'. This is where determinist and structuralist arguments seem to be reasonable.

However, through awareness and agency, a human subject does have some influence over their own constitution, but it requires an enactive approach, a participation of the aware self in how we choose to engage within an intricately complex dance. Our attention and intention towards any specific relation engages our agency; allowing us to influence the relation. What we do not pay attention to can become increasingly determining in our lives (i.e., influencing without our being aware). Our awareness acts as our own internal panopticon, a central aspect that can be directed towards any of our many relations, though it is impossible to be aware of all our relations at once.

Without the entanglement of agency and awareness, we would simply be determined systems, not (at least partially) self-governed through our agency, but rather constructed by an assemblage of constituting relations. Our lives are truly a dance of agency (Pickering, 1995, 2005), one where we can be continually led by the assemblages of our relations, or choose to participate in the dance through our own agency. Barad (2007) describes agency as 'a matter of intra-acting; it is an enactment, not something that someone or something has' (178).

Another subgroup of the mind is identity, which, as mentioned, is heavily influenced by culture. However, the basic concept of having an identity—a 'self' and a 'me'— is the part of the subject that is referred to here, the ability to identify as a subject. However, as Stuart Hall (2013) notes, 'Though they seem to invoke an origin in a historical past with which they continue to correspond, actually identities are about questions of using the resources of history, language and culture in the process of becoming rather than being' (4). In other words, identity is comprised of an aspect of the mind that is deeply entangled with culture.

The relational group 'mind' can help us focus on specific constituting relations of the mind and investigate how they enable and constrain us through the I-mind-world mediation formula. For instance, I can look into how my relational identities—as a practicing naturalist and as a nature photographer—can compete with each other. As a naturalist I might not want to disturb the behavior of the birds I am trying to photograph, especially if it is mating season and the bird in front of me is an endangered species. However, as a nature photographer my photos can help bring awareness to protecting this endangered species. These senses of identity compete with each other, and my awareness is split between them, attempting to find an acceptable compromise. Identifying the various relations of the mind and paying attention to how we are constituted by them increases our agency and ability to interact in a more informed way with our lifeworlds.

Space and Time

Having now described the more human-created relations of sociocultural and technological relations, as well as the core relations of mind and body, I now come to the more infrastructural relations of space and time. In physics these are understood as the first four dimension of reality. Space and time are the ultimate background, the tapestry upon which our universe exists. They are contextualizing relations. As John Urry (2005a) suggest, they are '"internal" to the processes by which the physical and social worlds themselves operate, helping to constitute their powers' (4). Both space and time can be considered mediums through which we relate, and I investigate how we are constituted through those relations.

In Chapter 3 I discuss how Harold Innis (2008) studies the space-time bias of mediums of communication. Shaun Moores (2005) also develops an entire book on media studies around time and space, claiming 'it is necessary to appreciate the complex ways in which media of communication are bound up with wider institutional, technological and political processes in the modern world' (3). He advocates for understanding 'media as operating in the wider temporal and spatial arrangements of society, but also as contributing, reciprocally, to the creation, maintenance or transformation of social time and space' (4).

Anthony Giddens (1979) argues the need to realize 'the time-space relations inherent in the constitution of all social interaction' (3). In this chapter, I am also advocating that space and time can and should be understood as relations, which impact the human subject's continual constitution. By naming them, we can analyze the specificity of those relations and bring to the foreground how they contribute to our own constitution in our everyday[5] lives.

Space Relations: I-Space-World

We can think of space as a medium within which we exist and to which we relate. Space defines the physical location, the embeddedness and situatedness of our location in the world. This section investigates the proximal effect of our physical surroundings. Space includes the natural world, as well as the human-made world. Space includes the Earth, air, clouds, atmosphere, and the vastness of outer space. Space is a medium and contributes to our own constitution through our relations with it. John Peters (2015) describes how these elements can be understood as mediums, affecting the species that exist within them. However, space is resistant to being understood singularly. It is easily entangled with other groups of relations such as technology and culture.

Using space as a relation tethers us to the physical world. While our minds and imaginations can get overly immersed in exploring the intricacies of sociocultural relations of power or issues surrounding representation and misrepresentation through the lens of social justice, it is the materiality and tangibility of our immediate surrounding that helps ground us in the here and now. The effects of the different mediums of space are clearly evident in communications. For instance, communicating underwater is vastly different than communicating through air (cf. Peters, 2015), which is vastly different than communication in outer space, in the absence of air. All of these particular elemental mediums are gathered in the general grouping of 'space'. This creates a way to locate and bring spatial relations to the

5 Alfred Schütz (cf.; Schütz & Luckmann, 1973) uses spatial arrangements as the foundation to his structure of everyday life, followed by temporal and then social arrangements. See also Laurence Claeys (2007, chapter 6) for a helpful schematic and description of Schütz's conceptual framework.

foreground in order to analyze and recognize their influence on our own constitutionality.

Spatial Entanglements with Other Groups. Rather than discussing subgroups of space, I will present several ways that space can combine with some of the other relational groups. The first is the combination of space and mind, where I investigate the spatial effects on perspective. Space can have a profound effect on a person's mental state. An example of this is what Frank White (2014: 2) refers to as the Overview Effect:

> The Overview Effect is a cognitive shift in awareness reported by some astronauts and cosmonauts during spaceflight, often while viewing the Earth from orbit, in transit between the Earth and the moon, or from the lunar surface. It refers to the experience of seeing firsthand the reality that the Earth is in space, a tiny, fragile ball of life, 'hanging in the void', shielded and nourished by a paper-thin atmosphere. The experience often transforms astronauts' perspective on the planet and humanity's place in the universe. Some common aspects of it are a feeling of awe for the planet, a profound understanding of the interconnection of all life, and a renewed sense of responsibility for taking care of the environment.

White also posits, 'mental processes and views of life cannot be separated from physical location. Our "worldview" as a conceptual framework depends quite literally on our view of the world from a physical place in the universe' (1). Space and mind are thus entangled. What is physically surrounding us can profoundly affect our mind and our perception of the world.[6]

Media and technology have historically had a profound effect on our understanding of space. Technology has a way of reducing space. For instance, it would take a moderately healthy person 2 ½ days to cover the space between Brussels and Paris by walking, while the train can travel the distance between the two cities in about 1 ½ hours, effectively shrinking our perception of the space since it takes less time to travel between them. Technology has also created virtual space, shaking up the idea of space. Current ICTs are changing aspects of proximity by allowing a virtual proximity. For the most part, the most common virtual space uses two of the five traditional senses (vision and hearing). Video conferencing and video calls are quite common.

---

6 For another excellent study on the impact of the visual image of Earth from space, see Sheila Jasanoff (2001).

However, though our other senses of smell, touch, and taste have not entered mainstream usage, there are development attempts underway (cf. Harley et al., 2018).

Being limited to the two senses, virtual proximity is not as engaging as actual proximity, where all of our senses can participate. However, virtual space still dramatically influences our contemporary world, and there are many authors who have investigated how this impacts our lifeworld (see Adams & Thompson, 2016; Lewis, 2020; Meyrowitz, 1985; Rauch, 2018; Turkle, 2011; Van Dijck, 2013; Wellner, 2016). However, virtual proximity tends to disembody a subject, which 'messes with *whereness.* In cyberspace you are everywhere and somewhere and nowhere, but almost never *here* in the positivist sense' (Stone, 1994: 180, italics in original). Virtual space demonstrates how two of the relational groups can combine together into a seemingly singular relation.

While space comprises the human-made (technological) world, it also comprises the natural world. However, the concept of nature is a social construction (Cronon, 1995). It is not possible to experience nature outside of the socioculturally sedimented values and experiences that have built up in our lifetimes. This does not mean that there is not a 'natural world', we simply experience this natural world through a sociocultural filter rather than directly. That said, the natural world does mediate and contribute to our constitution. For instance, researchers are exploring the benefits of spending time in nature and how it can increase both our physical and mental health (Faber Taylor & Kuo, 2006; Louv, 2008; Vitalia, 2013).

Spatial and bodily relations are also entangled. We are always somewhere, embedded and embodied physically. Coeckelbergh (2019) draws attention toward how the body moves through space, pointing out that the embodied relation within postphenomenology 'does not move enough' (19). A moving body is necessarily moving through both space and time. And, Maurice Merleau-Ponty (2002) explores how a 'bodily space can be differentiated from an external space' (115).

Space is also entangled with sociocultural relations. The idea of personal space—the distance between me and another person in a crowded room—can vary by culture. I am affected by how close someone is to me, not only because of the amount of personal space I prefer, but also because of my sociocultural upbringing. Additionally, Erving

Goffman (1956) explores the interaction between the performance of self and space, looking into how these issues of public and private spaces affect our behavior. These are all examples of the entanglement of spatial and sociocultural relations.

Recent Foregrounding of Space Relations. I am writing this during the global pandemic caused by COVID-19, which has caused spatial relations between people to become globally foregrounded. The main response to halt the spread of the virus has been through social distancing: working from home, massively reducing global travel, staying around two meters away from other people, and shutting many national borders. All of these measures involve shifting the use of space in order to stop the transmission of the virus until a vaccine (a technological response) can be first created and then disseminated throughout the global population. This is one of the rare times that proximity moves from the background to the foreground. It is likely that this pandemic has shifted nearly every person's personal awareness and experience of space on the planet.

Time Relations: I-Time-World

Time is the final group of relations. Time brings unique characteristics and can be challenging to pin down and define.[7] We are forever in the present, but both the past and future have mediating affects. Up until now I have discussed the groups of relations as they primarily mediate us in the present moment. I-technology-world, I-sociocultural-world, I-mind-world, I-body-world, and I-space-world all represent mediations in the moment of being mediated. But the present moment is affected by both the past and the future. As Barad (2007: 181) describes:

> The past matters and so does the future, but the past is never left behind, never finished once and for all, and the future is not what will come to be in an unfolding of the present moment; rather the past and the future are enfolded participants in matter's iterative becoming.

In this section I investigate time as a relation in order to understand how the past and future transform the way we presently perceive the world.

7 See Canales (2016) for a discussion on the debate between Einstein and Bergson concerning time.

Time is the relation that brings movement to life. Time is a flow—a process or an action—that affords the becomingness of humans. This flow is one directional. Complexity theory views time as being irreversible,[8] an arrow of time. As we are transformed by our experiences, we cannot go back to the way we were. We are always in the present, but we are simultaneously mediated by both past and future. Graham Harman (2007) suggests that for Heidegger, 'time is the ultimate concealed layer of everything' (48). In *Being and Time,* Heidegger (2010) counters the concept of presence,[9] which is predicated on the Aristotelian concept of time and which situates the present as separate from the historical past and the future that has not yet come to pass (§6 and §26). Instead, Heidegger believes that a more authentic understanding of time is as a unity of past, present, and future, an 'ecstatic openness' (Sheehan 2014: 266).

My sense of time, which is influenced by sociocultural relations, influences my interaction with the world in that moment. For instance, I am late leaving for work in the morning, causing me to rush and do everything quickly. I am affected by both the past (maybe I have been late already twice this week and my boss has let her displeasure known) and the future (I am imagining what will happen if I arrive late again). These are direct relations that I am experiencing with the past-present-future duration of time.

Relating to the Future through Potentiality. Asle Kiran's (2012) investigates one type of direct relation with a future orientation through the concept of potentiality, which he develops with regard to technological relations. Kiran describes how the future potential of technologies mediates our present experiences, stating that we are 'directed towards the future, and any kind of planning [...is] performed because we presuppose that we have certain possibilities to do something with our lives' (88). He looks beyond 'technologies in-use' (78) and broadens the mediating influence of technology, stating: 'technological shaping of the lifeworld happens in terms of possible technical mediations, not just actual technical mediations' (79). This potentiality adds a way of leveraging the future as a relation.

8 This concept of time rejects the part of Newtonian mechanics that views time as being reversible.

9 See also Derrida (1982).

Relating to the Past through Sedimentation. Another way of describing relations with time relates less directly *to* time and instead relates more *because of* time. This aspect expands upon the concept of sedimentation, which is the idea that our past experiences with a phenomenon influence each subsequent experience of the same phenomenon (Husserl, 1973; Merleau-Ponty, 2002). For example, our experiences with technologies become sedimented within us the more we use them, eventually causing the object to recede into the background of our attention. Sedimentation is often described by focusing on the use of actual technologies, such as using a hammer, driving a car, or a blind person using a cane to detect things while they are walking. However, sedimentation does not have to be an experience with the actual technology. As soon as awareness of a technology enters a person's lifeworld, sedimentation begins to be developed within the subject. For instance, consumer marketing advertises the latest technological gadget with the hope of transforming people into wanting to buy and incorporate the object into their lives. If the advertising is successful, the consumer will imagine owning the new technological device, already incorporating the idea of the device into their lifeworld.

We interact with the world in the present, but without past and future there would only be the here-and-now relations mediating the subject and world. Even given this predilection, this is not how our lifeworld works. In any present moment, we are connected with both our history and our future. While in some ways the past and future might not exist in the present, they do exist through their connection within our selves and their transformational abilities. Or, as Braidotti (2017) states, 'To do justice to the complexity of our times, we need to think of the posthuman present as *both* the record of what *we are ceasing to be* (the actual) and the seed of *what we are in the process of becoming* (the virtual)' (10). This entanglement of past and future acting upon someone in the present is more thoroughly described by intrasubjective mediation.

Adding Intrasubjective Mediation to the Framework

Having described the grouped relations within the framework, I now bring in the concept of intrasubjective mediation. One way to understand intrasubjective mediation (ISM) is by using postphenomenology's concept of the embodied relation. This is because intrasubjective mediation reflects the non-neutrality of the transformations from our relations that have taken place within the subject, which thus mediate our perceptions of the world as we engage with the world *through* them. Portraying the intrasubjective mediating relation using the embodied relation formula looks like the following:

$$(\text{I-}\mathit{ISM}) \rightarrow \text{world}$$

We perceive through our relational transformations as a type of embodied relation. We are mediated through our sedimented transformations and perceive the world (and our current relations) differently because of this perception. Therefore, looking specifically at technological mediation discussed in Chapter 3, the equation can be updated from I-technology-world to: (I-ISM)-technology-world. However, intrasubjective mediation represents the transformations from all of the relations identified by the framework, not just the technological. Figure 5.2 reflects a way to visualize the expanded technological mediation formula that includes intrasubjective mediation.

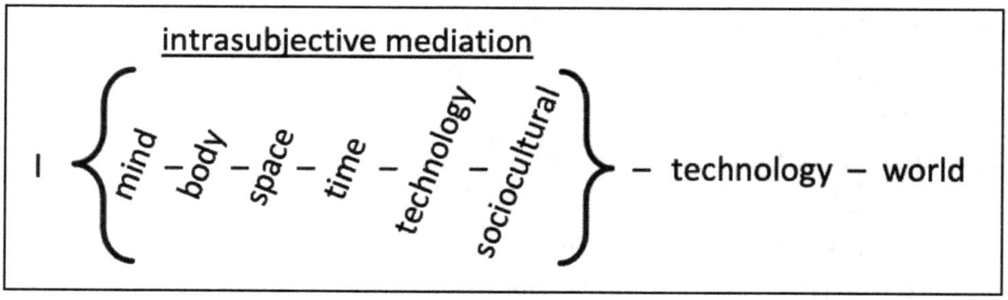

Fig. 5.2 *The Formula for Intrasubjective Mediation with Technology.* Image by author (2019), CC BY 4.0.

Intrasubjective mediation does not discount or ignore all of the other mediating relations, but rather is an additional mediating layer to whatever relations we are in at the present moment. A technological example of this is when I use a camera to take nature photographs. The more I use the camera, the more the camera becomes transparent, receding into the background as my sedimentation grows with use. The more that I use the camera, the more my relation with the camera influences my own constitution, transforming my perception of, and relation with, the world. However, even when I am out in nature without my camera, I notice that I perceive and frame nature through the filter of what would make a good photograph. This can be thought of as a 'technological gaze' (Lewis, 2020), which both enables me to be more aware of my surroundings—specifically looking for owls, raptors, and other wildlife, as well as noticing the light and interplay of shadows—but it also limits how I perceive the natural world around me. I end up looking *for* things, not just looking. I do not experience the natural world around me immediately; rather, I experience the natural world as intrasubjectively mediated through a residual aspect of the photograph based upon my previous experiences.

Intrasubjective Mediation versus 'I'

Intrasubjective mediation acknowledges how all of our relations both constitute us in the moment and continue to transform us, continuously changing how we perceive and engage with the world. These transformations are not separate from the subject; they *are* the subject. They are the multiplicity of the human becoming. All relations are mediated through intrasubjective mediation. This enables us to better understand the human subject as an assemblage of the transformations that have occurred through their relational experiences, as well as all of the relations they are experiencing in the present moment. This begs the question, Are humans anything besides intrasubjective mediation? What is the 'I' that is still preceding the intrasubjective mediation in the above formula?

My belief is that the 'I' includes (and is mediated by) the constituting relations in the person's life and all the relations that the person has experienced, as well as the potentiality that the person can imagine. The consciousness that is 'I' is still part of the mind, which is a part of the mediating whole. Therefore, instead of trying to reductively locate some essential aspect of the subject that we can identify, we can move in the opposite direction and open the idea of the subject as inclusive of all of our relations, current and past.[10] Human subjects are greater and more connected than the idea of the standalone human. We can therefore

10 The future is also included in the present through the concept of potentiality discussed previously.

unite the 'I' with intrasubjective mediation, referring to our selves as intrasubjectively mediated subjects.

One more step in visually demonstrating a comprehensive framework is to take Figure 5.2 and add the other groups of relations to the technological. This is shown in Figure 5.3, which includes all six relational groups plus the concept of intrasubjective mediation. There is no relation of the human subject that is not intended to be a part of the groupings of relations in Figure 5.3, though there might be relations that I have unintentionally missed (or that have not yet been discovered). It is also important to keep in mind that there are unknown and unknowable relations that also affect us. For example, there could be an unknown toxin near the physical location of your home, which detrimentally affects both your body and mind. While this is potentially knowable if identified, you could live with it for many years without ever knowing. There are also the theoretically unknown and unknowable relations.

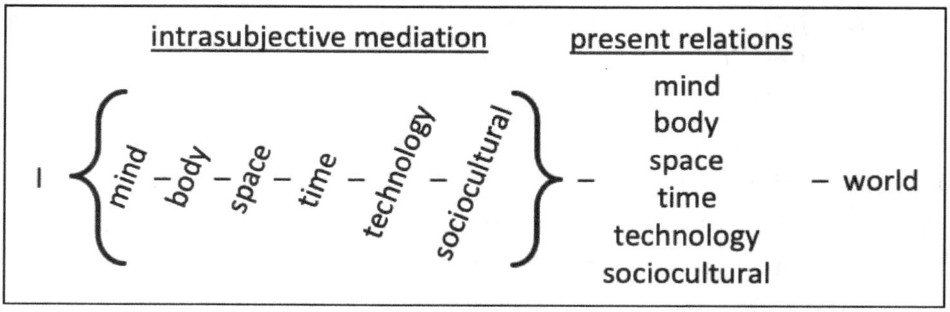

Fig. 5.3 *The Formula for an Inclusive Intrasubjective Mediation.* Image by author (2019), CC BY 4.0.

The intrasubjective mediating framework helps demonstrate that these groups of relations mediate our perception and engagement with the world, moving us beyond focusing on a single group of relations in isolation. By understanding intrasubjective mediation as an embodied relation through which we relate to the world, we can visually demonstrate how intrasubjective mediation mediates the relations we have in our lifeworld.

Even if our focus is on the effects of any one particular group of relations, the framework reminds us that those relations are situated and entangled with multiple other groups of concurrent relations. No one group is privileged in its effect on our own becoming at any one moment in time. The framework describes both the present constituting relations, as well as the aspect of how the transformations from those relations continue to mediate all of our relations as we move through time.

However, Figure 5.3 is clearly still built upon postphenomenology's I-technology-world formula. While I have expanded the first two parts of the formula, the 'world' has not received much attention by me,[11] or, indeed, by most postphenomenologists. I believe the formula is helpful in analyzing specific relations and how they mediate and constitute us. However, this process is a teasing apart of reality, or the world, as a whole. By keeping a larger perspective, we can approach understanding our own worlds as being made up of all of our relations and interrelations, which I will describe in more detail in the next chapter. This leaves less reason to retain a world 'placeholder' after the list of relations. And yet dropping it removes it as an effective formula for understanding our constitution through our interrelations. Therefore, the next step is integrating the framework into a complex interrelational system of the human becoming.

Intrasubjective Mediation: A Dance of Complexity

> To understand just one life, you have to swallow the world. (Rushdie, 2006: 145)

The final part of the human becoming process involves the system of our complex interrelationality. It is this interrelational complexity that gives the sense that in order to understand anything, you must understand everything (see Rushdie quote above). Up until now I have looked at either singular or a combination of mediating relations, showing how the subject is transformed by any of the various groups of relations, as well as intrasubjective mediation. However, human subjects cannot be boiled down to a linear causal algorithm, where all that is needed is to add up the various enabling and constraining relations and end up with a predictive model for the human becoming. In order to understand 'who and what we are actually in the process of becoming' (Braidotti, 2013: 12), we need to understand *how* we are becoming. The relational

11 I thank Alberto Romele for first pointing this out to me.

transformations described by intrasubjective mediation are not discrete transformations that can be added together to create a composite of the human subject. Instead, these transformations are entangled and interrelational, producing an emergent human becoming through a complex process.

The Complexity of Interrelating Relations

We are not simply relational or even multi-relational. Rather, we are a system of complex interrelationality, continually being transformed. Each of our relations is open to being influenced (enabled or constrained) by each of our other relations. These interrelations co-constitute each other. Mapping this complex interrelationality helps us to better understand and situate any one constituting relation within this broader, emergent system. This is an effort to re-envision the subject through a cartography-in-progress and should not be thought of as dogmatic. On the contrary, it is a partially new topic introduced into a conversation that has been going on for centuries, modifying the question, 'who are we?' to 'what are we and how are we becoming?' Complexity theory provides three insights: 1) we are open systems; 2) we are in a state of non-linear equilibrium; and 3) we are emergent.

Complex systems are open systems. Being complex, humans are open systems as well. We bring in matter and energy and also produce waste that leaves our 'system' (Capra, 2005). We are connected with, and constituted by, all of the relations in our lives, making us interconnected beings with no hard boundaries of separation. We are not singularly complex, but are assemblages of nested complex systems (Capra, 1996), from our biological bodies to our complex extended minds.

Complexity theory highlights the near impossibility of predicting how any particular relation will influence the overall constitution of a subject. This is because we are in a state of non-linear equilibrium. While we are in a continual state of being constituted, we are often in a generally stable, if non-linear, equilibrium. However, occasionally we experience major life-changing moments (called bifurcations in complexity theory), which can be caused by a very small nudge from any one of our multitude of relations. This continually changing state can be understood through probabilities but eludes any predictability.

Because of the interrelationality between all the groups of relations, any relation can affect any other relation. Therefore, rather than perceiving relations as summative (adding up all relations to get a final sum of influence), they should be thought of as being interrelated in a complex evolving web.

The final concept that aids our understanding of our selves as systems is the idea of emergence. In complexity theory, this is generally referred to as autopoiesis. However, as mentioned, Haraway (2016) has a more succinct way of referring to this process: *sympoiesis*. This term means making-with rather than the self-making concept of autopoiesis. This way of referring to the process of emergence moves away from the idea of the autonomous self and more accurately reflects how we are mutually being constituted with everything around us. This complex entanglement increases our resilience as no one relation determines us. Each relation's effect on us is enabled and constrained by many of our other relations, all happening in a sympoietic moment that emerges through time. While I began this chapter by introducing the groups of relations separately, the groupings are not meant to keep relations apart, but rather to allow the analysis of similarities and the ability to identify aspects of what contributes to our constitution.

Agency, Education, and Literacy: Understanding Degrees of Influence

Relating back to media literacy, how can the framework enhance our awareness concerning the effects of our media relations? Increasing our awareness allows us greater agency, without which we risk living as beings determined by the technologies in our lives (Puech, 2016: 173). One goal in philosophy of technology is in enhancing our awareness of the effects of technology. As Yoni Van Den Eede (2016) argues, 'From McLuhan to Heidegger to Ihde to Latour to Feenberg, [...] a thread can be said to run, uniting them in one great perceptual project: the spotting of blind spots, and the accompanying attempt of remedying them' (108). In order to become media-literate, we need to better understand our own complex interrelational becoming, which allows us to situate how our media relations interrelate with our other relations. In other words, this framework provides a cartography that enables us to become self-literate, becoming aware of all of our interrelationality, which then allows us to become more media literate.

What contributes to the amount of influence a particular relation has at any particular moment? While we are being constituted through a complex ecosystem of relations, all influencing each other in small and large ways, they also can be affected by our agency and our awareness, giving us the ability to—at least partially—manipulate the process of our own becoming. We are dynamic assemblages of relations, most of which we pay little or no attention to. However, many of these relations are available to us to become aware of, which allows us the opportunity to have some influence upon them.

Some relations in our lives have a great impact upon us, while others do not. This is often identified only in hindsight, though we cannot be certain that we ever truly know the full extent of the impact of any relation. For example, a person's ability to earn money derives from many possible influences: the situation they were born into, their upbringing, their immediate location, their level of education, their culture, race, gender, or simply being in the right place at the right time. Some relations are more difficult to change by a subject's agency. This does not mean, however, that a subject is completely determined. The subject has agency in how they interpret or understand this less flexible relation. This is Foucault's (Foucault et al., 1987) point about awareness of power: we cannot do much to change the fact that there is a power relation, but we can change how we perceive and relate to the power relation.

Ideally, this new framework will help us better understand and utilize our own agency, similar to the later Foucault. Tamar Sharon (2014: 168) summarizes some of Foucault's ideas:

> Rather, freedom here is the possibility of modifying the impact of power on one's subjectivity, it is a practice of actively engaging with one's relationship to power and so a practice of subject constitution. Freedom is not about escaping structures of power but of interacting with them. Because there is no authentic or natural self that can be liberated, freedom lies in the dynamic, aesthetic and experimental self-creation undertaken in the practices of the self.

Sharon's take on Foucault situates the subject between being completely independent and autonomous in relation to the world and being completely determined by the structures of power that make up that world. This is a very constructive starting point from which to think about how humans can relate to the technological—as well as other—relations that constitute them. This interrelating framework enables us to create a perspective in order to better understand the relations of influence. I prefer to use 'relations of influence' rather than 'relations of power', as I feel it is a more inclusive and descriptive way to portray these relations and their effects on us. These relations of influence are not just between the thing of influence and the subject, there are also interactions between the various relations.

For example, in my role as a nature photographer I can look for the interrelations that affect my photography: the physical place where I am (the landscape, the weather, the lighting, etc.), as well as my sense of identity (both mind-related and sociocultural). Also, my body (hunger level, brain chemistry, physical ability to manipulate the camera technology, etc.), and my historical experience with both the technology and the place (have I been there before, do I know where I am going or what I am trying to find) all influence me. Additionally, the future intention of what I am trying to accomplish—my imagined potentiality for the final image and my plans for that image, such as selling it, sharing it with my social network, entering it for a competition, etc.—all influence the photograph that I take. This is a very brief list of some of the relations that comprise the interrelationality of my experience taking nature photographs. In the next chapter I will use the framework to analyze the relations and interrelations that I experienced in the moment of taking a museum selfie, developing an instrument in the process that can be generalized and used for media literacy.

Concluding Thoughts

Leveraging the concept of technological mediation and turning the concept into a more inclusive and situating framework helps us to circumvent our attachment to a specific group of relations, such as focusing solely on the technological or the sociocultural. The intrasubjective mediating framework helps deterritorialize the concept of the individual, reterritorializing it into an interrelated human becoming. In summary, there are three parts that make up the systemic intrasubjective mediating framework:

1. The transformations that occur from the relations in our lives are not neutral, and they continue to mediate us as we perceive and engage with the world through them. This is intrasubjective mediation.
2. All of the relations in our lives can be gathered into six groups: technology, sociocultural, mind, body, space, and time.
3. Human subjects can be understood as open and complex systems whose constituting relations are constantly interrelating in non-linear and emergent ways.

There can be a tendency to view how a specific technology influences us in a singular manner. Even with the concept of multistability, we may consider that only one variant is acting upon us at a time, co-constituting our selves and our lifeworlds. This framework enables us to reflexively comprehend specific effects that technologies have, allowing us to more intentionally decide which technologies we invite into our lives and how we use them. We are an inter- and intra-connected complex assemblage moving through space and time, constantly becoming. This framework helps to broaden our understanding that there is a complexity of entangled relations, which constitute us. We experience our being-in-the world as a complex, entangled experience of relations, all influencing us whether we pay attention to them or not. Foregrounded or backgrounded, a multitude of relations exist, and it is impossible to disentangle them.

This new framework enables the ability to identify the multiplicity of relations that all contribute to our human experience of becoming. We can think of the six groups as different mediums through which we become. The framework can help us better understand the constituting factors that contribute to our human becoming across cultures and across time, aiding research in the social sciences by providing a situating cartography. The framework helps researchers move beyond a deterministic view, where subjectivity is determined by a single group or subgroup (be it power, economy, class, gender, nature, nurture, etc.)

and beyond an 'agency' view, where the subject has full agency and other things like technology and culture are simply neutral.

Variations on Relations

While the framework includes what I consider to be an inclusive and comprehensive organization of the differing relations that affect us, I leave room for the unknown and even unknowable (cf. Fig. 5.1). One of the main goals of postphenomenology and media ecology, as well as several media literacy approaches, is to help us become aware of the 'ground' in the figure/ground concept. In other words, to help us to perceive things that influence us but of which we are typically unaware. Adding a placeholder for the unknown/unknowable keeps our awareness open to the limits of what we know and helps compel us to continue seeking new influencing relations.

Additionally, I have been discussing the relations in our lives through a positive lens, meaning relations that we are engaged with. However, not having a relation is, in effect, a relation as well. Judith Butler (1993) critiques Foucault's notions of discourse and materiality by saying they 'fail to account for not only what is excluded from the economies of discursive intelligibility that he describes, but what has to be excluded for those economies to function as self-sustaining systems' (35). In other words, both our relations and our lack of relations—relations we may not have access to for a myriad of reasons—constitute us. We therefore can consider the absence of a relation as still a relation.

What does it mean to be 'human' in this age of ubiquitous digital communication? How can we contextualize and situate both the benefits and drawbacks of the transformative effects that ICTs have on humans as subjects? Our communication mediums are transforming more quickly than we as subjects and societies can completely adjust to. These changes transform us in important ways that need to be evaluated alongside of the changing media technologies. In other words, to fully become media literate we need an ability to be self-literate—to understand that a change in media technology causes a transformation in both our selves and our lifeworlds. By better understanding how we are interrelatedly constituted, we will be better able to judge new media and be better equipped to decide if and how we invite them into our lives.

This is the agency that media literacy and this intrasubjective mediating framework can enhance. However, how exactly can media literacy leverage this framework? An instrument is needed to assist with the pragmatic use of the framework in order to better situate the effects of media technologies. In order to develop such an instrument, in Chapter 6 I return to my experience taking a museum selfie and use it to engage with the framework.

6

Instrument for Facilitating Critical Reflection and Media Engagement

With the intrasubjective mediating framework now explained, the next step is to develop it into a practical instrument that can be used to facilitate critical reflection and engagement with media. In order to do so, I return to a museum selfie that I took while conducting a postphenomenological study (Lewis, 2017). It was this experience that inspired my desire to find a more inclusive framework beyond postphenomenology's focus on technological relations. I begin this chapter with a description of this event and then investigate the museum selfie through the development of an instrument that helps identify the broad range of influencing relations that contributed to both my own and the selfie's constitution. I then generalize the instrument into an exercise[1] that can be used to teach media literacy.

It was January 2017, and I was at the Art and History Museum[2] in Brussels to experience the fourth annual Museum Selfie Day, an event started by London blogger and museum advocate, Mar Dixon.[3] This event occurs annually around the third week in January. Museum goers are encouraged to upload their selfies to Twitter, Instagram, or other social media sites and tag the images with the hashtags #MuseumSelfie

1 You may download the exercise by going to the 'Additional Resources' tab at https://doi.org/10.11647/OBP.0253#resources

2 The museum was called the Cinquantenaire Museum when I visited but is now called the Art and History Museum.

3 Dixon identifies as a digital and social innovator. She has created and runs other social media campaigns, such as Ask a Curator Day and Love Theatre Day. She currently resides in the U.S.

or #MuseumSelfieDay. From Mar Dixon's blog she describes it as *'a FUN DAY to encourage people to visit museums and participate a bit with art or collections'.*[4] This event now spans the globe, taking place mostly on Instagram and Twitter. There are increasing numbers of museums that participate. In January, 2019, Turkey made it legal for people to take museum selfies in more than 300 sites because of the museum selfie day.

I became involved with museum selfie day because I had been studying the effects of technology on museum visitor's experiences, specifically using a philosophical style of analysis within philosophy of technology called postphenomenology, which emphasizes how to (pragmatically) understand the way technologies co-constitute both our selves and our world (cf. Chapter 3). I decided to participate in the event in order to experience how the selfie would contribute to both my constitution as well as the museum's. While postphenomenology helped me understand the technological relations of my museum selfie experience, I also felt that there was something missing. The technological mediation of taking and viewing selfies seemed to be only one aspect of a larger complexity of mediating relations. I felt that I needed a more comprehensive framework to fully understand what I was experiencing, both technologically and otherwise, as I took my museum selfies. This led to the framework I presented in the previous chapter.

Creating the Instrument

One challenge with theoretical ideas, even ones that are described as 'frameworks', is the ability to implement them in a practical and usable manner.[5] In this chapter I translate the framework into a concrete instrument by using a museum selfie as a way to situate media literacy. Specifically, I use the general groupings from the framework in order to identify the specific relations and their effects that existed when I created a museum selfie. This is done through a two-stage spreadsheet. The first stage enables me to identify the multiple relations in each group or subgroup that were involved when taking the museum selfie.

---

4 http://mardixon.com/

5 Postphenomenology has a history of creating philosophical case studies in order to ground their investigations in the 'real world'. This pragmatism has inspired my desire to create a practical instrument.

The second stage helps me to identify what I perceive to be the amount that each of the identified relations was influenced by the other groups and subgroups. By doing this, the phenomenon of the museum selfie in Figure 6.1 is uncovered to reveal the complex interrelationality that occurred—as analyzed autoethnographically—at a particular moment in time. Even though the instrument uses numbers that can have a semblance of objectivity, it is important to understand that these numbers all reflect a subjective analysis.

Fig. 6.1 *Meditating on Mediation.* Author with *Head of a Buddha,* from Ayutthaya, Thailand, seventeenth century. Art and History Museum, Brussels. Image by author (2017), CC BY-NC 4.0.

Identifying the Multiplicity of Relations

Rather than primarily focusing on the technological thing (the selfie) or the constitution of the subject (myself), the framework stresses how the relations and interrelations constitute both. I refer to this phenomenon as the selfie-subject constitution, what Karen Barad (2007) identifies as intra-action and postphenomenology calls co-constitution. While there can be a tendency to view the subject-selfie phenomenon in a singular or gestalt manner, the framework affords the ability to tease apart (but not separate) the phenomenon in order to reveal the complex interrelations. To begin with, every relation is a multi-relation. There is no 'technological relation' without a multiplicity of sociocultural, bodily, mind, temporal, and spatial relations. The gestalt of a technological relation is actually a unity of many relations as the example in Figure 6.2 demonstrates. This figure updates the original co-constituting relation from Figure 3.1. We perceive these multiple relations all at once, in a mostly singular/gestalt manner. Figure 6.2 demonstrates a way of visualizing the unpacking of this 'singularity' into the different groups of relations that occur during the museum selfie.

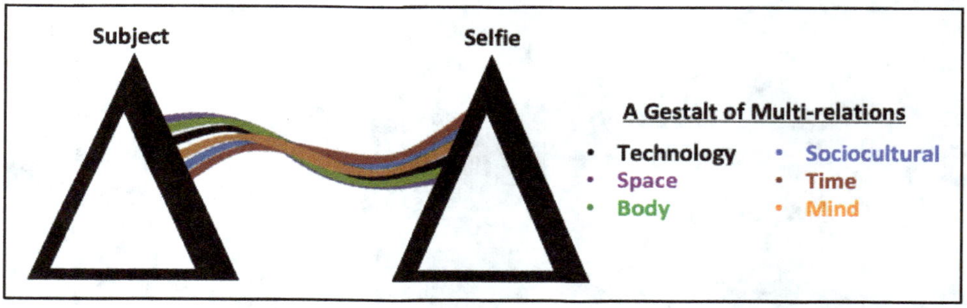

Fig. 6.2 *Multi-relationality of the Museum Selfie.* Image by author (2020), CC BY-NC 4.0.

The first questions for the instrument to help answer are: What are the relations that were involved in this subject-selfie constitution; and How much influence did they have? I use a spreadsheet (Table 6.1) in order to brainstorm as many specific relations in each grouping that I can think of that were influencing me at the moment when I took the museum selfie. This step identifies the multiplicity of relations that contribute in the 'singular' moment of taking a selfie. The spreadsheet is organized to use the framework as a facilitating cartography for self-inquiry, with the groups and subgroups helping me to focus on a narrower portion of the entirety of relations that could be contributing at the specific moment.

After listing the relations in Table 6.1, I then provide a rating for how much the relation influenced the subject-selfie constitution. I use a very basic scale to do so. The numbers in the light blue cells represent this influence as interpreted by me at a specific point in time, giving a three for the most influencing and going down to a zero for relations with no discernable influence. This interpretation is specific and changeable over time (emphasizing why time is also a group of relations), as I discovered when I went through the numbers months later. Totaling the average influences for each group offers a general comparative sense of how much each group impacts the subject-selfie constitution—again, not in an objective sense—but in a subjectively interpretive sense as a way to ask, How do I think and feel each of these groups influenced me at the moment I took this museum selfie?

3 = Heavy influence
2 = Moderate influence
1 = Light influence
0 = No discernable influence

	Relation's influence on subject-selfie constitution	
Mind	See museum object and imagine possible selfie	3
	Direction of my awareness: selfie, others, museum?	3
	The specific self I am trying to construct	3
	My desire to learn	3
	My interest in following the curatorial information	1
	Perceive object thru its history, curator, or my own lens	3
	Attention towards my senses: hearing, smelling, feeling	2
	My intention for visiting: academic, amusement, social	3
	My intention/desire for taking the selfie: object relation	3
	My state of with mind regards to time: hurried, relaxed	3
	Mind_Average	**2.7**
Temporality	Ideas from other museum selfies I've seen	3
	My own experience taking selfies w/ phone	3
	Past experience of museums	2
	History of the specific object	2
	Past experience as a photographer	3
	How much have I been using social media?	2
	What is my future goal for taking the selfie?	2
	Who will I share it with?	3
	Time_Average	**2.5**
Sociocultural	Who is judging me?	3
	Who am I disturbing?	3
	Is this my culture, am I a foreigner or tourist?	2
	Are others taking selfies as well?	3
	What would my family think of me?	2
	Class pressures: high class=museum, low class=selfie?	2
	Can I read the descriptions in my language?	1
	Pressure from norms or power not to take a selfie?	3
	Am I a privliged/entitled race, or an 'othered' minority?	2
	Is there a guard around?	3
	Sociocultural_Average	**2.4**

	Relation's influence on subject-selfie constitution	
Body	Am I hungry? Or tired?	2
	How is my formerly broken heel doing?	2
	Am I too hot or cold?	2
	Can my eyes see the screen very well?	3
	Is my body chemistry in balance?	2
	How distracting is my headache?	2
	What is my sense of smell detecting?	1
	Is it loud or are there distracting sounds?	2
	Are there visual distractions?	2
	Does my bodily appearance attract attention?	1
	Body_Average	**2**
Space	How close can I get?	3
	How many people are around me?	3
	What is the physical space around the object?	3
	Is there a frame or case?	2
	Enough light to show both me and the object?	3
	How far away do I hold the camera phone?	2
	How is the lack of nature affecting me?	2
	What is the overall feeling of the space?	2
	Space_Average	**2.5**
Technology	Are my clothes restricting or comfortable?	2
	Is my camera/phone charged?	2
	Do I know how to turn off flash?	2
	Do I set a filter/edit now or use FB/Instagram?	3
	Do I have cell reception?	1
	Is the phone sensitive enough for poor light?	3
	Upload to social media or edit first?	2
	Do I tag friends or limit sharing?	2
	Is the camera lens clean?	1
	Need for reading glasses to see the screen?	2
	Technology_Average	**2.0**
	Total_Average	**2.3**

Table 6.1 *Relational Influences on Subject-selfie Constitution.* Table by author (2020).

For the purpose of this research, I briefly analyze the groups and subgroups that had an effect on the subject-selfie constitution. I do not go into depth as to why I have given certain ratings and why I have identified these specific relations. Instead, the emphasis is to develop an instrument that can be used to encourage critical awareness of what happens when I engage with a specific media technology. I believe that this critical self-awareness is the key to helping people increase their media literacy. The instrument provides an autoethnographic process that people can use to investigate more deeply their relations with technologies. I now examine the various groups and subgroups and explain my thinking process for each in regards to the subject-selfie constitution.

Mind

I begin discussing the instrument by inquiring about the relations that are connected with the mind. I identify subgroups of imagination, identity, and awareness/perception to help narrow the focus and facilitate uncovering influencing relations. While these are not the only three subgroups that can make up the mind, I find them to be useful in identifying relations that I experienced while taking the museum selfie. After filling out Table 6.1, it is clear that the mind had the largest impact upon the subject-selfie constitution according to my evaluation.

Imagination

My imagination is the key relation that enables me to perceive the possibility of taking the selfie with the bust. The creative ability of my imagination is essential, a word not used lightly, especially in postphenomenological circles.[6] First, I use my imagination in order to notice a potential selfie that combines both the museum object and myself. I also have the desire to create a selfie with some aesthetics; a certain amount of artistic quality. My imagination is assimilating many variables in order to combine what I am seeing in order to create an artistic selfie worthy (in my mind) of representing me, one that I want

6 Postphenomenology is avidly anti-essentialist, primarily using the concept of multistability to resist considering that technologies have any essential aspect to them. Additionally, it is the imagination that is the source for our ability to recognize technology (see Chapter 5).

to share with my social group (which is middle-income, predominantly white, from U.S. or Europe, politically liberal, and educated).

Identity

I next discuss the subgroup of identity. The construction of one's own identity is, as John Falk (2009) notes, the main reason that visitors go to museums. The selfie is a very effective tool for identity construction (cf. Kozinets et al., 2017; Rettberg, 2014). Some questions of identity for me include: Am I being, or constructing, an academic self? Do I want to be funny or amusing for my friends? Am I trying to learn and follow the curatorial framing of the museum objects? For me, for this particular selfie, I am primarily being affected by my self-image as a photographer, and I am attempting to create a selfie that has artistic merit. In part, I want the selfie to demonstrate to an academic audience that selfies are not necessarily superficial or narcissistic, but rather a vehicle for identity construction.

Another identity-influencing factor for this specific selfie comes from my own experience. I studied Buddhism in Nepal for several months and this particular bust of a meditating Buddha connects with my own practice of meditation. This connection inspires me to compare myself with the bust. I take the selfie to juxtapose my own path to enlightenment while being present in the moment of taking a selfie, something that I have conflicting feelings about. This conflict is likely why my own face does not reflect the same peaceful state as that of the Buddha.

Perception/Awareness

The last subgroup of the mind that I use to analyze the selfie is that of perception or awareness. My mind's directed perception (awareness) is on creating artistic selfies. This excludes, or diminishes, my ability to perceive other things or other aspects of my surroundings in the museum. I am not paying close attention to the curatorial signage, except occasionally when an object especially strikes my interest, or when I want the name and title of the object because I have taken a selfie with it. While my goal is primarily to make an artistic and aesthetically pleasing selfie, my awareness is also directed toward my own experience.

I attempt to watch and take note of my experiences using the selfie-as-technology, in a phenomenological manner.

However, my awareness is usurped by the other museum visitors because I am sensitive to how others might be perceiving me if they see me taking a selfie. I have the sense that I am alienating the people in my immediate proximity by what Galit Wellner (2016) calls the wall/window aspect of smartphones. These phones can open a window to a virtual social group but also create a wall for the surrounding people in the area. I am concerned with alienating those around me, and this focuses my attention on watching for other visitors while also looking for possible selfies. The impact of the people around me is the most unexpected aspect of my experience in the museum. This in part might have to do with being in a different culture (Belgium instead of the U.S.) and not wanting to draw attention to myself or make a cultural faux pas.

Body

While I evaluate my mind's relations as the most influencing group, my body's relations were the least influencing. This was likely because my body, though just over fifty years old at the time of the selfie, was still in decent shape and had no major physical impediments. The most significant bodily challenge I experienced was my need for reading glasses and the fact that my smartphone screen was quite small. My eyes were no longer able to focus well on things that were close to my face, causing me to rely on using reading glasses in order to see things in detail that are near to me. I experienced this in the darkened museum while attempting to take selfies. For the most part I chose not to keep taking my reading glasses out of my coat pocket, even though my compromised vision kept the technology from receding into the background as I strained to see what was on the screen. This also dissuaded me from doing any editing or using any filters or even sending out any of the selfies that I took while in the museum.

By the time I took the selfie with the bust I had been in the museum for several hours. I was getting hungry and my feet were beginning to ache. I broke my heel many years before, and after several hours of walking I develop a significant amount of pain. Both the hunger and the pain contributed to a desire to leave the museum. Therefore, at the point where I took the bust selfie, I was beginning to hurry, bypassing some museum objects that could potentially make for good selfies. However, the opportunity with the bust and my imaginative ability to see the potential of the selfie was able to overcome my bodily desire to keep walking to the exit.

Time

Temporal relations include the direct past and future relations. An example of the direct past relation in my experience of taking a museum selfie is my consideration of the head of the Buddha being from the seventeenth century and wonder at how it had come through all of the years to wind up at the museum. Much of what is in museums is geared toward objects and cultures from the past.

The future-directedness is also an influence. My desire to create a selfie is one of the most influential aspects in how I perceive and relate with the museum as I walk around. I am less focused on the objects for what they are and more focused on how they can make an interesting and artistic selfie. One of my goals is to share the selfie online with the hashtag #museumselfieday. This inspires me to take a selfie that I can be proud of, one that has artistic merit in my eyes and hopefully the eyes of others. I am also using the experience as an academic investigation for my research. Therefore, I am being self-reflexive, as I am analyzing my own experience as I experience it.

The future also affects the present because I have something to do after the museum visit, and by the time I arrive at the Buddha sculpture I am 'running out of time'. This, along with my bodily fatigue, contributes to my sense of rushing through the last part of the museum. Alternatively, if I had no plans and was using the museum to 'pass time', then I would experience the opposite effect. I would likely linger longer at objects that seemed interesting.

Space

One of the main influencing relations regarding proximity that affected taking the museum selfie was how close I could get to the museum artifact. Many of the objects in the temporary Ukiyo-E exhibit were encased in glass or separated from the public by ropes. I found that, especially with the dim lighting, I needed to get quite close to the objects in order to create a good selfie. For this particular selfie (see Fig. 6.1) the object was simply on a pedestal, and I was able to get quite close and therefore able to juxtapose my head with the statue. The other proximity factor, which I have already alluded to, was the proximity of other people (cf. above and below).

Though nature did not play an active role in the creation of the museum selfie, it often plays a significant role in many other situations. However, the role it played in the museum selfie constitution was one of absence. The lack of nature and natural light can also be a significant, if subtle, relation. Our disconnection with nature affects us. After being inside a completely constructed and controlled environment for many hours it was a pleasure to leave and enter the park surrounding the museum.

Sociocultural

This grouping of relations contains many relevant subgroups. If I am performing a primarily critical media literacy investigation, this group would be one of the most extensive sections in my analysis. There are various normative relations that can be identified. I ask myself the predominant question: Who is judging me? As a foreigner living in Brussels, there is the question of belonging. Even though Brussels is a very international city and the majority of people are not native to the city, as a non-European citizen there is a part of me that does not quite feel like I belong. This is a much smaller element of self that arises than if I lived in another city such as Paris, where there is a stronger sense of cultural identity, which leads those who are not originally from the culture to feel othered by those who are. Also, if other people are taking selfies, I potentially feel less uncomfortable. Or, if I am a person who is an active selfie taker, I likely would feel less self-imposed judgment.

Sociocultural - Normativity

My biggest surprise was my own feeling of self-consciousness for taking selfies. While this was 'museum selfie day', there were no other people that I came across who were taking selfies. For this particular museum, the day was not being promoted, so I did not feel any official approval for taking selfies. While there was no demonstrable hostility towards me, I did my best not to be noticed taking selfies. This was not a small concern but an intrusive feeling that greatly impeded my selfie taking. The influence of this particular relation was more determining than any other relation that day, and one that came as a surprise as I was expecting to mainly be concentrating on how the technological relations were influencing me. This demonstrated my own too-narrow approach when I went to engage with my research.

Sociocultural - Language

Language plays a significant role in how we are constituted and is deeply connected with our sociocultural relations. As a native English speaker and a person who has a passable amount of French, I can understand most of the museum signage and explanations. Most of the other visitors do not speak English and, if they do speak French, I do not attend to what they are saying. There are times when language, or lack of language, can play a more influential role. There is also a way of using language as a dominant approach to understanding how we are constituted (cf. Coeckelbergh, 2017 for a study on language and technology). However, in an attempt to limit the scope of my investigation, I create a placeholder for this topic but I do not fully engage with it here.

Sociocultural - Power/Politics

I have visited many museums over the course of my life, so I feel quite comfortable in the role of a museum visitor. I do not feel out of place, except for while I am taking selfies. This can be a combination of two cultural aspects. The first I describe above under normativity. The second is more along the lines of Foucault's perspective of power relations and the control of institutions like museums upon the society. I have been brought up (and this relates to my own sedimented experience with museums) with the idea that museums are the epitome of culture and they hold a certain reverence for me. Analyzing the research, it is clear that selfies are not just one thing; they can be both powerful and significant vehicles to construct or share one's identity (Abidin, 2016;

Dinhopl & Gretzel, 2016; Hess, 2015; Kozinets et al., 2017; Rettberg, 2014; Risam, 2018; Senft & Baym, 2015). There are now many genres of selfies, some of which include: refugee, political, gender-diverse, and other genres that help bring marginalized groups a way to be seen.

While selfies enable identity construction, they also reflect a disruption in the museum experience (Clines, 2017; Kozinets et al., 2017; Lewis, 2017; Russo et al., 2008). As Mar Dixon's definition of museum selfie day demonstrates, selfies have a bias towards fun and entertainment, which does not mean they cannot be used for serious matters, only that one of their primary uses has been geared toward amusement. This can conflict with the traditional approach to museums, which has had a more serious and austere presence, one directed more towards education than entertainment. Even though education and entertainment need not be mutually exclusive, one of the challenges is the expectation of museum visitors. People wanting a quiet and reflective moment with an object may likely object to other 'less serious' visitors who simply want to capture an interesting selfie to share with their friends. I experience a conflicting, or at least ambiguous, feeling while taking museum selfies. I recognize an internal judgment and question if I am being disrespectful towards these cultural objects, wondering if I am belittling their cultural past and their present cultural role within the museum.

Sociocultural - Museum Effect

There is a sociocultural phenomenon called the *museum effect.* Valerie Casey (2003) is one of several researchers who analyzes museum visitor-object relationships and describes the museum itself as having an effect on everything, both people and objects, which enter through its doors. Museums re-contextualize objects from their origins through specific narratives, proximity to other objects, the use of labels, and through contextualizing meta-language. However, Casey (2003) and others (cf. Malraux, 1967; Kirshenblatt-Gimblett, 1998; Henning, 2006; and Alpers, 1991) point out that objects also become meaningful just by entering through the doors of the museum. They become identified as culturally important by virtue of being chosen by a museum. Again, the idea of enabling and constraining is raised. The importance of the object might be enabled, but seeing the object for its original purpose—or even in new ways by the visitor without the filter of the museum—is now constrained (Lewis, 2017: 95).

Technology

There are both simple and complicated technologies that contribute to the subject-selfie constitution. However, if artificial intelligence (AI) software is developed for smartphone cameras, then it may not be too long before complex technologies can also play a role in museum selfies. Until then, I can integrate AI through Google's Deep Dream Generator[7] to manipulate photos. Figure 6.3 is an example of this hybrid human-AI collaboration. While I supply the original photo (see Fig. 6.1), the Deep Dream Generator uses its own AI algorithm in order to manipulate the original. I still have some control in deciding which type of manipulation I want and how much I want it manipulated, but otherwise the AI accomplishes the actual process.

The smartphone is a very complicated device with many functions. For selfies, I see through the smartphone screen, meaning there is an embodied relation happening. And, while I could be using the phone's black and white filter (the final selfie is in black and white), I take the selfie in color, knowing I can alter it with software on my home computer at a later time. As I situate myself next to the bust that I want my selfie to be with, I look through the iPhone screen, which shows me how my selfie will turn out thanks to the front-facing camera. While this enables me to compose the selfie, it also constrains my depth perception and the wider area around me, cutting out a visual chunk of reality. This constraint has, unfortunately, contributed to the damage of several museum objects such as a statue of St. Michael in Lisbon (Lewis, 2017).

While I could take advantage of the digital image, which affords the possibility—unlike a print photograph—to immediately upload the selfie to social networks, allowing my friends to more temporally share in the actual moment with me, I choose to wait until later to do so. This is in part due to my difficulty focusing on the small screen of my phone, but it also allows me to take my time in making adjustments to the images using the software and larger screen on my laptop.

---

7 https://deepdreamgenerator.com

Fig. 6.3 *Museum Selfie and AI Hybrid*. Manipulation created using Deep Dream Generator. Image by author (2020), CC BY-NC 4.0.

In my experience taking a museum selfie, there are also many simple technologies at work. For instance, the bust sits upon a pedestal, which is lucky for me as it allows me to get close. In contrast, other museum objects have ropes keeping visitors from approaching too close to the museum objects. If we think of technology as a continuum, moving from simple to complicated to complex, my clothes might be considered as being between simple and complicated technology; they influence my movement, what I can carry in pockets, and if I am warm or cool in temperature. Museum lighting also influences taking the selfie and can be considered on the continuum between simple and complicated. Other simple aspects related to technological relations concern things like my glasses and the phone's camera lens being clean or needing to be cleaned.

Intrasubjective Mediation and the Relational Groups

Besides the direct relations just explained, I experience a lot of intrasubjective mediation (ISM) related to previous experiences. This is captured by the question, How do my past experiences mediate the selfie-subject constitution? To demonstrate the influence of intrasubjective mediation, I briefly review how my past experiences with each group of relations influence the subject-selfie constitution intrasubjectively.

Mind and ISM

Before going to the museum, I conducted research on museums, selfies, and museum selfies in particular. There were many different types of selfies, and exploring the range of some of what had come before gave me ideas of how I could potentially frame myself with the museum object. These possible framings allowed me to overlay them with the museum objects I was coming across. In addition, my experience as a semi-professional photographer influenced my ability to imagine and compose the selfies that I was taking.

Body and ISM

The primary temporal effect on my bodily relations was the sedimented action of taking selfies with my smartphone, which involved physically manipulating not only the settings of the camera phone, but also situating my body in relation to the camera, myself, and the museum object—holding the camera in such a way that I could then take the selfie when everything was aligned. This was awkward to do at first, but eventually the action became more embodied and the manipulation of the technology became more transparent.

Space and ISM

While I had been in many museums throughout my life, I had never been in the Art and History Museum. This made me unsure of the layout of the museum and somewhat hesitant as I explored. I did not know what there was to see or even how much there was to see. This lack of experience made me unsure and a bit unsettled in my mind as

I attempted to navigate beyond the main Ukiyo-e exhibit and enter the permanent collection area.

Sociocultural and ISM

Because I have had many experiences in European museums, I felt comfortable being there. And, because of my limited amount of experience taking selfies in public, I did not feel comfortable doing that. Part of this stemmed from my own upbringing. As a child, I was taught not to disturb others when in public and to not draw undue attention to my self. I have also run across U.S. citizens in Europe who, unfortunately, fell into a stereotype of being loud and seemingly oblivious to the culture around them. Not behaving in that way has always been a goal of mine, especially when in another culture.

Technology and ISM

Part of this relation was explained with the body-ISM section above. My use of taking photos with my smartphone, not just selfies, contributed to my ability to manipulate the technology in order to take the museum selfie. My past experience with social media also gave me ideas about how I might want to use filters or hashtags when I uploaded the selfie to social media.

This concludes the overview of the first step in using the instrument to identify and evaluate some of the relevant relations that exist when I take a selfie (see Fig. 6.1). However, the experience is more complex than simply a multiplicity of these *primary* relations. The term 'primary' is used here to indicate the direct relation between a subject and whatever they are relating with, no matter what relational grouping is involved. However, there are *secondary* interrelations that affect these primary relations. These are discussed next.

Interrelationality

The direct relations discussed above are both enhanced or constrained by other relations. There are no standalone relations. While all relations and interrelations happen in one moment of co-constitution, we can gently pull apart the phenomenon of this interrelating moment in order to identify some of the complex entanglement. Therefore, the next step consists of analyzing how relations from other groups affect the relations listed previously. The instrument is one way to engage with the framework in order to provide clarity without removing the complexity altogether. The goal of the instrument is to create a practical way to leverage the framework for a specific situation. The framework itself should be viewed in an open way, available for creative interpretation by whomever is using it.

While Table 6.1 demonstrates each specific relation's influence on the subject-selfie constitution, it is Table 6.2 that captures the interrelations that occur. This table shows the relations in Table 6.1 and then adds how I felt (at the time) each group or subgroup of relations influenced each specific relation. This table reflects the entanglement of the interrelations that contribute to the constitution of the subject-selfie. As with most quantifiable representations of reality, the numbers should only be considered a snapshot in time and are embedded with bias and interpretation. However, my intent is less to show the specific detail of exactly how each group interrelates and influences each other than to portray the broader effect of interrelationality in order to emphasize the fact that any situation is comprised of not just one relation, even though we experience an event in a gestalt manner.

The right-hand columns should be read in a downward direction, reflecting how the relations in that group or subgroup influence the direct relations listed on the left. For example, the far-right column 'Technology' is listed as affecting the first direct relation: 'See museum object and imagine possible selfie' with a moderate influence (value=2). By filling out this spreadsheet, the media user can be guided to reflexively identify many underlying relations that they may not have noticed and also analyze the interrelating influences from a variety of sources. The spreadsheet is a way to realize how media are situated within an entanglement of relations, all interrelating and influencing each other.

After assigning a value for each interrelating relation, I create an average for the group or subgroup for each section. I then take this average (or the largest subgroup average) and create Table 6.3. This table reflects the significant interrelating impact of one group on another group. This table should be read left to right. For instance, the first line shows that relations from the mind group have a significant impact of

3 = Heavy influence
2 = Moderate influence
1 = Light influence
0 = No discernable influence

	Relation's influence on subject-selfie constitution		Mind_Imagination	Mind_Identity	Mind_Awareness	Body	Time_Past	Time_Future	Space	Cultural_Normative	Cultural_Language	Cultural_Politics	Technology
Mind	See museum object and imagine possible selfie	3	3	1	1	2	2	3	3	2	0	0	2
Mind	Direction of my awareness: selfie, others, museum?	3	3	2	1	1	3	2	2	2	0	0	2
Mind	The specific self I am trying to construct	3	3	3	3	1	3	3	1	3	0	2	2
Mind	My desire to learn	3	3	3	3	1	3	2	0	3	0	1	1
Mind	My interest in following the curatorial information	1	1	2	3	0	2	2	2	3	1	1	1
Mind	Perceiving object thru its history, curator, or my own lens	3	2	3	3	0	2	2	3	3	1	2	2
Mind	Attention towards my senses: hearing, smelling, feeling	2	2	1	0	3	2	1	3	2	1	1	2
Mind	Intention for visiting: academic, amusement social?	3	2	3	3	1	3	2	1	3	1	2	1
Mind	My intention/desire for taking the selfie: object relation	3	2	3	3	2	3	3	0	3	1	2	2
Mind	My state of mind regards to time: hurried, relaxed	3	3	2	1	1	2	3	1	2	0	0	1
	Mind_Average	**2.7**	**2.4**	**2.3**	**2.1**	**1.2**	**2.5**	**2.3**	**1.6**	**2.6**	**0.5**	**1.1**	**1.6**
Body	Am I hungry? Or tired?	2	2	1	0	3	2	2	0	1	0	0	0
Body	How is my formerly broken heel doing?	2	2	1	0	3	2	2	0	2	0	0	0
Body	Am I too hot or cold?	2	2	1	0	3	2	2	3	2	0	0	3
Body	Can my eyes see the screen very well?	3	1	1	1	3	1	1	3	1	0	0	3
Body	Is my body chemistry in balance?	2	3	2	1	3	2	1	1	2	0	0	2
Body	How distracting is my headache?	2	2	1	1	2	1	0	1	1	0	0	2
Body	What is my sense of smell detecting?	1	3	2	3	3	1	1	1	2	0	0	1
Body	Is it loud or are there distracting sounds?	2	2	1	3	3	1	1	2	3	0	0	2
Body	Are there visual distractions?	2	2	1	2	3	1	1	3	2	0	0	2
Body	Does my bodily appearance attract attention?	1	3	1	3	3	2	1	3	3	0	0	2
	Body_Average	**1.9**	**2.2**	**1.2**	**1.4**	**2.9**	**1.5**	**1.2**	**1.7**	**1.9**	**0.0**	**0.0**	**1.7**
Temporality	Ideas from other museum selfies I've seen	3	3	1	1	2	3	2	0	2	1	1	3
Temporality	My own experience taking selfies w/ phone	3	2	2	2	2	3	1	0	3	0	1	3
Temporality	Past experience of museums	2	2	3	3	0	3	1	0	3	0	0	2
Temporality	History of the specific object	2	2	2	3	0	3	0	0	2	0	2	2
Temporality	Past experience as a photographer	3	2	3	3	2	3	1	0	2	0	1	3
Temporality	How much have I been using social media?	2	2	2	2	1	3	1	0	3	0	1	3
Temporality	What is my future goal for taking the selfie?	2	3	2	1	1	1	3	1	3	0	0	2
Temporality	Who will I share it with?	3	3	2	1	1	2	3	0	3	0	0	2
	Time_Average	**2.5**	**2.4**	**2.1**	**2.0**	**1.1**	**2.6**	**1.5**	**0.1**	**2.6**	**0.1**	**0.8**	**2.5**

Column group heading: Affecting Interrelations (Mind_Imagination through Technology)

3 = Heavy influence
2 = Moderate influence
1 = Light influence
0 = No discernable influence

	Relation's influence on subject-selfie constitution		Mind_Imagination	Mind_Identity	Mind_Awareness	Body	Time_Past	Time_Future	Space	Cultural_Normative	Cultural_Language	Cultural_Politics	Technology
			Affecting Interrelations										
Space	How close can I get?	3	1	1	1	2	0	2	3	3	0	3	3
	How many people are around me?	3	2	1	0	1	1	1	3	3	0	1	2
	What is the physical space around object?	3	3	1	1	2	0	0	3	2	0	1	3
	Is there a frame or case?	2	1	0	1	1	1	0	3	1	0	1	3
	Is there enough light to show both me and the object?	3	3	1	1	2	2	1	3	3	0	1	3
	How far away do I hold the camera phone?	2	2	0	1	2	1	2	2	2	0	1	3
	How is the lack of nature affecting me?	2	2	1	1	2	2	1	2	2	0	0	3
	What is the overall feeling of the space?	2	2	1	2	2	2	1	3	3	0	1	3
	Space_Average	**2.5**	**2.0**	**0.8**	**1.0**	**1.8**	**1.1**	**1.0**	**2.8**	**2.4**	**0.0**	**1.1**	**2.9**
Sociocultural	Who is judging me?	3	3	3	3	2	3	3	0	3	0	2	2
	Who am I disturbing?	3	3	3	3	1	3	2	2	3	0	1	2
	Is this my culture, am I a foreigner or tourist?	2	3	3	3	2	3	2	1	3	0	2	2
	Are others taking sefies as well?	3	2	2	2	0	1	1	2	3	0	1	2
	What would my family think of me?	2	3	3	3	1	3	3	0	3	0	2	2
	Class pressures: high class=museum, low class=selfie?	2	3	3	3	1	3	2	0	3	0	3	2
	Can I read the descriptions in my language?	1	2	2	2	1	3	1	1	3	3	1	2
	Pressure from norms or power not to take a selfie?	3	3	3	3	1	3	3	1	3	0	1	2
	Am I a privliged/entitled race, or an 'othered' minority?	2	2	3	3	1	3	2	0	3	0	3	2
	Is there a guard around?	3	3	2	1	2	2	3	2	3	0	3	2
	Sociocultural_Average	**2.4**	**2.7**	**2.7**	**2.6**	**1.2**	**2.7**	**2.2**	**0.9**	**3.0**	**0.3**	**1.9**	**2.0**
Technclogy	Are my clothes restricting or comfortable?	2	2	2	2	3	2	1	1	3	0	1	3
	Is my camera/phone charged?	2	2	1	0	1	3	3	0	2	0	0	3
	Do I know how to turn off flash?	2	2	1	0	0	2	2	0	3	0	2	3
	Do I set a filter/edit now or use FB/Instagram?	3	3	2	1	1	2	3	0	3	0	1	3
	Do I have cell reception?	1	1	1	1	0	0	0	2	0	0	0	3
	Is the phone sensitive enough for poor light?	3	2	1	0	1	2	2	0	1	0	0	3
	Upload to social media or edit first?	2	2	2	2	0	2	2	1	3	0	1	3
	Do I tag friends or limit sharing?	2	2	2	2	1	2	3	0	3	0	1	3
	Is the camera lens clean?	1	1	1	1	0	1	1	1	2	0	0	3
	Need for reading glasses to see the screen?	2	2	3	3	3	2	3	0	3	0	1	3
	Media-Tech_Average	**2.0**	**1.9**	**1.6**	**1.2**	**1.0**	**1.8**	**2.0**	**0.5**	**2.3**	**0.0**	**0.7**	**3.0**
	Total_Average	**2.3**	**2.3**	**1.8**	**1.7**	**1.5**	**2.1**	**1.7**	**1.3**	**2.5**	**0.2**	**0.9**	**2.3**

Table 6.2 *Interrelational Influences on Subject-selfie Constitution.* Table by author (2020).

2.2 upon the direct relations in the body group. The averages allow us to reflect on the asymmetry involved between the groups, meaning one group might affect another group significantly but is not significantly affected in return. For example, reversing the mind to body example just used, the body only has a slight influence of 1.1 upon the direct relations involving the mind. Reviewing the table also is a chance to question the results. For instance, the table reflects that technology greatly influences spatial relations (2.9). At the same time, spatial relations only slightly influence technological relations (.5). Is this true? Can I analyze this result to bring up counter relations that disprove this outcome?

	Mind	*Body*	*Time*	*Space*	*Sociocultural*	*Tech*
Mind	2.4	2.2	2.4	2	2.7	1.9
Body	1.1	2.9	1.1	1.8	1.2	1
Time	2.5	1.5	2.6	1.1	2.7	2
Space	1.6	1.7	.1	2.8	.9	.5
Sociocultural	2.6	1.9	2.6	2.4	3	2.3
Technological	1.6	1.7	2.5	2.9	2	3

Table 6.3 *Interrelational Average Influences* (3=strong, 2=medium, 1=weak). Table by author (2020).

The summary of averages in Table 6.3 is not to be used to indicate general truisms between groups, but rather it reflects the media user's specific experience of interrelations concerning a specific selfie at a specific time. Since the table is filled out on the micro level of specific relations, the averages enable me to check the results on a macro level. This can help facilitate a deeper investigation and help me potentially think of relations that I did not at first consider. I present this table in order to demonstrate various ways researchers can use the framework and instrument in order to engage with interrelational influences for specific research investigations.

Complexity

Interrelationality rests upon a foundation of complexity (cf. Chapter 4). It is not actually possible to come up with an objective number that represents the influence of any one relation. While this subjective analysis might rankle a reader looking for objective truth, that is not the goal of this framework or instrument. The goal is to better understand the human subject. An important aspect of complexity relating to the evaluation of this instrument is that, as complex systems, we are emergent, non-linear, and open systems.

Complexity can be understood historically, but it is unable to predict the impact of future relations. When we rate our relations, we are doing so after that fact, meaning that we are rating our perception of the actual effect that the relation caused. For example, before I went to the museum it did not even occur to me that the proximity of other people would affect me. However, this relation was the most significant of all influences. An interesting experiment would be to complete a version of the instrument before actually participating in an event, and then complete another one after the event in order to compare expectations and the actual experience. I explore various ways of generalizing the framework and instrument in the next section.

The culminating spreadsheet (Table 6.2) was, in a way, an endpoint to my beginning. I began investigating technological relations by experiencing taking museum selfies and comparing that experience to the postphenomenological approach that I was studying. However, what I experienced was not completely captured by postphenomenology, and so I began to expand my search in an attempt to more fully connect theory and practice. This led to asking about the 'I' that was experiencing and gathering concepts from various fields of study in order to bring them altogether. Looking back shows a clear path, but when I was going forward through this experience it was an open process without the intention of creating a framework or tool that could help with media literacy. This reflected the complex process that was emergent and not predictable.

Even if they happen to be virtual interactions, our interactions with media and media technologies happen in 'real life'. In order to understand the complexity that is involved, it is helpful to investigate some of the specific interrelations involved in order to then have a better understanding of how the media relations are situated and interconnected within our own lifeworld. While domestication theory (cf. Chapter 2) makes the important step to include the context of the media use, the intrasubjective mediating framework attempts to situate our media use even further. The next section continues implementing the theory by investigating how the theory and instrument discussed in this section might be pragmatically used for enhancing media literacy.

Generalizing the Framework and Instrument for Media Literacy

Now that the intrasubjective mediating framework and instrument have been developed through the analysis of a museum selfie, I begin exploring how they could be generalized for media education. I do this by imagining the instrument being used in a university-level media studies or media literacy course. I am not presenting a fully formed curriculum, but simply a possible way to practically implement this posthuman approach. Though it can be used in other ways, for example with younger students, I believe starting with the university level is a good initial choice as younger students would likely need the instrument to be re-worked and simplified.

I had the good fortune to be able to lead a small group of Master's level students through a course designed around this posthuman approach. This allowed me to perform a small initial usability study for the framework and instrument, which provided valuable feedback and a chance to generalize the instrument and create an exercise just before the publication of this book. The instructions for the exercise are below. Updated instructions, as well as a generalized and simplified spreadsheet, are available on the listing for this book on Open Book Publishers' website.[8]

It is through the process of doing the exercise that students will more fully grasp the academic ideas discussed so far. Through my work at Prescott College in the U. S., I have found that experiential education is one of the strongest pedagogical tools that a teacher can employ. The exercise below can allow students to experience the concepts for themselves, allowing the learning to become more deeply embodied.

My hope is that many teachers will find a seed of inspiration in this approach to media literacy and will continue developing unique ways

8 Look under the 'Additional Resources' tab at https://www.openbookpublishers.com/product/1405

to leverage the framework as a pedagogical instrument. Douglas Kellner and Jeff Share (2005) note, 'Computer and multimedia technologies demand novel skills and competencies and if education is to be relevant to the problems and challenges of contemporary life, engaged teachers must expand the concept of literacy and develop new curricula and pedagogies' (369–70).

This autoethnographic approach can specifically help people reflect on the influences involved when they engage with media in order to become more aware of how media is situated within a complexity of interrelations. The media affect and are affected by these interrelations. As Kellner and Share (2005) also point out, 'Individuals are often not aware that they are being educated and constructed by media culture, as its pedagogy is frequently invisible and unconscious' (372). The posthuman approach acts as a cartography to help reveal these influences.

Posthuman Approach Exercise: Learning by Doing

How can we critically evaluate the effects of technologies in order to decide if and how to engage with them?

The goal of this exercise is to help students reflect on the complexity of influences involved when they engage with technologies in order to become more aware of how they are situated within a complexity of interrelations. All technologies affect and are affected by these interrelations. This exercise is used to reveal (foreground) the many relations that are simultaneously happening when we engage with technologies. This posthuman approach acts as a cartography to help reveal these hidden influences, bringing us to the point of being able to critically decide how we want to engage with them.

The term 'engagement' refers to the student's *phenomenological* experience with a specific innovative technology. The student here puts aside their judgement and strives to become aware of the various relations that are occurring at the time of their experience with the technology. The first step of deciding which technology to engage with (and exactly how) is critical, as some types of technologies may work well and others may not. Modification and improvements, in discussion with the instructor, are welcomed.

A conceptual review:

- The relations in our lifeworld transform us through a continual interrelating process, enabling and constraining our selves and each other.
- The relations can be gathered into loose groupings, though not all relations can be known or are knowable.
- These relations interrelate—enhancing and constraining each other—in complex (potentially non predictive) ways.

Through awareness of these points, we have the ability to increase our agency.

Step One: Identify

Identify a technology that you want to engage with. Be specific in what you will experience. This will be an autoethnographic investigation, as you will be analyzing yourself engaging with a specific technology in a specific way during a specific time. For instance, instead of investigating 'how Instagram affects teenage youths', narrow it down to investigating 'Recording and sharing my exercise workout through fitness selfies on Instagram'. It would also be possible to compare two similar experiences, one using a recent technology and another using a technology it replaced. For example, compare the exploration of a new city through a GPS based smartphone app to experiencing a new city with a paper map.

The instructor should approve the idea before continuing. The instructor may also want the student to do some background research about the technology. This can help the student become more familiar and understand what preceding technologies transformed into the one they are studying. For instance, the smartphone evolved from the phone, the camera, the GPS navigation system, and the computer (to name a few). The student will describe the specific engagement chosen on the spreadsheet (cf. Table 6.4), recording: Date, time, and duration of engagement. Also, include the location and conditions (busy, rainy, etc.)

Step Two: Framework

Review the framework (Fig. 5.1), understanding the six interconnected groups and the concept of intrasubjective mediation. To review, intrasubjective mediation is the idea that every relation transforms us in some manner, and that these transformations continue to affect the way we perceive and engage with the world (these transformations can be thought of as embodied relations). If there is a need or compelling reason, identify specific subgroups, or even a specific group for extra attention. Most students will likely use the framework as is. The framework is the foundation for the instrument.

Step Three: Pre-assessment

This is a general inquiry as to what the student believes will be the most influencing relations when they engage with the technology. The student should identify at least two or three possible relations (or questions to ask themselves) in each group in order to begin thinking about the different relations and specific relations. This allows the student to begin exploring the identification of relations.

Step Four: Engage

Intentionally engage with the event. Focus on being aware of the various relations involved. Approach the event as a phenomenological experience, attempting to bracket your own biases and judgement to become aware of all of the various relations that are involved. In other words, you will be engaging with the technology and, at the same time, opening your awareness to the often-hidden background relations. Think about the groups and subgroups to help guide your awareness to these background relations.

Depending upon the event, it could be helpful to have a field journal to take notes and write down the specific relations. This will depend upon the event and how it is orchestrated. Writing down the relations helps acknowledge them without needing try and remember them. Patiently stay with the event, giving it time for new relations to surface. It is likely helpful to focus on one grouping of relations at a time and keep asking yourself what types of relations are happening that relate to that particular group.

Influence: 3-heavy, 2-medium, 1-light, 0-none

1. Describe your engagement with technology here: When, How long, Where, What, etc...			6. Affecting Interrelations					
5. Influencing relations on subject-tech constitution			Mind	Body	Time	Space	Sociocultural	Technology
Mind								
Mind_Average		###	###	###	###	###	###	###
Body								
Body_Average		###	###	###	###	###	###	###

Table 6.4 *Example of Posthuman Spreadsheet.* Table by author (2021), CC BY 4.0.

Step Five: Identifying and Evaluating Direct Relations

Now it is time to fill in the relations on the spreadsheet. Brainstorm all the relations that you can think of, taking advantage of the groups and subgroups to focus your inquiry. Write them down in column B. Remember that you can use, or modify, any of the pre-assessment relations you had written down in Step Three. You can write these as questions (how did the rain affect me?) or statements (I was affected by the rain). Ask yourself, what are all the possible relations within this group/subgroup that had an influence on the constitution of my self or the event being analyzed? These can be thought of as 'direct' relations. Analyze how they had influence upon the co-constitution of you and the technological event you engaged with. Use a 3 for highly influencing; 2 for moderately influencing; 1 for slightly influencing; and 0 for no discernable influence. It is not necessary to overthink these evaluations (unless you have a compelling reason to do so).

A note about the 'PH Instrument' spreadsheet: The spreadsheet (see Table 6.4) has formulas built into it which automatically average the ratings you will enter in Steps Five and Six. It also contains an 'Analysis' worksheet that incorporates the averages of the interrelations for Step Seven. Therefore, be careful to not delete these cells. They will show '###' until you enter numbers into the cells above them. If you have lost one of the cells that averages, you can copy an adjacent cell that has the formula and try pasting. Or, you can download a new spreadsheet and start over. If you would like to modify the spreadsheet in some way (for instance, adding subgroups), check with the instructor.

Come up with 8–10 relations for each main group. Consider if there are any subgroups that you want to focus on specifically. If you are not finding enough relations, you might look at a general relation you listed and see if you can break it into more specific parts. For example, instead of listing that 'the physical museum affected my experience', I could break that into how the museum's lighting affected me, how the rope barriers between me and the art affected me, how the glass cases housing museum artefacts affected me, etc. Some groups will be easier than others to come up with 8–10 relations, but stick with it. You should also look for slightly influencing relations, not just ones that had a significant influence.

Some possible questions for each group that you can ask yourself in order to uncover more relations are:

Mind:

- What are your intentions?
- How is your mind directing your awareness/perception?
- What is the state of your mind (relaxed, stressed, etc.)?
- Which senses are you focusing on?
- How is your imagination engaged?

Body:

- What is the current state of your body (tired, hungry, temperature, any pains, etc.)?
- How are your bodily abilities enabling/constraining you?
- What bodily skills are you engaged with?
- How are your bodily sense organs being affected: sounds, smells, tastes, feelings, vision?

Space:

- What is immediately surrounding you, and how is it affecting you?
- What attributes of the physical space are enabling and constraining?
- How is the space around you specifically affecting your engagement with the media?
- What is the composite of the space between 'natural' and 'human made'?
- If you are outside, what is the weather and how is it affecting you?

Time:

- What is the history of the media you are engaged with?
- Have your own experiences with the specific media changed how you interact with it? If so, how?

- What future plans are involved, and how do they affect your use?
- What other past experiences have contributed to the current engagement?

Sociocultural:

- What normative influences are you experiencing?
- Are you feeling judged or judging yourself?
- How is language playing a role?
- Are there any gender, class, power, or racial influences?
- Are you feeling empowered or marginalized?

Technological:

- What are the basic technologies that are affecting you (such as glasses, clothes, etc.)?
- What different technological relations are you experiencing (embodied, hermeneutic, alterity, or background)?
- How are the various technological mediums influencing you?
- What are the technological infrastructures in place for you to experience the media (wireless technology, servers, corporations, electricity/batteries...)?

<u>Draft Due</u>: Before proceeding to Step Six, the instructor should review the student's work up until this point. This is a chance to make sure the student understands how to identify and describe the various relations that are occurring. Are the relations in the proper groups? Are the relations clearly articulated? Are there also relations listed with low influence? Do all the relations fit under the specific engagement or are there some unrelated relations mentioned? The student should revise their work before going onto the next step.

Step Six: Evaluating Interrelations

The next step is to evaluate the interrelations that affected the direct relations noted above. The right-most columns (E through J) on the spreadsheet provide you the space to evaluate how the other relations influenced each direct relation listed in Step Five. Keep the specific relation listed in column B in your mind and then ask if it was affected in any way by relations within the interrelational group you are evaluating. Use the most influential relation you can think of for each group and rate it from 3 to 0. The general purpose here is to identify and demonstrate the interconnections that occur, reflecting the complexity of interrelationality.

For instance, if my direct relation was 'See museum object and imagine a possible selfie' then I would ask myself how much the Mind relations affected this relation. Clearly, they had a lot of influence, so I put a 3 under the Mind group. How about Body relations? At the current time my body was beginning to get tired, so I would put down a 2. However, if there was something more significantly wrong with me, either my eyesight was failing, or I had another condition going on, this could have been a 3. How about Time relations? Well, my experiences seeing other museum selfies did affect me a bit, but the future potential relation really affected my engagement, so I would list a 3 under Time. Space was also a 3 since I was being mediated by the museum setup in how close I could get and how well lit the object was. Sociocultural relations were affecting me either as a 2 or 3 depending upon how many people were around me. And the technology itself was also affecting me as a 2 or 3 as I had to manipulate my smartphone in order to take the selfie.

What we are trying to do is to quantify complex relations. While this is ultimately impossible in any objective sense, we are simply trying to give approximate numbers to an interpretation of an interrelation at a particular point in time, and our evaluation will be influenced by many things. Do not worry about getting things exactly right. Instead, it is okay to simply give a subjective number that is 'good enough' to represent the particular scenario you have in your mind at that moment. There will be many ways that each group will interrelate with the specific relation you are looking at. Simply choose the most influential one that you can think of.

Step Seven: Analyze

After finishing step 6, take a step back from the details you have recorded and reflect if they make sense in a broader perspective. At the bottom of each group's column are the averages, showing summative data. Looking at the tabs on the bottom of the worksheet (Fig. 6.4), you will notice that you have been working in the 'PH Instrument' tab. There is also an 'Analysis' tab. Click on this tab and you will be able to see in Table 1 (see Fig. 6.5) the averages for each group's direct relations (total averages for each group from column C) as well as Table 2 that shows the interrelational averages (see Fig. 6.5).

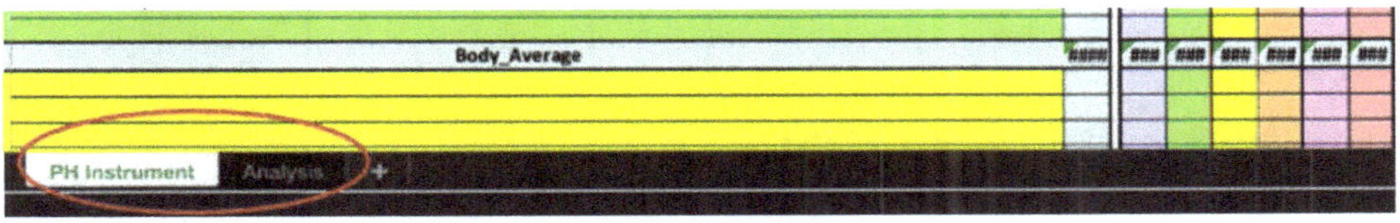

Fig. 6.4 *Worksheet tabs for switching between PH Instrument and Analysis*. Image by author (2021), CC BY 4.0

The first step is to analyze the average numbers for each group's direct influence on your engagement with the technology in Table 1. The total averages allow for a quick glance and a chance to analyze the numbers to see if they make sense to you. This is an opportunity for questioning and critique. Look especially at the highest and lowest averages. Does this seem to reflect your overall sense of your engagement with the technology? These results reflect how we are perceiving the situation at the moment we record the numbers. Can we change our perception? How are our own biases influencing these results? If there are things that do not seem right, can you think of either additional relations or ways of modifying the direct relations you evaluated in order for the average to better represent your experience?

Now, look at Table 2. This table is read from left to right. This reflects how influential the groups on the left were in co-influencing the direct relational groups on the right. This directionality can be interesting. To help explore the table, find the group that is most different from its reverse. For example, the Sociocultural group on the left might show a 2.5 influence over the Time group on the right, but the Time group on the left might only have a 1.0 influence over the Sociocultural group on the right. Do the results make sense? Are you surprised by any of the results?

We can also perform a general evaluation of the entire process. Are there other influences not captured by this worksheet, and if so, do they

Table 1. Average of each group's direct influence on the subject-technology engagement

Mind	2,1
Body	2,2
Time	2,0
Space	2,1
Sociocultural	2,4
Technology	2,6

Table 2. Average totals of each group's interrelational influence. Direction of interrelational influence →

→	Mind	Body	Time	Space	Sociocultural	Technology	Overall Total
Mind	2,6	1,6	2,1	2,0	2,8	2,3	2,2
Body	1,3	2,2	1,1	1,8	0,5	0,8	1,3
Time	1,7	1,6	2,8	1,5	1,3	0,3	1,6
Space	1,4	2,0	1,1	3,0	0,6	2,3	1,7
Sociocultural	2,2	1,3	2,3	1,6	0,6	2,3	2,0
Technology	2,4	1,4	1,5	1,8	3,0	1,5	1,9

Fig. 6.5 *Tables 1 and 2 for analysis.* Image by author (2021), CC BY 4.0.

fit somewhere or is another group or subgroup needed? For the lowest-rated groups, might there be relations that have not been considered within the group? Or, might it be necessary to enter a disclaimer stating that a particular group or subgroup was not focused on, acknowledging that there could be significant relations that had influence but lay outside the scope of the specific analysis? And finally, acknowledge the fact that we cannot know all of the relations that affect us. Not only are there some that are unknown, but there are those that are simply unknowable. Being aware that there are unknowable relations helps us keep a more realistic perspective on our own becomingness.

Step Eight: Critical Assessment

The first seven steps are all about increasing our own awareness of a relation we have with a specific technology. We did this by attempting to set aside our judgement in order to simply become aware of how we were engaging with technology. Now is the time to bring the judgement back and critically (and affirmatively) evaluate your relation with the media technology you engaged with. Your agency and empowerment reside in taking the 'uncovered' relational affects and deciding what you want to do about this new awareness. What kind of lifeworld do you want to co-create? Describe both positive and negative aspects of engaging with this specific technology. Do this for both your own perspective (how it is for you), and then more broadly for society as a whole. What are some of the broader ramifications of this technology? What would you recommend people keep in mind when engaging with it? What are ways to mitigate its negative effects and hang onto its positive effects?

Concluding Thoughts

The museum selfie is an entanglement of culture (power, normativity, and language), history, space, time (both past and future), the mind (identity, imagination, memory), and technology. While I created a quantitative instrument to better understand this entanglement, I also thought about how I could represent the underlying complexity in a gestalt manner, visually displaying the general complexity of interrelations that have an effect upon taking the museum selfie. To do so, I used a program called Circos (http://circos.ca/) to create a background for the museum selfie. I took the data in Table 6.2 and, after many hours of experimenting, created the visual gestalt of Figure 6.6. While this visually displays the complexity of interrelationality behind the museum selfie, it of course loses much of the specific details.

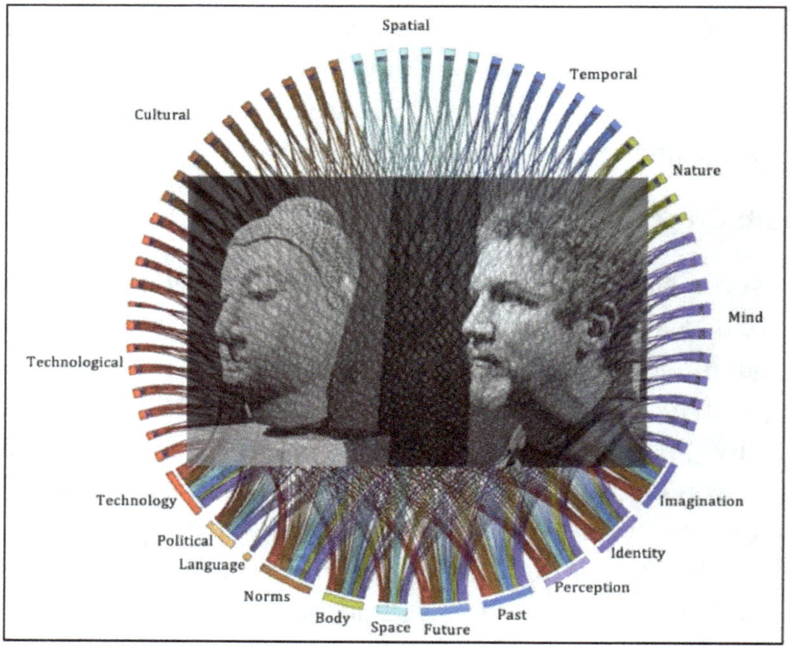

Fig. 6.6 *The Museum Selfie as a Complex Assemblage of Interrelations*. Image created using Circos. Image by author (2019), CC BY-NC 4.0.

Something similar could be added to the exercise above. For students, it would be an interesting task to creatively represent their own experience, something beyond the spreadsheet. This would allow them to engage with their experience in a more creative manner, giving them another chance to think about the complexity of relations that are involved when they engage with technology.

The benefit of the instrument developed in this chapter is how it can help us become aware by foregrounding the many relations that are occurring at any given moment. For media literacy, this allows us to better situate any media or media event that we are interested in investigating, interconnecting the event with the broad spectrum of constituting relations. The framework and instrument together can act as a facilitating cartography, helping to direct our inquiry both broadly and specifically in a posthuman approach.

7

Summary and Conclusions

The primary aim of this study was to create a way to situate and contextualize media literacy in order to better understand how we are affected by the ubiquitous media technologies that comprise our daily existence. This study first investigated the current state of media literacy and then took an interdisciplinary approach in order to leverage useful concepts from the fields of postphenomenology, media ecology, and philosophical posthumanism. The intent was to create a posthuman approach consisting of a framework and instrument that could be used by media literacy to facilitate our understanding of how the human subject is influenced by media technologies, thereby increasing our agency and helping us decide which media technologies we want in our lives.

This results in a facilitating cartography for both students and researchers to retain a broad perspective while investigating the unique relations that contribute to a subject's continual constitution as they move through their life. In this conclusion, I summarize my findings concerning how to expand media literacy. I then reflect on strengths and weaknesses of the study. I conclude with further recommendations for how the posthuman approach could be used outside of media literacy.

Summary of Main Findings

My main findings involve understanding how media literacy should be expanded to include a focus on the medium, as well as on the broader context within which media relations are situated. I found that it was first necessary to clarify a contemporary understanding of what a human subject is and how it is continually being constituted through its relations. Following this, I developed the concept of an intrasubjective mediating framework and instrument that can then help us explore our use of specific media through identifying the interrelated constituting relations that are concurrently involved.

Expanding Media Literacy

The first main finding reveals that while media literacy is helpful in many of its various approaches, it in general has a couple limitations that could be improved in order to make it more effective in helping people understand the effects of our daily use of ICTs. The first limitation is that most media literacy approaches do not focus on the biases of the medium itself. Each communication medium—be it newspaper, television, or smartphone—has its own biases, enabling some things while constraining others. Making sure that the medium is included in media literacy investigations helps keep the focus from solely being on issues of content and representation (which are still important).

In addition, media literacy can benefit by including the broader environment within which the media use takes place. This is supported by the non-media-centric approach to media literacy advocated by Shaun Moores (2016) and David Morley (2007). This contextualizing move de-centers the focus on media and attends to the broader lifeworld where media happens. This is a critical component upon which I build, creating a practical approach that helps situate and identify the various relations that affect and are affected by our relations with specific media technologies.

The Human Becoming

In order to understand the effects of media literacy on the human subject, we need to have a contemporary understanding of the human subject, one that counters a traditionally humanist understanding of an idealized autonomous and standalone individual—a concept with roots in the eighteenth-century Enlightenment. Instead, we are relational, and it is through our relations that we are constituted. Rather than viewing our selves as human *beings,* it is more appropriate to call our selves human *becomings.* We are in a state of constant becoming in a complex and sympoietic manner, evolving and transforming through the myriad of relations that are also constantly changing in our lives.

The concept of complexity is key to understanding the human becoming as it shifts the gestalt from an individual subject to a complex posthuman subject. We are always and already in relations, not only with other humans but also with technologies and the world. These relations are complex, situated, dynamic, and emergent. How these relations influence a subject continually changes, and the ability to bring one's awareness to a particular relation can affect the amount of influence the relation has.

Intrasubjective Mediation: Framework and Instrument

The key to creating a new framework in order to situate media literacy and the human becoming is to build upon postphenomenology's formula of technological mediation: I-technology-world. This helps us to (pragmatically) understand how we, as human subjects, are constituted through our relations. However, focusing only on technological relations limits our ability to understand and situate the broader relations that affect and are affected by media technologies. Therefore, in order to gain a more comprehensive understanding, we can include the other relations that are constituting our selves as well as influencing (enabling and constraining) the effects of the technological relations. This is where the intrasubjective mediating framework comes into play.

Intrasubjective mediation describes the process of how the transformations that occur to the human subject through technological, sociocultural, mind, body, time, and space relations mediate—and continue to mediate through time—how the subject perceives and engages with the world. Intrasubjective mediation enables the ability to understand how all of our relations continue to mediate our experiences with our lifeworld, creating a way to investigate both the current and continuing impact from relations. In the case of ICTs, this helps us to become more media literate by understanding their broader and ongoing effects.

The intrasubjective mediating framework and instrument is designed to enable a media user to better understand how media technologies are situated within a complexity of interrelations, all of which affect the user on an intrasubjective level. This framework and instrument provide a facilitating cartography for the human subject to become more aware through an autoethnographic process, guiding the investigator to analyze six groupings of relations. Additionally, the investigator then identifies and rates the effects of interrelations that influence the direct relations, leading to a clearer understanding of the complexity of interrelating factors that occur during any engagement with media. Through this broader understanding, the investigator enhances their own agency, empowering them to make better-informed choices concerning which media they invite into their lives.

Strengths and Weaknesses of the Study

Roger Silverstone (2006) points out, 'All concepts are metaphors. They stand in place of the world. And in so doing they mask as well as reveal it' (229). This holds true for the framework and instrument described in this book. On the one hand, the approach can help facilitate the investigation into identifying the interrelating effects of media technologies within the broader frame of all constituting relations. The approach has been designed with the media user in mind—either as a consumer, user, or producer of media. The goal of the approach is to enable a broader perspective on how we are—in part—constituted by the media technologies in our lives. However, it is impossible to identify all of the mediating relations that influence us. While the framework and instrument can help broaden our perspective, they can only facilitate our own inquiry into revealing a portion of the complexity of interrelations that affect us. And, attempting to create a comprehensive approach can give a person using it the false sense that they are actually being completely comprehensive. I first comment on the significance of the findings and then discuss some of their limitations.

Significance and Implications of Findings

These findings are significant because they provide media literacy a practical way for situating the effects of specific media use in a broader context, allowing for a more comprehensive understanding of the complexity and interrelationally of our media relations. The findings balance broad interdisciplinary theories concerning humans and technology and then connect them to a practical framework and instrument that can be used for media education. Not only are these findings based on solid, contemporary philosophical thought; they are also—most importantly—used to build a practical instrument for media literacy. I say importantly because while academic scholarship is often helpful for the academic world, in order to improve the everyday lives of people using media technologies, it is critical to do more than create academic theories. Through developing the theory into a usable instrument, there is an increased likelihood that there can be some positive effect on individuals and society. The framework and instrument are beneficial for researchers and educators of media literacy as well as users who engage with media.

Limitations of the Study

The limitations of this study stem, in part, from the intrasubjective framework and instrument not yet being fully tested. While I have used the intrasubjective framework and instrument to analyze a museum selfie, as well as using it with a small group of students, further application and field research is necessary in order to ascertain possible limitations and make further revisions.

How the instrument will work in other settings and contexts is still left to be seen. In addition, while I have validated many aspects through interaction with my peers (through discussions, papers, and conference presentations), I have not yet reached out to very many media literacy teachers and researchers who work in the field. I believe that further usability testing is necessary in order to generate feedback by students and instructors as they use the instrument to conduct their own investigations into specific media relations.

Critical Considerations

When should criticism enter into the dialogue? Throughout this book I have kept from focusing too much on how to critically evaluate our media relations. Before being able to pass judgement on a technology and its effects on our lives, I believe we should have a credible understanding of the complexity of the situated technology. This is what the posthuman approach supplies, allowing us to be in a better position for us to judge whether we should or should not invite specific technologies into our lives, and how we should engage with the technologies that are already in our lives. This critical assessment is absolutely necessary. It is also easier to accomplish on the personal/micro level rather than on a societal/macro level. However, it is the second part of the process, and the primary focus of this book is in exploring the first part.

Recommendations

In Chapter 6, I demonstrated how the framework could be employed to investigate and reveal the interrelations that I experienced taking a museum selfie. Additionally, I created a generic exercise that can be used for media literacy, which is now ready for media literacy instructors to experiment with. Up until now, I have been working mostly alone on the creation and implementation of the framework. This limits the likelihood of identifying what still needs improvement.

As indicated in the above section, the instrument will benefit through continued usability testing. I imagine students using it to conduct their own investigations into specific media relations. This will help revise the framework and instrument. As Paul Cilliers (2005: 259) states,

> There is no stepping outside of complexity (we are finite beings), thus there is no framework for frameworks. We choose our frameworks. This choice need not be arbitrary in any way, but it does mean that the status of the framework (and the framework itself) will have to be continually revised. Our knowledge of complex systems is always provisional.

I believe that continuing to use the framework and instrument with university undergraduates and graduate students who are studying media education and media literacy will be very beneficial. Graduate students in information literacy and the library sciences could also benefit by experimenting with the instrument, both in order to understand their own media relations but also as a way to educate others about media literacy. Through continued studies with older students, potential issues can further be remedied before having educators modify the instrument in a manner that is tailored for younger students.

Another recommendation for the field of media literacy is a policy type of recommendation. In Chapter 2, I discussed several organizations focused on media literacy (such as the Center for Media Literacy, the National Association for Media Literacy Education, and the Association for Media Literacy in Canada). These are very helpful resources for media educators, and they all have their own unique approach to, and definition of, media literacy. My recommendation is for these organizations to incorporate more of a focus on the importance of understanding: 1) the biases of particular mediums; and 2) how the specific context and interrelations influence, and are influenced by, our relations with media. These recommendations allow media literacy organizations to retain the strength of focusing on media relations while also including the broader context, allowing for a more inclusive and situated understanding.

Extrapolating to Other Fields

Looking to the future, I wish to share my enthusiasm for the potential of using this posthuman approach for the broader fields of humanities and social sciences. The framework and instrument is a useful way to understand our selves as subjects who are continually being constituted through a complexity of interrelations. I believe that research in the various fields within the social sciences can benefit from leveraging the posthuman approach in order to situate and bring perspective to the specific research being conducted. I believe that it can even be used with a non-technological engagement. For example, using it to better understand one's experience marching in a political protest.

This approach provides perspective, which in turn helps us understand the interconnections and broader context of whatever research is being conducted. For instance, social science research focusing on the issue of race could use the framework in order to help situate the specific race relations, demonstrating how they affect and are affected by many of the other relations, all of which are interrelated in a complex existence. This keeps researchers from being too narrow in their approach, and can help demonstrate how race importantly interrelates and affects other relations more broadly.

This posthuman approach is an effective first step toward a comprehensive situating framework. One of its strengths is in its interdisciplinary nature, having been created by bringing concepts together from different fields that have not necessarily interacted much previously. This cross-fertilization can now have benefits by introducing the approach back into some of the original fields of study. While the approach attempts to be inclusive and holistic, it is meant to be static. Both students and researchers in various disciplines can use it to investigate more deeply into any of the already defined groups and subgroups—or even create new groups and subgroups. To begin describing what this might look like, I will briefly explore how philosophical posthumanism, postphenomenology, and transhumanism might find the framework and instrument useful.

Philosophical Posthumanism

Posthumanism has an excellent, broad perspective, creating a post-anthropocentric, post-humanist, and post-binary outlook in order to understand the complex and emergent human subject. However, while posthumanism excels at keeping a broad perspective of what constitutes a posthuman subject, it is less clear exactly how to implement the posthuman concepts into an everyday living of one's lifeworld. Most helpful to posthumanism are the contributions in the field that implement the broader theoretical concepts into practical applications (for examples, see Adams & Thompson, 2016; Bayley, 2018). I believe that the intrasubjective mediating framework and instrument presented has the potential to be used in such a manner as practical tool for implementing posthumanist concepts relating to complexity as well as a non-humanist and a non-binary focus. The design of the framework leverages the broad concepts into a facilitating cartography that can be specifically applied to a broad range of research.

Postphenomenology

Postphenomenology's concept of technological mediation and the co-constitutionality of the I-technology-world formula is one of the main foundations upon which the framework and instrument are built. The framework can be useful in broadening postphenomenological research to include the other constituting groupings of relations. This inclusion helps keep postphenomenological research from being limited by its predominant focus on technology and allows the broader context of relations to also be addressed. Since the framework already uses many concepts from postphenomenology, it should be relatively easy to leverage it into the research within the field. This can also help the field address some of the criticisms that have been made against it in the past, specifically with regard to not incorporating cultural relations along with the technological relations (Scharff, 2006).

Transhumanism

While transhumanism is a forward-looking discipline, it is hampered by its foundation in rational humanist and Enlightenment concepts, dating back to the seventeenth and eighteenth centuries (Hughes, 2010a; More, 2013). As a discipline, it generally views the world and the human condition as complicated but solvable, allowing for an engineering approach to resolve many of humanity's issues. While its goals center on improving the human condition through contemporary and future technologies, transhumanism would benefit by taking a critical look into the philosophy it is built upon.

I argue that by leaving rational humanism (and the debate with bioconservatives) behind and incorporating intrasubjective mediation—with its foundation based on a complex, post-humanist subject—transhumanism has a better chance at positively improving not only the human species, but all living organisms on the planet. Therefore, I suggest that transhumanism evolve three of its perspectives: 1) the idea of a standalone individual to an interrelated and continually emergent subject; 2) the perception of human enhancement as complicated to understanding it as complex; and 3) a neutral view of technology to an understanding that technology is transformative and non-neutral. By changing transhumanist's theoretical foundation based in humanism to a combination of posthumanism, postphenomenology, and complexity theory, transhumanism can become more contemporary and bring a more balanced and grounded expectation for the future of humans, technologies, and the world.

Non-Western Cultures

The scope of this research has remained embedded in the contemporary Western culture. However, as I conclude, it can be useful to think how this proposed posthuman approach might be used in non-Western cultures or to make comparisons between cultures. The framework is setup in such a way as to be useful in researching any culture, as well as being helpful in better understanding differences between cultures. For instance, some cultures might have a more developed sense of social interconnectedness, such as the idea of Ubuntu, which is roughly translated as I am because you are (Lief & Thompson, 2015). While much of this book has been focused on overcoming a strong sense of individuality that permeates much of the contemporary Western world, a culture based on the concept of Ubuntu can give rise to a vastly different lifeworld.

But rather than idealize or in some way *other* such a culture, the framework provides a way to look at the embedded and situated interrelations that exist within these cultures. We can use the framework to better understand what is enabled and what is constrained across all the various groupings of relations. The framework provides a cartography to bring the various relations and interrelations to the foreground of our awareness and to see on balance how all the groupings of relations co-exist.

Final Thoughts

While marketing departments spend a lot of money trying to convince us otherwise, there is no ideal technology that can do everything. Each enables some abilities while constraining others. Most ICTs, as technological objects, are closed systems. However, in their relations with humans they become a part of a complex living system. These complex systems and environments are emergent and dynamic, usually fairly stable in any one moment but dynamic over time.

The approach presented here allows a systematic analysis of the many influences happening in the moment one is engaged with a specific media technology. The approach also helps a media user to more clearly understand that they are immersed in, and part of, an interrelated environment. Changing any one relation can have wide ranging effects on the other relations.

One might ask the question, so what? My response is to point out that an increase in understanding—an increase in self-literacy—allows us to be more aware and better informed when we choose what ICT or technological medium we decide to engage with, thus helping us to regain agency with regard to all the relations within our lifeworld. To emulate John Culkin (1967), we shape our media environments and in turn our media environments shape us. Using this posthuman approach can help us more clearly understand the interplay of media relations in our lives, allowing us the chance to shape them to our best advantage.

References

Abidin, C. 2016. '"Aren't These Just Young, Rich Women Doing Vain Things Online?" Influencer Selfies as Subversive Frivolity', *Social Media + Society*, 2(2), https://doi.org/10.1177/2056305116641342

Achterhuis, H. J. 2001. *American Philosophy of Technology: The Empirical Turn* (Minneapolis: Indiana University Press).

Adam, G. S. 2008. 'Foreword', in *Communication as Culture, Revised Edition: Essays on Media and Society*, ed. by J. W. Carey (New York: Routledge), pp. ix-xxiv.

Adams, C., & Thompson, T. L. 2016. *Researching a Posthuman World: Interviews with Digital Objects* (London: Springer), https://doi.org/10.1057/978-1-137-57162-5

Adolf, M. 2011. 'Clarifying Mediatization: Sorting through a Current Debate', *Empedocles: European Journal for the Philosophy of Communication*, 3(2), 153–75, https://doi.org/10.1386/ejpc.3.2.153_1

Ahn, J. 2013. 'What Can We Learn from Facebook Activity? Using Social Learning Analytics to Observe New Media Literacy Skills', in *Proceedings of the Third International Conference on Learning Analytics and Knowledge*, ed. by Dan Suthers et al. (Leuven: ACM), pp. 135–44, https://doi.org/10.1145/2460296.2460323

Allenby, B. R., & Sarewitz, D. 2011. *The Techno-Human Condition* (Cambridge: MIT Press), https://doi.org/10.7551/mitpress/8714.001.0001

Alpers, S. 1991. 'The Museum as a Way of Seeing', in *Exhibiting Cultures: The Poetics and Politics of Museum Display*, ed. by I. Karp & S. Lavine (Washington: Smithsonian Institution Press), pp. 25–32.

Alvermann, D. E., Moon, J. S., & Hagood, M. C. 2018. *Popular Culture in the Classroom: Teaching and Researching Critical Media Literacy* (New York: Routledge), https://doi.org/10.4324/9781315059327

Andersen, N., & Arcus, C. 2017. 'Agency', *Journal of Media Literacy*, 64(1–2).

Anton, C. 2006. 'History, Orientations, and Future Directions of Media Ecology', in *Mass Media Research: International Approaches*, ed. by Y. Pasadeos & D. Dimitrakopoulou (Athens: Athens Institute for Education and Research), pp. 299–308.

Anton, C. 2016. 'On the Roots of Media Ecology: A Micro-History and Philosophical Clarification', *Philosophies*, 1(2), 126–32, https://doi.org/10.3390/philosophies1020126

Arute, F., et al. 2019. 'Quantum Supremacy Using a Programmable Superconducting Processor', *Nature*, 574(7779), 505–10, https://doi.org/10.1038/s41586-019-1666-5

Aufderheide, P. 1993. *Media Literacy. A Report of the National Leadership Conference on Media Literacy* (Queenstown: Aspen Institute), https://eric.ed.gov/?id=ED365294

Austin, W., Park, C., & Goble, E. 2008. 'From Interdisciplinary to Transdisciplinary Research: A Case Study', *Qualitative Health Research*, 18(4), 557–64, https://doi.org/10.1177/1049732307308514

Bachmair, B., & Bazalgette, C. 2007. 'The European Charter for Media Literacy: Meaning and Potential', *Research in Comparative and International Education*, 2(1), 80–87, https://doi.org/10.2304/rcie.2007.2.1.80

Badmington, N. 2011. 'Posthumanism', in *The Routledge Companion to Literature and Science*, ed. by B. Clarke and M. Rossini (London: Routledge), pp. 374–84, https://doi.org/10.4324/9780203848739.ch32

Barad, K. 2007. *Meeting the Universe Halfway: Quantum Physics and the Entanglement of Matter and Meaning* (Durham: Duke University Press), https://doi.org/10.1215/9780822388128

Barker, C. & Jane, E. A. 2016. *Cultural Studies: Theory and Practice*, 5th ed. (Los Angeles: Sage).

Bauwens, J., Thorbjornsson, G. B., & Verstrynge, K. 2019. 'Unplug your Life: Digital Detox through a Kierkegaardian Lens', *Kierkegaard Studies Yearbook*, 24(1), 415–36, https://doi.org/10.1515/kierke-2019-0017

Bayley, A. 2018. *Posthuman Pedagogies in Practice: Arts Based Approaches for Developing Participatory Futures* (New York: Springer).

Beck, B. B. 1980. *Animal Tool Behavior: The Use and Manufacture of Tools by Animals* (New York: Garland STPM Publishing).

Benjamin, W. 2008. *The Work of Art in the Age of Mechanical Reproduction* (London: Penguin Books).

Bennett, T. 1998. *Culture: A Reformer's Science* (London: Sage).

Bentley-Condit, V. K., & Smith, E. O. 2010. 'Animal Tool Use: Current Definitions and an Updated Comprehensive Catalog', *Behaviour*, 147(2), 185–221, A1-A32, https://doi.org/10.1163/000579509x12512865686555

Bergen, J. P., & Verbeek, P.-P. 2020. 'To-Do Is to Be: Foucault, Levinas, and Technologically Mediated Subjectivation', *Philosophy & Technology*, 1–24, https://doi.org/10.1007/s13347-019-00390-7

Bergson, H. 1965. *Duration and Simultaneity* (Indianapolis: Bobbs-Merrill Company).

Berker, T., Hartmann, M., Punie, Y., & Ward, K. 2006. *Domestication of Media and Technology* (Maidenhead: Open University Press).

Blackford, R. 2011. 'Trite Truths about Technology: A Reply to Ted Peters', in *H+/-: Transhumanism and Its Critics*, ed. by R. Hansell & W. Grassie (Philadelphia: Metanexus Institute), pp. 176–88.

Blond, L., & Schiølin, K. 2018. 'Getting to Grips with Multistable Technology in an Apparently Stable World', in *Postphenomenological Methodologies: New Ways in Mediating Techno-Human Relationships*, ed. by J. Aagaard, J. K. B. Friis, J. Sorenson, O. Tafdrup, & C. Hasse (Lanham: Lexington Books), pp. 151–67.

Boltin, L. 2017. 'Sublime Embodiment of the Media', in *Postphenomenology and Media: Essays on Human–Media–World Relations*, ed. by S. O. Irwin & G. Wellner (Lanham: Lexington Books), pp. 168–84.

Borgmann, A. 2015. 'Stability, Instability, and Phenomenology', in *Postphenomenological Investigations: Essays on Human-Technology Relations*, ed. by R. Rosenberger & P. -P. Verbeek (Lanham: Lexington Books), pp. 247–52.

Bosanquet, T. 2006. *Henry James at Work* (Ann Arbor: University of Michigan Press), https://doi.org/10.3998/mpub.98996

Bostrom, N. 2005. 'A History of Transhumanist Thought', *Journal of Evolution and Technology*, 14(1), 1–25.

Bostrom, N. 2013. 'Existential Risk Prevention as Global Priority', *Global Policy*, 4(1), 15–31, https://doi.org/10.1111/1758-5899.12002

Bostrom, N. 2014. *Superintelligence* (Oxford: Oxford University Press).

Box, G. E. 1979. 'Robustness in the Strategy of Scientific Model Building', in *Robustness in Statistics*, ed. by R. L. Launer & G. N. Wilkinson (New York: Academic Press), pp. 201–36, https://doi.org/10.1016/b978-0-12-438150-6.50018-2

Braidotti, R. 2002. *Metamorphoses: Towards a Materialist Theory of Becoming* (Cambridge: Polity Press).

Braidotti, R. 2011. *Nomadic Theory: The Portable Rosi Braidotti* (New York: Columbia University Press).

Braidotti, R. 2013. *The Posthuman* (Cambridge: Polity Press).

Braidotti, R. 2016a. 'Posthuman Critical Theory', in *Critical Posthumanism and Planetary Futures*, ed. by D. Banerji & M. R. Paranjape (London: Springer), pp. 13–32, https://doi.org/10.1007/978-81-322-3637-5_2

Braidotti, R. 2016b. 'The Contested Posthumanities', in *Conflicting Humanities*, ed. by R. Braidotti & P. Gilroy (New York: Bloomsbury), pp. 9–25, https://doi.org/10.5040/9781474237574.ch-001

Braidotti, R. 2017. 'Posthuman, All Too Human: The Memoirs and Aspirations of a Posthumanist', *Tanner Lectures on Human Values at the Whitney Humanities Center*, Yale University (March 1), Lectures 1–2, https://rosibraidotti.com/2019/11/21/memoirs-of-a-posthumanist/

Byrne, D. S., & Callaghan, G. 2014. *Complexity Theory and the Social Sciences: The State of the Art* (London: Routledge), https://doi.org/10.4324/9780203519585

Buckingham, D. 2006. 'Defining Digital Literacy', *Digital Kompetanse*, 4(1), 263–76.

Burnett, C., & Merchant, G. 2011. 'Is There a Space for Critical Literacy in the Context of Social Media?', *English Teaching: Practice and Critique*, 10(1), 41–57.

Butler, J. 1993. *Bodies that Matter: On the Discursive Limits of Sex* (New York: Routledge).

Cafaro, P. 2015. 'Three Ways to Think about the Sixth Mass Extinction', *Biological Conservation*, 192, 387–93, https://doi.org/10.1016/j.biocon.2015.10.017

Callon, M., & Latour, B. 1981. 'Unscrewing the Big Leviathan: How Actors Macro-Structure Reality and How Sociologists Help Them to Do So', in *Advances in Social Theory and Methodology: Toward an Integration of Micro-and Macro-Sociologies*, ed. by K. Knorr-Cetina & A. V. Cicourel, vol. 1 (Boston: Routledge), pp. 277–303, http://www.bruno-latour.fr/sites/default/files/09-LEVIATHAN-GB.pdf

Canales, J. 2016. *The Physicist and the Philosopher: Einstein, Bergson, and the Debate that Changed our Understanding of Time* (Princeton: Princeton University Press), https://doi.org/10.1515/9781400865772

Capra, F. 1996. *The Web of Life: A New Scientific Understanding of Living Systems* (New York: Anchor Books).

Capra, F. 2002. *The Hidden Connections: Integrating the Hidden Connections among the Biological, Cognitive, and Social Dimensions of Life* (New York: Doubleday).

Capra, F. 2005. 'Complexity and Life', *Theory, Culture & Society*, 22(5), 33–44, https://doi.org/10.1177/0263276405057046

Carey, J. W. 2008. *Communication as Culture, Revised Edition: Essays on Media and Society* (New York: Routledge), https://doi.org/10.4324/9780203928912

Carpenter, E. 1973. *Oh, What a Blow that Phantom Gave Me!* (New York: Holt, Rinehart & Winston).

Casey, V. 2003. 'The Museum Effect: Gazing from Object to Performance in the Contemporary Cultural-History Museum', *Archives & Museum Informatics*, 2, 1–21.

Castelvecchi, D. 2017. 'IBM's Quantum Cloud Computer Goes Commercial', *Nature News*, 543(7644), 159, https://doi.org/10.1038/nature.2017.21585

Center for Humane Technology. (n.d.). 'Problem', *Center for Humane Technology*, http://humanetech.com/problem

Center for Media Literacy. 2019. 'Media Literacy: A Definition and More', *CML*, http://www.medialit.org/media-literacy-definition-and-more

Chen, S. 2017. 'Sampling as Secondary Orality Practice and Copyright's Technological Biases', *Journal of High Technology Law*, 17(2), 206–72.

Chouliaraki, L. 2013. 'Re-Mediation, Inter-Mediation, Trans-Mediation: The Cosmopolitan Trajectories of Convergent Journalism', *Journalism Studies*, *14*(2), 267–83, https://doi.org/10.1080/1461670x.2012.718559

Chouliaraki, L. 2017. 'Symbolic Bordering: The Self-representation of Migrants and Refugees in Digital News', *Popular Communication*, 15(2), 78–94, https://doi.org/10.1080/15405702.2017.1281415

Cilliers, P. 2005. 'Complexity, Deconstruction and Relativism', *Theory, Culture & Society*, 22(5), 255–67, https://doi.org/10.1177/0263276405058052

Claeys, L. 2007. 'ICT in the Daily Life: An Interpretive Approach to Equal Opportunities in the Network Society' (PhD thesis, Ghent University).

Clark, L. S. 2009. 'Theories: Mediatization and Media Ecology', in *Mediatization: Concept, Changes, Consequences*, ed. by K. Lundby (New York: Peter Lang), pp. 85–100.

Clark, A., & Chalmers, D. 1998. 'The Extended Mind', *Analysis*, 58(1), 7–19.

Clines, F. X. 2017. 'A Starry Night Crowded with Selfies', *New York Times* (September 23), https://www.nytimes.com/2017/09/23/opinion/sunday/starry-night-van-gogh-selfies.html

Coeckelbergh, M. 2013. *Human Being@ Risk: Enhancement, Technology, and the Evaluation of Vulnerability Transformations* (New York: Springer Science & Business Media).

Coeckelbergh, M. 2017. *Using Words and Things: Language and Philosophy of Technology* (New York: Routledge), https://doi.org/10.4324/9781315528571

Coeckelbergh, M. 2019. *Moved by Machines: Performance Metaphors and Philosophy of Technology* (New York: Routledge), https://doi.org/10.4324/9780429283130

Consalvo, M. 2004. 'Borg Babes, Drones, and the Collective: Reading Gender and the Body in Star Trek', *Women's Studies in Communication*, 27(2), 177–203, https://doi.org/10.1080/07491409.2004.10162472

Courtois, C., Mechant, P., Paulussen, S., & De Marez, L. 2012. 'The Triple Articulation of Media Technologies in Teenage Media Consumption', *New Media & Society*, 14(3), 401–20, https://doi.org/10.1177/1461444811415046

Courtois, C., Verdegem, P., & De Marez, L. 2013. 'The Triple Articulation of Media Technologies in Audiovisual Media Consumption', *Television & New Media*, 14(5), 421–39, https://doi.org/10.1177/1527476412439106

Craig, R. T. 1999. 'Communication Theory as a Field', *Communication Theory*, 9(2), 119–61, https://doi.org/10.1111/j.1468-2885.1999.tb00355.x

Cronon, W. 1995. *Uncommon Ground: Toward Reinventing Nature* (New York: W. W. Norton).

Culkin, J. M. 1967. 'A Schoolman's Guide to Marshall McLuhan', *The Saturday Review* (March), 51–53, 70–72.

Deetz, S. A. 1994. 'Future of the Discipline: The Challenges, the Research, and the Social Contribution', in *Communication Yearbook 17*, ed. by S. A. Deetz (Thousand Oaks: Sage), pp. 565–600.

Deleuze, G., & Guattari, P. F. 1987. *A Thousand Plateaus. Capitalism and Schizophrenia* (Minneapolis: University of Minnesota Press).

Derrida, J. 1982. *Margins of Philosophy*, trans. by Alan Bass (Chicago: University of Chicago Press).

Dewey, J. 1997. *Democracy and Education* (New York: Free Press).

Dinhopl, A., & Gretzel, U. 2016. 'Selfie-Taking as Touristic Looking', *Annals of Tourism Research*, 57, 126–39, https://doi.org/10.1016/j.annals.2015.12.015

Donati, A. R., Shokur, S., Morya, E., Campos, D. S., Moioli, R. C., Gitti, C. M., ... & Brasil, F. L. 2016. 'Long-Term Training with a Brain-Machine Interface-Based Gait Protocol Induces Partial Neurological Recovery in Paraplegic Patients', *Scientific Reports*, 6(1), 30383, https://doi.org/10.1038/srep30383

Doudna, J. A., & Sternberg, S. H. 2017. *A Crack in Creation: Gene Editing and the Unthinkable Power to Control Evolution* (Boston: Houghton Mifflin Harcourt).

Dreyfus, H. L. & Dreyfus, S. E. 1986. 'From Socrates to Expert Systems: The Limits of Calculative Rationality', in *Philosophy and Technology II*, ed. by Carl Mitcham & Alois Huning (New York: Springer), pp. 111–30.

Duncan, B. 2010. 'Voices of Media Literacy: International Pioneers Speak', http://www.medialit.org/sites/default/files/Voices_of_ML%20Barry%20 Duncan.pdf

Ehret, C., & D'Amico, D. 2019. Why a More Human Literacy Studies Must Be Posthuman, in *Affect in Literacy Learning and Teaching: Pedagogies, Politics and Coming to Know*, ed. by K. M. Leander & C. Ehret (New York: Routledge), pp. 147–69, https://doi.org/10.4324/9781351256766-12

Ellul, J. 1964. *The Technological Society* (New York: Vintage Books).

Engel, S. 1999. *Context Is Everything: The Nature of Memory* (New York: W. H. Freeman).

European Commission. 2018. *Standard Eurobarometer 88: Autumn 2017: Media use in the European Union*, https://doi.org/10.2775/116707

Faber Taylor. A., & Kuo. F. E. 2006. 'Is Contact with Nature Important for Healthy Child Development? State of the Evidence', in *Children and Their Environments*, ed. by C. Spencer & M. Blades (Cambridge: Cambridge University Press), pp. 124–40, https://doi.org/10.1017/cbo9780511521232.009

Falk, J. H. 2009. *Identity and the Museum Visitor Experience* (New York: Routledge).

Feenberg, A. 1999. *Questioning Technology* (New York: Routledge).

Feenberg, A. 2017. *Technosystem* (Cambridge: Harvard University Press), https://doi.org/10.4159/9780674982109

Ferrando, F. 2013. 'Posthumanism, Transhumanism, Antihumanism, Metahumanism, And New Materialisms', *Existenz*, 8(2), 26–32.

Ferrando, F. 2019. *Philosophical Posthumanism* (New York: Bloomsbury), https://doi.org/10.5040/9781350059511

Fiske, J. 1990. *Introduction to Communication Studies* (London: Routledge).

Fleming, C. 2004. *René Girard: Violence and Mimesis* (Cambridge: Polity Press).

Folke, C. 2006. 'Resilience: The Emergence of a Perspective for Social–Ecological Systems Analyses', *Global Environmental Change*, 16(3), 253–67, https://doi.org/10.1016/j.gloenvcha.2006.04.002

Foucault, M. 1970. *The Order of Things: An Archaeology of the Human Sciences* (London: Routledge).

Foucault, M. 1988. *Michel Foucault: Politics, Philosophy, Culture: Interviews and Other Writings*, ed. by L. Kritzman (London: Routledge).

Foucault, M. 1995. *Discipline and Punish: The Birth of the Prison* (New York: Vintage Books).

Foucault, M., Fornet-Betancourt, R., Becker, H., Gomez-Müller, A., & Gauthier, J. D. 1987. 'The Ethic of Care for the Self as a Practice of Freedom: An Interview with Michel Foucault on January 20, 1984', *Philosophy & Social Criticism*, 12(2–3), 112–31.

Fragoso, V., Gauglitz, S., Zamora, S., Kleban, J., & Turk, M. 2011. 'TranslatAR: A Mobile Augmented Reality Translator', in *2011 IEEE Workshop on Applications of Computer Vision (WACV)* (Kona: IEEE), pp. 497–502, https://doi.org/10.1109/WACV.2011.5711545

Francis, M. 2016. 'Investigating Approaches to Media Literacy: An Analysis of Media Literacy Organizations' (PhD thesis, Florida Atlantic University), https://fau.digital.flvc.org/islandora/object/fau%3A33450/datastream/OBJ/view/Investigating_Approaches_to_Media_Literacy__An_Analysis_of_Media_Literacy_Organizations.pdf

Franklin, U. 2004. *The Real World of Technology* (Toronto: House of Anansi).

Frost, S. 2016. *Biocultural Creatures: Toward a New Theory of the Human* (Durham: Duke University Press), https://doi.org/10.1515/9780822374350

Fukuyama, F. 2002. *Our Posthuman Future: Consequences of the Biotechnology Revolution* (New York: Farrar, Straus and Giroux).

Fukuyama, F. 2004. 'Transhumanism', *Foreign Policy*, 144, 42–43, https://doi.org/10.2307/4152980

Gergen, K. J. 2009. *Relational Being: Beyond Self and Community* (Oxford: Oxford University Press).

Giddens, A. 1979. *Central Problems in Social Theory: Action, Structure, and Contradiction in Social Analysis* (London: Macmillan).

Giddens, A. 1990. *The Consequences of Modernity* (Cambridge: Polity Press).

Girard, R. 1978. *Des choses cachées depuis la fondation du monde* (Paris: Grasset & Fasquelle).

Giroux, H. 2002. 'Neoliberalism, Corporate Culture, and the Promise of Higher Education: The University as a Democratic Public Sphere', *Harvard Educational Review*, 72(4), 425–63, https://doi.org/10.17763/haer.72.4.0515nr62324n71p1

Gilster, P. 1997. *Digital Literacy* (New York: Wiley Computer).

Goffman, E. 1956. *The Presentation of Self in Everyday Life* (Edinburgh: Social Sciences Research Centre).

Grabham, E., Cooper, D., Krishnadas, J., & Herman, D. (Eds.). 2009. *Intersectionality and Beyond: Law, Power and the Politics of Location* (London: Routledge).

Gray, D. 2009. 'Complicated vs. Complex', *Communication Nation* (November 25), http://communicationnation.blogspot.com/2009/11/

Grishakova, M. 2019. 'The Predictive Mind, Attention, and Cultural Evolution: A New Perspective on Narrative Dynamics', in *Narrative Complexity: Cognition, Embodiment, Evolution*, ed. by M. Grishakova & M. Poulaki (Lincoln: University of Nebraska Press), pp. 367–90, https://doi.org/10.2307/j.ctvhktjh6.21

Gyongyosi, L., & Imre, S. 2019. 'A Survey on Quantum Computing Technology', *Computer Science Review*, 31, 51–71, https://doi.org/10.1016/j.cosrev.2018.11.002

Habermas, J. 2003. *The Future of Human Nature* (Cambridge: Polity Press).

Haddon, L. 2007. 'Roger Silverstone's Legacies: Domestication', *New Media & Society*, 9(1), 25–32, https://doi.org/10.1177/1461444807075201

Hall, S. 1980. 'Encoding/decoding', in *Culture, Media, Language*, ed. by S. Hall, D. Hobson, A. Love, & P. Willis (London: Hutchinson), pp. 128–38.

Hall, S. 2013. 'Introduction: Who Needs "Identity"?', in *Questions of Cultural Identity*, ed. by S. Hall & P. du Gay (London: Sage), 1–17, https://doi.org/10.4135/9781446221907.n1

Han, S. 2008. *Navigating Technomedia: Caught in the Web* (Lanham: Rowman & Littlefield).

Han-Pile, B. 2010. 'The "Death of Man": Foucault and Anti-humanism', in *Foucault and Philosophy*, ed. by T. O'Leary & C. Falzon (Oxford: Blackwell), pp. 118–42, https://doi.org/10.1002/9781444320091.ch6

Hansell, G. R. & Grassie, W. (Eds). 2011. *H+/-: Transhumanism and Its Critics* (Philadelphia: Metanexus Institute).

Hansen, M. B. N. 2004. *New Philosophy for New Media* (Cambridge: MIT Press).

Harari, Y. N. 2016. *Homo Deus: A Brief History of Tomorrow* (London: Random House).

Haraway, D. J. 1985. 'A Manifesto for Cyborgs: Science, Technology, and Socialist Feminism in the 1980s', *Socialist Review*, 15(2), 65–107.

Haraway, D. 1988. 'Situated Knowledges: The Science Question in Feminism and the Privilege of Partial Perspective', *Feminist studies*, 14(3), 575–99, https://doi.org/10.2307/3178066

Haraway, D. J. 2016. *Staying with the Trouble: Making Kin in the Chthulucene* (Durham: Duke University Press), https://doi.org/10.1215/9780822373780

Harley, D., Verni, A., Willis, M., Ng, A., Bozzo, L., & Mazalek, A. 2018. 'Sensory Vr: Smelling, Touching, and Eating Virtual Reality', in *Proceedings of the Twelfth International Conference on Tangible, Embedded, and Embodied Interaction* (New York: Association for Computing Machinery), pp. 386–97, https://doi.org/10.1145/3173225.3173241

Harman, G. 2007. *Heidegger Explained. From Phenomenon to Thing* (Chicago: Open Court Publishing).

Harris, T. 2019. 'Optimizing for Engagement: Understanding the Use of Persuasive Technology on Internet Platforms (Testimony to the U.S. Senate)', *U.S. Senate Committee on Commerce, Science, and Transportation*, https://www.commerce.senate.gov/2019/6/optimizing-for-engagement-understanding-the-use-of-persuasive-technology-on-internet-platforms

Harris, T. 2020. 'Tristan Harris — Congressional Hearing January 8, 2020 — Statement Plus Highlights', *YouTube*, 24 January, posted by Center for Humane Technology, 11:16, https://www.youtube.com/watch?v=LUNErhONqCY

Hartley, J. 2002. *Communication, Cultural and Media Studies: The Key Concepts* (New York: Routledge), https://doi.org/10.4324/9780203136379

Hartmann, M. 2006. 'The Triple Articulation of ICTs. Media as Technological Objects, Symbolic Environments and Individual Texts', in *Domestication of Media and Technology*, ed. by T. Berker, M. Hartmann, Y. Punie, & K. Ward (Maidenhead: Open University), pp. 80–102.

Hayles, N. K. 1990. *Chaos Bound: Orderly Disorder in Contemporary Literature and Science* (Ithaca: Cornell University Press).

Hayles, N. K. 1991. 'Introduction: Complex Dynamics in Literature and Science', in *Chaos and Order: Complex Dynamics in Literature and Science*, ed. by N. K. Hayles (Chicago: University of Chicago Press), pp. 1–33.

Hayles, N. K. 1995. 'Searching for Common Ground', in *Reinventing Nature? Responses to Postmodern Deconstruction*, ed. by M. E. Soulé & G. Lease (Washington, DC: Island Press), pp. 47–64.

Hayles, N. K. 1999. *How We Became Posthuman: Virtual Bodies in Cybernetics, Literature, and Informatics* (Chicago: University of Chicago Press).

Hayles, N. K. 2014. 'Cognition Everywhere: The Rise of the Cognitive Nonconscious and the Costs of Consciousness', *New Literary History*, 45(2), 199–220, https://doi.org/10.1353/nlh.2014.0011

Heidegger, M. 1977. 'The Question Concerning Technology', in *The Question Concerning Technology and Other Essays*, trans. by W. Lovitt (New York: Garland), pp. 3–35.

Heidegger, M. 2010. *Being and Time* (Albany: State University of New York).

Heim, M. 1987. *Electric Language: A Philosophical Study of Word Processing* (New Haven: Yale University Press).

Henning, M. 2006. *Museums, Media and Cultural Theory* (Maidenhead: Open University Press).

Hershock, P. D. 2003. 'Turning Away from Technotopia: Critical Precedents for Refusing the Colonization of Consciousness', in *Technology and Cultural Values: On the Edge of the Third Millennium*, ed. by P. D. Hershock, M. Stepaniants, & R. T. Ames (Honolulu: Hawaii University Press), pp. 587–600.

Hess, A. 2015. 'The Selfie Assemblage', *International Journal of Communication*, 9(18), 1629–46.

Hill, K. 2019. 'Goodbye Big Five', *Gizmodo*, http://gizmodo.com/c/goodbye-big-five

Hirsch, P. D., Adams, W. M., Brosius, J. P., Zia, A., Bariola, N., & Dammert, J. L. 2011. 'Acknowledging Conservation Trade-Offs and Embracing Complexity', *Conservation Biology*, 25(2), 259–64, https://doi.org/10.1111/j.1523-1739.2010.01608.x

Hjarvard, S. P. 2013. *The Mediatization of Culture and Society* (New York: Routledge), https://doi.org/10.4324/9780203155363

Hjarvard, S. P. 2014. 'From Mediation to Mediatization: The Institutionalization of New Media', in *Mediatized Worlds: Culture and Society in a Media Age*, ed. by A. Hepp & F. Krotz (Basingstoke: Palgrave), pp. 123–39.

Hobbs, R. 2010. *Digital and Media Literacy: A Plan of Action. A White Paper on the Digital and Media Literacy Recommendations of the Knight Commission on the Information Needs of Communities in a Democracy* (Washington, DC: Aspen Institute), https://www.aspeninstitute.org/wp-content/uploads/2010/11/Digital_and_Media_Literacy.pdf

Hobbs, R., & Jensen, A. 2009. 'The Past, Present, and Future of Media Literacy Education', *Journal of Media Literacy Education*, 1(1), 1.

Horst, H. A. 2012. 'New Media Technologies in Everyday Life', in *Digital Anthropology*, ed. by H. Horst & D. Miller (London: Berg), pp. 61–79, https://doi.org/10.4324/9781003085201-5

Hughes, J. 2004. *Citizen Cyborg: Why Democratic Societies Must Respond to the Redesigned Human of the Future* (New York: Basic Books).

Hughes, J. 2010a. 'Contradictions from the Enlightenment Roots of Transhumanism', *Journal of Medicine and Philosophy*, 35(6), 622–40, https://doi.org/10.1093/jmp/jhq049

Hughes, J. 2010b. 'Problems of Transhumanism: Introduction', *Institute for Ethics and Emerging Technologies.*

Hughes, J. 2012. 'The Politics of Transhumanism and the Techno-Millennial Imagination, 1626–2030', *Zygon*, 47(4), 757–76, https://doi.org/10.1111/j.1467-9744.2012.01289.x

Humphrey, C. S. 2013. *The American Revolution and the Press: The Promise of Independence* (Evanston: Northwestern University Press), https://doi.org/10.2307/j.ctv47wcc8

Husserl, E. 1973. *Experience and Judgment: Investigations in a Genealogy of Logic*, trans. by J. S. Churchill & K. Ameriks (Evanston: Northwestern University Press).

Ihde, D. 1990. *Technology and the Lifeworld: From Garden to Earth* (Bloomington: Indiana University Press).

Ihde, D. 2002. *Bodies in Technology* (Minneapolis: University of Minnesota Press).

Ihde, D. 2003. 'If Phenomenology is an Albatross, Is Post-Phenomenology Possible?', in *Chasing Technoscience: Matrix for Materiality*, ed. by Don Ihde & Evan Selinger (Bloomington: Indiana University Press), pp. 131–44.

Ihde, D. 2009. *Postphenomenology and Technoscience: The Peking University Lectures* (Albany: SUNY Press).

Ihde, D. 2011. 'Of Which Human are We Post?', in *H+/-: Transhumanism and Its Critics*, ed. by R. Hansell & W. Grassie (Philadelphia: Metanexus Institute), pp. 123–35.

Ihde, D. 2012. *Experimental Phenomenology: Multistabilities* (Albany: SUNY Press).

Ihde, D, & Malafouris, L. 2018. '*Homo Faber* Revisited: Postphenomenology and Material Engagement Theory', *Philosophy & Technology*, 35, 195–214, https://doi.org/10.1007/s13347-018-0321-7

Ihde, D., & Selinger, E. 2003. *Chasing Technoscience: Matrix for Materiality* (Bloomington: Indiana University Press).

Ingold, T. 2013. 'Prospect', in *Biosocial Becomings: Integrating Social and Biological Anthropology*, ed. by T. Ingold & G. Pálsson (Cambridge: Cambridge University Press), pp. 1–21, https://doi.org/10.1017/cbo9781139198394.002

Ingold, T., & Pálsson, G. (Eds.). 2013. *Biosocial Becomings: Integrating Social and Biological Anthropology* (Cambridge: Cambridge University Press), https://doi.org/10.1017/cbo9781139198394

Innis, H. A. 2008. *The Bias of Communication* (Toronto: University of Toronto Press).

Irwin, S. O. 2014. 'Technological Reciprocity with a Cell Phone', *Techné: Research in Philosophy and Technology*, 18, 10–19, https://doi.org/10.5840/techne201461613

Irwin, S. O. 2016. 'Media Ecology and the Internet of Things', *Explorations in Media Ecology*, 15(2), 159–71, https://doi.org/10.1386/eme.15.2.159_1

Irwin, S. O. 2017. 'Multimedia Stabilities: Exploring the GoPro Experience', in *Postphenomenology and Media: Essays on Human–Media–World Relations*, ed. by Y. Van Den Eede, S. O. Irwin, & G. Wellner (Lanham: Lexington Books), pp. 103–22.

Jandrić, P. 2019. 'The Postdigital Challenge of Critical Media Literacy', *The International Journal of Critical Media Literacy*, 1(1), 26–37, https://doi.org/10.1163/25900110-00101002

Jasanoff, S. 2001. 'Image and Imagination: The Formation of Global Environmental Consciousness', in *Changing the Atmosphere: Expert Knowledge and Environmental Governance*, ed. by P. N. Edwards (Cambridge: MIT Press), pp. 309–37, https://doi.org/10.7551/mitpress/1789.003.0013

Jiang, J., & Vetter, M. A. 2020. 'The Good, the Bot, and the Ugly: Problematic Information and Critical Media Literacy in the Postdigital Era', *Postdigital Science and Education*, 2(1), 78–94, https://doi.org/10.1007/s42438-019-00069-4

Jolls, T., & Johnsen, M. 2017. 'Media Literacy: A Foundational Skill for Democracy in the 21st Century', *Hastings Law Journal*, 69, 1379–408.

Jolls, T., & Wilson, C. 2014. 'The Core Concepts: Fundamental to Media Literacy Yesterday, Today and Tomorrow', *Journal of Media Literacy Education*, 6(2), 68–78.

Kalmar, I. 2005. 'The Future of "Tribal Man" in the Electronic Age', in *Marshall McLuhan: Critical Evaluations in Cultural Theory, Vol. II: Theoretical Elaborations*, ed. by G. Genosko (New York: Routledge), pp. 227–32.

Kellner, D., & Share, J. 2005. 'Toward Critical Media Literacy: Core Concepts, Debates, Organizations, and Policy', *Discourse: Studies in the Cultural Politics of Education*, 26(3), 369–86, https://doi.org/10.1080/01596300500200169

Kellner, D., & Share, J. 2007. 'Critical Media Literacy, Democracy, and the Reconstruction of Education', *Media Literacy: A Reader*, 3–23.

Kellner, D., & Share, J. 2019. *The Critical Media Literacy Guide: Engaging Media and Transforming Education* (Boston: Brill), https://doi.org/10.1163/9789004404533

Kim, K. Y. 2015. 'The Everydayness of Mobile Media in Japan', in *The Routledge Handbook of New Media in Asia*, ed. by L. Hjorth (London: Routledge), pp. 445–57.

Kiran, A. H. 2012. 'Technological Presence: Actuality and Potentiality in Subject Constitution', *Human Studies*, 35(1): 77–93, https://doi.org/10.1007/s10746-011-9208-7

Kiran, A. 2015. 'Four Dimensions of Technological Mediation', in *Postphenomenological Investigations: Essays on Human-technology Relations*, ed. by R. Rosenberger & P.-P. Verbeek (Lanham: Lexington Books), pp. 123–40.

Kirshenblatt-Gimblett, B. 1998. *Destination Culture: Tourism, Museums, and Heritage* (Berkeley: University of California Press).

Kittler, F. A. 1999. *Gramophone, Film, Typewriter* (Redwood City: Stanford University Press).

Koltay, T. 2011. 'The Media and the Literacies: Media Literacy, Information Literacy, Digital Literacy', *Media, Culture & Society*, 33(2), 211–21, https://doi.org/10.1177/0163443710393382

Koltay, T. 2015. 'Data Literacy: In Search of a Name and Identity', *Journal of Documentation*, 71(2), 401–15, https://doi.org/10.1108/jd-02-2014-0026

Kopytoff, I. 1988. 'The Cultural Biography of Things: Commoditization as Process', in *The Social Life of Things: Commodities in Cultural Perspective*, ed. by A. Appadurai (Cambridge: Cambridge University Press), pp. 64–91.

Kozinets, R., Gretzel, U., & Dinhopl, A. 2017. 'Self in Art/self as Art: Museum Selfies as Identity Work', *Frontiers in Psychology*, 8, https://doi.org/10.3389/fpsyg.2017.00731

Krajina, Z., Moores, S., & Morley, D. 2014. 'Non-Media-Centric Media Studies: A Cross-Generational Conversation', *European Journal of Cultural Studies*, 17(6), 682–700, https://doi.org/10.1177/1367549414526733

Kranzberg, M. 1986. 'Technology and History: "Kranzberg's Laws"', *Technology and Culture*, 27(3), 544–60, https://doi.org/10.2307/3105385

Kroes, P., & Meijers, A. 2001. *The Empirical Turn in the Philosophy of Technology* (Amsterdam: JAI Press).

Kurzweil, R. 2005. *The Singularity is Near* (New York: Viking Books).

Kurzweil, R. 2012. *How to Create a Mind: The Secret of Human Thought Revealed* (New York: Viking Penguin).

Lamagna, J. 2011. 'Of the Self, by the Self, and for the Self: An Intra-Relational Perspective on Intra-psychic Attunement and Psychological Change', *Journal of Psychotherapy Integration*, 21(3), 280–307, https://doi.org/10.1037/a0025493

Latour, B. 1987. *Science in Action: How to Follow Scientists and Engineers through Society* (Cambridge: Harvard University Press).

Latour, B. 1993. *We Have Never Been Modern* (Cambridge: Harvard University Press).

Latour, B. 1999. *Pandora's Hope: Essays on the Reality of Science Studies* (Cambridge: Harvard University Press).

Lemke, J. 2006. 'Toward Critical Multimedia Literacy: Technology, Research, and Politics', in *International Handbook of Literacy and Technology: Volume Two*, ed. by M. C. McKenna, L. D. Labbo, R. D. Kieffer, & D. Reinking (Mahwah: Lawrence Erlbaum Associates), pp. 3–14.

Lemmens, P. 2017. 'Thinking through Media: Stieglerian Remarks on a Possible Postphenomenology of Media', in *Postphenomenology and Media: Essays on Human–media–world Relations*, ed. by Y. Van Den Eede, S. O. Irwin, & G. Wellner (Lanham: Lexington Books), pp. 185–206.

Lesage, F. 2013. 'Cultural Biographies and Excavations of Media: Context and Process', *Journal of Broadcasting & Electronic Media*, 57(1), 81–96, https://doi.org/10.1080/08838151.2012.761704

Levin, S. A. 1998. 'Ecosystems and the Biosphere as Complex Adaptive Systems', *Ecosystems*, 1(5), 431–36, https://doi.org/10.1007/s100219900037

Lewis, R. S. 2017. 'Turning our Back on Art: A Postphenomenological Study of Museum Selfies', *Kunstlicht*, 38(4), 92–99.

Lewis, R. S. 2018. 'Hello Anthropocene, Goodbye Humanity: Reassessing Transhumanism through Postphenomenology', *Glimpse*, 19, 79–87, https://doi.org/10.5840/glimpse2018198

Lewis, R. S. 2020. 'Technological Gaze: Understanding How Technologies Transform Perception', in *Perception and the Inhuman Gaze: Perspectives from Philosophy, Phenomenology and the Sciences*, ed. by A. Daly, F. Cummins, J. Jardine, & D. Moran (New York: Routledge), pp. 128–42.

Li, J., Yao, L., & Wang, J. Z. 2015. 'Photo Composition Feedback and Enhancement', in *Mobile Cloud Visual Media Computing*, ed. by G. Hua & X.-S. Hua (Cham: Springer International Publishing), pp. 113–44.

Liberati, N. 2018. 'The Borg–eye and the We–I. The Production of a Collective Living Body through Wearable Computers', *AI & Society*, 35(1), 39–49, https://doi.org/10.1007/s00146-018-0840-x

Lie, M., & Sørensen, K. H. (Eds.). 1996. *Making Technology our Own? Domesticating Technology into Everyday Life* (Oslo: Scandinavian University Press North America).

Lief, J., & Thompson, A. 2015. *I Am Because You Are: How the Spirit of Ubuntu Inspired an Unlikely Friendship and Transformed a Community* (New York: Rodale).

Livingstone, S. 2004. 'Media Literacy and the Challenge of New Information and Communication Technologies', *The Communication Review*, 7(1), 3–14, https://doi.org/10.1080/10714420490280152

Livingstone, S. 2007. 'On the Material and the Symbolic: Silverstone's Double Articulation of Research Traditions in New Media Studies', *New Media & Society*, 9(1), 16–24, https://doi.org/10.1177/1461444807075200

Livingstone, S. 2009. 'On the Mediation of Everything: ICA Presidential Address 2008', *Journal of Communication*, 59(1), 1–18, https://doi.org/10.1111/j.1460-2466.2008.01401.x

Livingstone, S. 2014. 'Developing Social Media Literacy: How Children Learn to Interpret Risky Opportunities on Social Network Sites', *Communications*, 39(3), 283–303, https://doi.org/10.1515/commun-2014-0113

Livingston, S. 2018. 'Media Literacy — Everyone's Favourite Solution to the Problems of Regulation', *Media Policy Project Blog* (May 8), https://blogs.lse.ac.uk/medialse/2018/05/08/media-literacy-everyones-favourite-solution-to-the-problems-of-regulation/

Livingstone, S., & Van der Graaf, S. (2008). 'Media literacy', *The International Encyclopedia of Communication*, ed. by W. Donsbach, https://doi.org/10.1002/9781405186407.wbiecm039

Logan, R. K. 2000. T*he Sixth Language: Learning a Living in the Internet Age* (Toronto: Stoddart).

Logan, R. K. 2011. 'Figure/ground: Cracking the McLuhan Code', *E-Compós Brasília*, 14, 1–13.

Logan, R. K. 2013. *McLuhan Misunderstood: Setting the Record Straight* (Toronto: Key Publishing House).

Logan, R. K. 2015. 'General Systems Theory and Media Ecology: Parallel Disciplines That Animate Each Other', *Explorations in Media Ecology*, 14(1), 39–51, https://doi.org/10.1386/eme.14.1-2.39_1

López, A. 2008. *Mediacology: A Multicultural Approach to Media Literacy in the 21st Century* (New York: Peter Lang).

López, A. 2014. *Greening Media Education: Bridging Media Literacy with Green Cultural Citizenshi*p (New York: Peter Lang).

Lorenz, E. 1972. 'Predictability: Does the Flap of a Butterfly's Wings in Brazil Set Off a Tornado in Texas?', Paper delivered at the American Association for the Advancement of Science, Washington, DC.

Louv, R. 2008. *Last Child in the Woods: Saving Our Children from Nature-Deficit Disorder* (Chapel Hill: Algonquin Books).

Luke, C. 1989. *Pedagogy, Printing and Protestantism: The Discourse on Childhood* (Albany: SUNY Press).

Lundby, K. (Ed.). 2014. *Mediatization of Communication* (Berlin: CPI books GmbH).

Malraux, A. 1967. *Museum without Walls* (Garden City: Doubleday).

Manovich, L. 2013. *Software Takes Command* (New York: Bloomsbury Academic).

Martin, H.-J., & Cochrane, L. G. 1994. *The History and Power of Writing* (Chicago: University of Chicago Press).

Mason, L. 2016. 'McLuhan's Challenge to Critical Media Literacy: The City as Classroom Textbook', *Curriculum Inquiry*, 46(1), 79–97, https://doi.org/10.1080/03626784.2015.1113511

Mason, L. E. 2019. 'Media Literacy and Pragmatism', *The International Encyclopedia of Media Literacy*, 1–5, https://doi.org/10.1002/9781118978238.ieml0119

Masterman, L. 1980. *Teaching about Television* (London: Macmillan), https://doi.org/10.1007/978-1-349-16279-6

Masterman, L. 1989. 'Media Awareness Education: Eighteen Basic Principles', *Center for Media Literacy*, https://www.medialit.org/reading-room/media-awareness-education-eighteen-basic-principles

Masterman, L. 2010. 'Voices of Media Literacy: International Pioneers Speak', http://www.medialit.org/sites/default/files/VoicesMediaLiteracyLenMasterman_1.pdf

Maturana, H. R., & Varela, F. J. 1972. *Autopoiesis and Cognition: The Realization of the Living* (Dordrecht: D. Reidel Publishing).

Mazzei, L. A. 2014. 'Beyond an Easy Sense: A Diffractive Analysis', *Qualitative Inquiry*, 20(6), 742–46, https://doi.org/10.1177/1077800414530257

McCall, L. 2009. 'The Complexity of Intersectionality', in *Intersectionality and Beyond: Law, Power and the Politics of Location*, ed. by E. Grabham, D. Cooper, J. Krishnadas, & D. Herman (London: Routledge), pp. 49–76.

McKibben, B. 2004. *Enough: Staying Human in an Engineered Age* (New York: Times Book).

McLuhan, E. 2008. 'Marshall McLuhan's Theory of Communication: The Yegg', *Global Media Journal — Canadian Edition*, 1(1), 25–43.

McLuhan, E. 2009. 'Literacy in a New Key', *Proceedings of the Media Ecology Association*, 10, 9–18.

McLuhan, E., & Zingrone, F. 1997. *Essential McLuhan* (London: Routledge).

McLuhan, M. 1955. 'A Historical Approach to the Media', *Teachers College Record*, 57(2), 104–10.

McLuhan, M. 1969. 'The Playboy Interview: Marshall McLuhan', *Playboy Magazine* (24 December 2009), http://www.nextnature.net/2009/12/the-playboy-interview-marshall-mcluhan/

McLuhan, M. 1970. *Culture Is Our Business* (New York: Ballantine Books).

McLuhan, M. 1994. *Understanding Media: The Extension of Man* (Cambridge: MIT Press).

McLuhan, M., Hutchon, K., & McLuhan, E. 1977. *City as Classroom: Understanding Language and Media* (Agincourt: The Book Society of Canada).

Media Ecology Association. 2019. *Media Ecology Association*, https://www.media-ecology.org/

Merleau-Ponty, M. 2002. *Phenomenology of Perception*, trans. by C. Smith (London: Routledge)

Meyrowitz, J. 1985. *No Sense of Place: The Impact of Electronic Media on Social Behavior* (Oxford: Oxford University Press).

Meyrowitz, J. 1994. 'Medium Theory', in *Communication Theory Today*, ed. by D. Crowley & D. Mitchell (Stanford: Stanford University Press), pp. 50–77.

Michelfelder, D. P. 2015. 'Postphenomenology with an Eye to the Future', in *Postphenomenological Investigations: Essays on Human-Technology Relations*, ed. by R. Rosenberger & P.-P. Verbeek (Lanham: Lexington Books), pp. 237–46.

Mitchell, M. 2009. *Complexity: A Guided Tour* (Oxford: Oxford University Press).

Moores, S. 2005. *Media/Theory: Thinking about Media and Communications* (Abingdon: Routledge).

Moores, S. 2012. *Media, Place and Mobility* (Basingstoke: Palgrave Macmillan).

Moores, S. 2016. 'Arguments for a Non-media-centric, Non-representational Approach to Media and Place', in *Communications/Media/Geographies*, ed. by P. C. Adams, J. Cupples, K. Glynn, A. Jansson, & S. Moores (New York: Routledge), pp. 144–72.

Moravec, H. 1988. *Mind Children: The Future of Robot and Human Intelligence* (Cambridge: Harvard University Press).

More, M. 2013. 'The Philosophy of Transhumanism', in *Transhumanist Reader: Classical and Contemporary Essays on the Science, Technology, and Philosophy of The Human Future*, ed. by M. More & N. Vita-More (Malden: Wiley-Blackwell), pp. 3–17.

More, M., & Vita-More, N. (Eds.). 2013. 'Transhumanist Declaration (2012)', in *Transhumanist Reader: Classical and Contemporary Essays on the Science, Technology, and Philosophy of The Human Future*, ed. by M. More & N. Vita-More (Malden: Wiley-Blackwell), pp. 54–55.

Morin, E. 2007. 'Restricted Complexity, General Complexity', in *Worldviews, Science and Us: Philosophy and Complexity*, ed. by C. Gershenson, D. Aerts, & B. Edmonds (Singapore: World Scientific), pp. 5–29, https://doi.org/10.1142/9789812707420_0002

Morley, D. 2007. *Media, Modernity and Technology: The Geography of the New* (London: Routledge), https://doi.org/10.4324/9780203413050

Morley, D. 2009. 'For a Materialist, Non-media-centric Media Studies', *Television & New Media*, 10(1), 114–16, https://doi.org/10.1177/1527476408327173

Morley, D., & Silverstone, R. 1990. 'Domestic Communication—Technologies and Meanings', *Media, Culture & Society*, 12(1), 31–55, https://doi.org/10.1177/016344390012001003

Naughton, J. 2012. *From Gutenberg to Zuckerberg* (London: Quercus Books).

Neely, R. M., Piech, D. K., Santacruz, S. R., Maharbiz, M. M., & Carmena, J. M. 2018. 'Recent Advances in Neural Dust: Towards a Neural Interface Platform', *Current Opinion in Neurobiology*, 50, 64–71, https://doi.org/10.1016/j.conb.2017.12.010

Nichols, T. P., & Stornaiuolo, A. 2019. 'Assembling "Digital Literacies": Contingent Pasts, Possible Futures', *Media and Communication*, 7(2), 14–24, https://doi.org/10.17645/mac.v7i2.1946

Nielsen. 2019. *The Nielsen Total Audience Report: Q3 2018* (New York: The Nielsen Company),https://www.nielsen.com/us/en/insights/report/2019/q3-2018-total-audience-report/

Okkonen, J., & Kotilainen, S. 2019. 'Minors and Artificial Intelligence — Implications to Media Literacy', in *Information Technology and Systems*, ed. by A. Rocha, C. Ferras, & M. Paredes (Cham: Springer), pp. 881–90.

Ong, W. J. 1977. *Interfaces of the Word: Studies in the Evolution of Consciousness and Culture* (Ithaca: Cornell University Press).

Ong, W. J. 2012. *Orality and Literacy* (New York: Routledge).

Onge, J. S. 2018. 'Teaching Media Literacy from a Cultural Studies Perspective', in *Handbook of Research on Media Literacy in Higher Education Environments*, ed. by Jayne Cubbage (Hershey: IGI Global), pp. 136–52, https://doi.org/10.4018/978-1-5225-4059-5.ch008

Onishi, B. 2011. 'Information, Bodies, and Heidegger: Tracing Visions of the Posthuman', *Sophia*, 50(1), 101–12, https://doi.org/10.1007/s11841-010-0214-4

Pearce, W. B. 1989. *Communication and the Human Condition* (Carbondale: Southern Illinois University Press).

Peters, J. D. 2015. *The Marvelous Clouds: Toward a Philosophy of Elemental Media* (Chicago: University of Chicago Press).

Pettitt, T. 2007. 'Before the Gutenberg Parenthesis: Elizabethan American Compatibilities', *Media in Transition 5, Creativity, Ownership and Collaboration in the Digital Age, Communications Forum*, Massachusetts Institute of Technology, Cambridge (April 27–29), http://web.mit.edu/comm-forum/legacy/mit5/papers/pettitt_plenary_gutenberg.pdf

Pettitt, T. 2012. 'Bracketing the Gutenberg Parenthesis', *Explorations in Media Ecology*, 11(2), 95–114, https://doi.org/10.1386/eme.11.2.95_1

Pickering, A. 1995. *The Mangle of Practice: Time, Agency, and Science* (Chicago: University of Chicago).

Pickering, A. 2005. 'Asian Eels and Global Warming: A Posthumanist Perspective on Society and the Environment', *Ethics and the Environment*, 10(2), 29–43, https://doi.org/10.1353/een.2005.0023

Pickering, A. 2010. *The Cybernetic Brain: Sketches of Another Future* (Chicago: University of Chicago Press).

Pickering, A. 2011. 'Brains, Selves and Spirituality in the History of Cybernetics', in *H+/-: Transhumanism and Its Critics*, ed. by R. Hansell & W. Grassie (Philadelphia: Metanexus Institute), pp. 189–204.

Plato. 2002. *Phaedrus*, trans. by R. Waterfield (Oxford: Oxford University Press).

Poli, R. 2013. 'A Note on the Difference between Complicated and Complex Social Systems', *Cadmus*, 2(1), 142–47.

Postman, N. 1970. 'The Reformed English Curriculum', in *High School 1980: The Shape of the Future in American Secondary Education*, ed. by A. C. Eurich (New York: Pitman), pp. 160–68.

Postman, N. 1974. 'Media Ecology: General Semantics in the Third Millennium', *General Semantics Bulletin*, 41–43, 74–78.

Postman, N. 2000. 'The Humanism of Media Ecology', *Proceedings of the Media Ecology Association*, 1(1), 10–16.

Postman, N. 2006. *Amusing Ourselves to Death: Public Discourse in the Age of Show Business*, 20th anniversary edition (New York: Penguin).

Potter, W. J. 2018. *Media Literacy* (Thousand Oaks: Sage Publications).

Poushter, J., Bishop, C., & Chwe, H. 2018. 'Social Media Use Continues to Rise in Developing Countries but Plateaus across Developed Ones', *Pew Research Center*, https://www.pewresearch.org/global/2018/06/19/social-media-use-continues-to-rise-in-developing-countries-but-plateaus-across-developed-ones/

Preston, C. J. 2018. *The Synthetic Age: Outdesigning Evolution, Resurrecting Species, and Reengineering Our World* (Cambridge: MIT Press).

Prigogine, I., & Stengers, I. 1984. *Order out of Chaos: Man's New Dialogue with Nature* (New York: Bantam Books).

Prigogine, I., & Stengers, I. 1997. *The End of Certainty: Time's Flow and the Laws of Nature* (New York: Free Press).

Puech, M. 2016. *The Ethics of Ordinary Technology* (New York: Routledge), https://doi.org/10.4324/9781315620282

Qvortrup, L. 2006. 'Understanding New Digital Media: Medium Theory or Complexity Theory?', *European Journal of Communication*, 21(3), 345–56, https://doi.org/10.1177/0267323106066639

Ralón, L. 2016. 'The Media Ecology — Philosophy of Technology Disconnect: A Matter of Perception?', *Explorations in Media Ecology*, 15(2), 113–28, https://doi.org/10.1386/eme.15.2.113_1

Ran, F. A., Hsu, P. D., Wright, J., Agarwala, V., Scott, D. A., & Zhang, F. 2013. 'Genome Engineering Using the CRISPR-Cas9 System', *Nature Protocols*, 8(11), 2281–308, https://doi.org/10.1038/nprot.2013.143

Rauch, J. 2018. *Slow Media: Why Slow Is Satisfying, Sustainable, and Smart* (Oxford: Oxford University Press).

Rettberg, J. W. 2014. *Seeing Ourselves through Technology: How We Use Selfies, Blogs and Wearable Devices to See and Shape Ourselves* (Basingstoke: Palgrave Macmillan).

Risam, R. 2018. 'Now You See Them: Self-Representation and the Refugee Selfie', *Popular Communication*, 16(1), 58–71, https://doi.org/10.1080/15405702.2017.1413191

Roco, M. C., & Bainbridge, W. S. (Eds.). 2003. *Converging Technologies for Improving Human Performance: Nanotechnology, Biotechnology, Information Technology and Cognitive Science* (Dordrecht: Springer Science & Business Media).

Roden, D. 2014. *Posthuman Life: Philosophy at the Edge of the Human* (London: Routledge), https://doi.org/10.4324/9781315744506

Romele, A. 2020. *Digital Hermeneutics: Philosophical Investigations in New Media and Technologies* (London: Routledge), https://doi.org/10.4324/9780429331893

Rosenberger, R. 2012. 'Embodied Technology and the Dangers of Using the Phone while Driving', *Phenomenology and the Cognitive Sciences*, 11(1), 79–94, https://doi.org/10.1007/s11097-011-9230-2

Rosenberger, R. 2014. 'Multistability and the Agency of Mundane Artifacts: From Speed Bumps to Subway Benches', *Human Studies*, 37(3), 369–92, https://doi.org/10.1007/s10746-014-9317-1

Rosenberger, R. 2017. *Callous Objects: Designs against the Homeless* (Minneapolis: University of Minnesota Press), https://doi.org/10.5749/9781452958538

Rosenberger, R., & Verbeek, P.-P. (Eds). 2015. *Postphenomenological Investigations: Essays on Human-Technology Relations* (Lanham: Lexington Books).

Rubin, D. C. 1988. 'Go for the Skill', in *Remembering Reconsidered: Ecological and Traditional Approaches to the Study of Memory*, ed. by U. Neisser & E. Winograd (Cambridge: Cambridge University Press), pp. 374–82.

Rushdie, S. 2006. *Midnight's Children* (London: Vintage Books).

Russo, A., Watkins, J., Kelly, L., & Chan, S. 2008. 'Participatory Communication with Social Media', *Curator: The Museum Journal*, 51(1), 21–31, https://doi.org/10.1111/j.2151-6952.2008.tb00292.x

Sandberg, A. 2013. 'Feasibility of Whole Brain Emulation', in *Philosophy and Theory of Artificial Intelligence*, ed. by V. C. Müller (Berlin: Spring), pp. 251–64.

Sargent, G., Zhang, H., Morgan, A., Van Camp, A., D'Arcy, A., Cassedy, A., Aspiras, T., Romstadt, E. Dicillo, V., & Asari, V. 2017. 'Brain Machine Interface for Useful Human Interaction via Extreme Learning Machine and State Machine Design', *2017 IEEE Symposium Series on Computational Intelligence (SSCI)* (November 27).

Scharff, R. C. 2006. 'Ihde's Albatross: Sticking to a 'Phenomenology' of Technoscientific Experience', in *Postphenomenology: A Critical Companion to Ihde*, ed. by E. Selinger (Albany: SUNY Press), pp. 131–44

Schütz, A., & Luckmann, T. 1973. *The Structures of the Life-World*, vol. 1 (Evanston: Northwestern University Press).

Schwab, K. 2017. *The Fourth Industrial Revolution* (Geneva: World Economic Forum).

Selinger, E. (Ed.). 2012. *Postphenomenology: A Critical Companion to Ihde* (Albany: SUNY Press).

Senft, T. M., & Baym, N. K. 2015. 'What Does the Selfie Say? Investigating a Global Phenomenon', *International Journal of Communication*, 9, 1588–606.

Shannon, C. E. 1948. 'A Mathematical Theory of Communication', *Bell System Technical Journal*, 27(3), 379–423.

Shannon, C. E., & Weaver, W. 1964/1949. *A Mathematical Model of Communication* (Urbana: University of Illinois Press).

Sharon, T. 2014. *Human Nature in an Age of Biotechnology: The Case for Mediated Posthumanism* (Cham: Springer).

Sheehan, T. 2014. 'What, after All, Was Heidegger about?' *Continental Philosophy Review*, 47(3–4), 249–74.

Silverstone, R. 1989. 'Television: Text or Discourse?', *Science as Culture*, 1(6), 104–23.

Silverstone, R. 1994. *Television and Everyday Life* (London: Routledge).

Silverstone, R. 2006. 'Domesticating Domestication: Reflections on the Life of a Concept', in *Domestication of Media and Technology*, ed. by T. Berker, M. Hartmann, Y. Punie & K. J. Ward (Maidenhead: Open University Press), pp. 229–48.

Silverstone, R., & Haddon, L. 1996. 'Design and the Domestication of Information and Communication Technologies: Technical Change and Everyday Life', in *The Politics of Information and Communication Technologies*, ed. by R. Mansell & R. Silverstone (Oxford: Oxford University Press), pp. 44–74.

Silverstone, R., Hirsch, E., & Morley, D. 1991. 'Listening to a Long Conversation: An Ethnographic Approach to the Study of Information and Communication Technologies in the Home', *Cultural Studies*, 5(2), 204–27.

Simon, H. A. 1962. 'The Architecture of Complexity', *Proceedings of the American Philosophical Society*, 106(6), 467–82.

Simons, D. J., & Chabris, C. F. 1999. 'Gorillas in Our Midst: Sustained Inattentional Blindness for Dynamic Events', *Perception*, 28(9), 1059–74.

Smith, D. 2015. 'Rewriting the Constitution: A Critique of "Postphenomenology"', *Philosophy & Technology* 28(4), 533–51.

Smith, D. 2018. *Exceptional Technologies: A Continental Philosophy of Technology* (London: Bloomsbury Publishing).

Smith, J., & Jenks, C. 2006. *Qualitative Complexity: Ecology, Cognitive Processes and the Re-emergence of Structures in Post-humanist Social Theory* (London: Routledge).

Smith, M. R. & Marx, L. 1994. *Does Technology Drive History? The Dilemma of Technological Determinism* (Cambridge: MIT Press).

Sontag, S. 1973. *On Photography* (London: Penguin Books).

Sorgner, S. 2019. 'Transhumanism: The Best Minds of Our Generation Are Needed for Shaping Our Future', *APA Newsletter on Philosophy and Computers*, 18(2).

Steffen, W., Crutzen, P. J., & McNeill, J. R. 2007. 'The Anthropocene: Are Humans Now Overwhelming the Great Forces of Nature', *AMBIO: A Journal of the Human Environment*, 36(8), 614–21.

Steffen, W., Grinevald, J., Crutzen, P., & McNeill, J. 2011. The Anthropocene: Conceptual and Historical Perspectives', *Philosophical Transactions of the Royal Society A: Mathematical, Physical and Engineering Sciences*, 369(1938), 842–67, https://doi.org/10.1098/rsta.2010.0327

Stember, M. 1991. 'Advancing the Social Sciences through the Interdisciplinary Enterprise', *The Social Science Journal*, 28(1), 1–14.

Stengers, I. 2008. 'A Constructivist Reading of Process and Reality', *Theory, Culture & Society*, 25(4), 91–110, https://doi.org/10.1177/0263276408091985

Stone, A. R. 1994. 'Split Subjects, Not Atoms: Or, How I Fell in Love with My Prosthesis', *Configurations*, 2(1), 173–90, https://doi.org/10.1353/con.1994.0016

Strate, L. 2014. *Amazing Ourselves to Death: Neil Postman's Brave New World Revisited* (London: Peter Lang).

Strate, L. 2017. *Media Ecology: An Approach to Understanding the Human Condition* (London: Peter Lang).

Swierstra, T., & Waelbers, K. 2012. 'Designing a Good Life: A Matrix for the Technological Mediation of Morality', *Science and Engineering Ethics*, 18(1), 157–72.

Thompson, P. 2006. 'Ihde and Technological Ethics', in *Postphenomenology: A Critical Companion to Ihde*, ed. by E. Selinger (Ithaca: SUNY Press), pp. 109–16.

Turkle, S. 2011. *Alone Together: Why We Expect More from Technology and Less from Each Other* (Philadelphia: Basic Books).

Turner, J. R., & Baker, R. M. 2019. 'Complexity Theory: An Overview with Potential Applications for the Social Sciences', *Systems*, 7(1), 4, https://doi.org/10.3390/systems7010004

Twenge, J. M. 2017. *IGen: Why Today's Super-connected Kids Are Growing Up Less Rebellious, More Tolerant, Less Happy — and Completely Unprepared for Adulthood — and What that Means for the Rest of Us* (New York: Simon and Schuster).

Twenge, J. M., Joiner, T. E., Rogers, M. L., & Martin, G. N. 2018. 'Increases in Depressive Symptoms, Suicide-Related Outcomes, and Suicide Rates among US Adolescents after 2010 and Links to Increased New Media Screen Time', *Clinical Psychological Science*, 6(1), 3–17, https://doi.org/10.1177/2167702617723376

Twenge, J. M., Martin, G. N., & Spitzberg, B. H. 2019. 'Trends in US Adolescents' Media use, 1976–2016: The Rise of Digital Media, the Decline of TV, and the (Near) Demise of Print', *Psychology of Popular Media Culture*, 8(4), 329–45, https://doi.org/10.1037/ppm0000203

Ugur, N. G., & Koc, T. 2015. 'Time for Digital Detox: Misuse of Mobile Technology and Phubbing', *Procedia-Social and Behavioral Sciences*, 195, 1022–31, https://doi.org/10.1016/j.sbspro.2015.06.491

Urry, J. 2003. *Global Complexity* (Cambridge: Polity Press).

Urry, J. 2005a. 'The Complexity Turn', *Theory, Culture & Society*, 22(5), 1–14.

Urry, J. 2005b. 'The Complexities of the Global', *Theory, Culture & Society*, *22*(5), 235–54.

Urry, J. 2007. 'Global Complexities', *Frontiers of Globalization Research*, ed. by I. Rossi (Boston: Springer), pp. 151–62, https://doi.org/10.1007/978-0-387-33596-4_6

Vanwynsberghe, H. 2014. 'How Users Balance Opportunity and Risk: A Conceptual Exploration of Social Media Literacy and Measurement' (PhD thesis, Ghent University).

Van Den Eede, Y. 2011. 'In between Us: On the Transparency and Opacity of Technological Mediation', *Foundations of Science*, 16(2–3), 139–59, https://doi.org/10.1007/s10699-010-9190-y

Van Den Eede, Y. 2012. *Amor Technologiae: Marshall McLuhan as Philosopher of Technology* (Brussels: VUB Press).

Van Den Eede, Y. 2015a. 'Where Is the Human? Beyond the Enhancement Debate', *Science, Technology, & Human Values*, 40(1), 149–62, https://doi.org/10.1177/0162243914551284

Van Den Eede, Y. 2015b. 'Tracing the Tracker: A Postphenomenological Inquiry into Self-tracking Technologies', in *Postphenomenological Investigations:*

Essays on Human-Technology Relations, ed. by R. Rosenberger & P.-P. Verbeek (Lanham: Lexington Books), pp. 143–58.

Van Den Eede, Y. 2016. 'Blindness and Ambivalence: The Meeting of Media Ecology and Philosophy of Technology', *Explorations in Media Ecology*, 15(2), 103–12, https://doi.org/10.1386/eme.15.2.103_1

Van Den Eede, Y. 2017. 'Concrete/abstract: Sketches for a Self-Reflexive Epistemology of Technology Use', *Foundations of Science*, 22(2), 433–42, https://doi.org/10.1007/s10699-015-9464-5

Van Den Eede, Y., Goeminne, G., & Van den Bossche, M. 2017a. 'The Art of Living with Technology: Turning over Philosophy of Technology's Empirical Turn', *Foundations of Science*, 22(2), 235–46.

Van Den Eede, Y., Irwin, S. O., Wellner, G. 2017b. 'Introduction: "What media do"', in *Postphenomenology and Media: Essays on Human–Media–World Relations*, ed. by S. O. Irwin & G. Wellner (Lanham: Lexington Books), pp. xvii-xxxii.

Van Dijk, J. A., & Van Deursen, A. J. 2014. *Digital Skills: Unlocking the Information Society* (New York: Palgrave Macmillan).

Van Dijck, J. 2013. *The Culture of Connectivity: A Critical History of Social Media* (Oxford: Oxford University Press).

Varela, F. J., Rosch, E., & Thompson, E. 1992. *The Embodied Mind: Cognitive Science and Human Experience* (Cambridge: MIT Press).

Verbeek, P.-P. 2005. *What Things Do: Philosophical Reflections on Technology, Agency, and Design* (University Park, PA: Pennsylvania State University Press).

Verbeek, P.-P. 2008. 'Cyborg Intentionality: Rethinking the Phenomenology of Human–Technology Relations', *Phenomenology and the Cognitive Sciences*, 7(3), 387–95.

Verbeek, P.-P. 2011. *Moralizing Technology: Understanding and Designing the Morality of Things* (Chicago: University of Chicago Press).

Verbeek, P.-P. 2012. 'Expanding Mediation Theory', *Foundations of Science*, 17(4), 391–95, https://doi.org/10.1007/s10699-011-9253-8

Verbeek, P.-P. 2015. 'Beyond Interaction: A Short Introduction to Mediation Theory', *Interactions*, 22(3), 26–31.

Vitalia, I.-L. 2013. 'Emotional Health, and Spending Time in Nature', *Current Trends in Natural Sciences*, 2(3), 100–03.

Wellman, S. M., Eles, J. R., Ludwig, K. A., Seymour, J. P., Michelson, N. J., McFadden, W. E., ... & Kozai, T. D. 2018. 'A Materials Roadmap to Functional Neural Interface Design', *Advanced Functional Materials*, 28(12), 1701269, 1–38, https://doi.org/10.1002/adfm.201701269

Wellner, G. 2016. *A Postphenomenological Inquiry of Cell Phones: Genealogies, Meanings, and Becoming* (Lanham: Lexington Books).

Wellner, G. 2017a. 'I-media-world', in *Postphenomenology and Media: Essays on Human–Media–World Relations*, ed. by S. O. Irwin & G. Wellner (Lanham: Lexington Books), pp. 207–27.

Wellner, G. 2017b. 'Do Animals Have Technologies?', *Studia Phaenomenologica*, 17, 265–82, https://doi.org/10.5840/studphaen20171713

White, F. 2014. *The Overview Effect: Space Exploration and Human Evolution* (Reston: The American Institute of Aeronautics and Astronautics).

Whitehead, A. N. 1978. *Process and Reality* (New York: Free Press).

Whyte, K. P. 2015. 'What is Multistability? A Theory of the Keystone Concept of Postphenomenological Research', in *Technoscience and Postphenomenology: The Manhattan Papers*, ed. by J. K. B. O. Friis & R. P. Crease (Lanham: Lexington Books), pp. 69–81.

Wilden, A. 1980. *System and Structure: Essays in Communication and Exchange* (London: Tavistock).

Williams, R. 2004. *Television: Technology and Cultural Form* (London: Routledge).

Wolfe, C. 2010. *What is Posthumanism?* (Minneapolis: University of Minnesota Press).

Wood, D. 2017. 'Technoprogressive Declaration Recommitment', TransVision 2017, Brussels.

Yan. (Ed.). 2019. 'Museum Selfie Day Marked in Turkey', *Xinhua* (1 January 2019), http://www.xinhuanet.com/english/2019-01/16/c_137749474.htm

Zhang, S., Yuan, S., Huang, L., Zheng, X., Wu, Z., Xu, K., & Pan, G. 2019. 'Human Mind Control of Rat Cyborg's Continuous Locomotion with Wireless Brain-to-brain Interface', *Scientific Reports*, 9(1), 1–12, https://doi.org/10.1038/s41598-018-36885-0

Zylinska, J. 2009. *Bioethics in the Age of New Media* (Cambridge: MIT Press), https://doi.org/10.7551/mitpress/9780262240567.001.0001

Zylinska, J. 2017. *Nonhuman Photography* (Cambridge: MIT Press), https://doi.org/10.7551/mitpress/10938.001.0001

Permissions

All chapters in this book were first published in TMLHS, by Open Book Publishers by Richard S. Lewis; hereby published with permission under the Creative Commons Attribution License or equivalent. Every chapter published in this book has been scrutinized by our experts. Their significance has been extensively debated. The topics covered herein carry significant information for a comprehensive understanding. They may even be implemented as practical applications or may be referred to as a beginning point for further studies.

We would like to thank the editorial team for lending their expertise to make the book truly unique. They have played a crucial role in the development of this book. Without their invaluable contributions this book wouldn't have been possible. They have made vital efforts to compile up to date information on the varied aspects of this subject to make this book a valuable addition to the collection of many professionals and students.

This book was conceptualized with the vision of imparting up-to-date and integrated information in this field. To ensure the same, a matchless editorial board was set up. Every individual on the board went through rigorous rounds of assessment to prove their worth. After which they invested a large part of their time researching and compiling the most relevant data for our readers.

The editorial board has been involved in producing this book since its inception. They have spent rigorous hours researching and exploring the diverse topics which have resulted in the successful publishing of this book. They have passed on their knowledge of decades through this book. To expedite this challenging task, the publisher supported the team at every step. A small team of assistant editors was also appointed to further simplify the editing procedure and attain best results for the readers.

Apart from the editorial board, the designing team has also invested a significant amount of their time in understanding the subject and creating the most relevant covers. They scrutinized every image to scout for the most suitable representation of the subject and create an appropriate cover for the book.

The publishing team has been an ardent support to the editorial, designing and production team. Their endless efforts to recruit the best for this project, has resulted in the accomplishment of this book. They are a veteran in the field of academics and their pool of knowledge is as vast as their experience in printing. Their expertise and guidance has proved useful at every step. Their uncompromising quality standards have made this book an exceptional effort. Their encouragement from time to time has been an inspiration for everyone.

The publisher and the editorial board hope that this book will prove to be a valuable piece of knowledge for students, practitioners and scholars across the globe.

Index